Born and raised in Surrey, Ashley Parkes' journey down the river of Life has generally passed through peaceful waters, periodically straying into more challenging tidal estuaries with the occasional white-water ride thrown in for good measure. His greatest adventure was a trip to the Falkland Islands at a time when most people, Ashley included, had never heard of the place, and his foremost achievement has been to raise two marvellous children, although to be honest, in this enterprise he played a support role to his wife who did most of the heavy lifting. He likes to play his guitar and listen to music, Pink Floyd and Leonard Cohen being particular favourites. Ashley prefers beer to wine, and enjoys being on, in or near the sea. His first book, 'The Same but Different', takes a light-hearted look at the way the world around him has changed since he first graced it with his presence in 1955.

For my dear wife and kids.

The Same
but
Different

ASHLEY PARKES

"…….unleash memories of your own."

Contents

1.

What's This All About Then?

Welcome. Come in. Take a seat. I guess you're wondering what this is all about, so let me explain. Way back when, during Covid lockdown, I celebrated my sixty-fifth birthday. The very nature of the event got me thinking; locked up while the sands of time inexorably drained away, I should be 'Doing Something'. After deep thought I came to the conclusion that writing a book was the answer; it can't be that hard after all, and it only remained for me to decide on the subject.

Bereft of ideas on topics for a novel, having no urge to research any serious subject in detail, and lacking any practical knowledge that could be imparted in a self-help manual, I floundered. It seemed the only thing I truly knew about was me; hardly a scintillating subject with no celebrity status or riotous lifestyle to celebrate.

Then again, I have been on this planet for approaching twenty-five thousand days, quite a long time really, and perhaps the many changes that I've witnessed during that time might provide material for a book. We hear a lot from the younger generation about how things are so much harder today, how the Oldies had it easy while at the same time managing to wreck everything for those following on, that life's so unfair, blah, blah, blah. Meanwhile, the Oldies moan about the kids of today; whining snowflakes who have it so easy and expect everything on a plate, don't know what a good day's work is, blah, blah, blah. This is hardly new; inter-generational differences and disappointments have been the norm for centuries. But surely someone must be wrong? So I thought that by looking back over my life at how things have changed just in those years, I might get a better idea of how we got to where we are today, and just might be able to come up with a more balanced view of where we stand. Then again…

I finished my project at the end of 2021 but then, in less than nine months, we celebrated 70 years of Queen Elizabeth being our longest ruling monarch before, months later, sadly witnessing the pomp and ceremony surrounding her state funeral. We saw King Charles take to the throne, breaking another record as the oldest person ever to take on the job, and we experienced three different Prime Ministers and a revolving door of ever-changing cabinets, all without an election. Russia invaded Ukraine resulting in unprecedented solidarity between western nations and renewed talk of a nuclear threat, and we are now experiencing a cost of living crisis, not just in the UK but globally. Latest official UN figures put the world population at 8 billion, Elon Musk has bought Twitter, allegedly to promote freedom of speech, and Just Stop Oil have recently knocked Extinction Rebellion from top of the charts of headline-grabbing groups seeking to change government policy on the environment. With so much change happening at such speed, I felt the need to blow the dust off and make a final update.

Consider just a few of the changes to have occurred in my time. The world population in 1955 was 2.8 billion, yet it now stands at around 8 billion; that's an increase of 5 billion or 5,000,0000,000, or 178% or simply, a lot in a very short time. Worse, UN predictions are for the number to rise to 10.9 billion by 2100. The population of little old UK alone has risen from 51 to 67 million. In 1955, the average life expectancy in the UK was 73.4 for women, and 67.7 for men; it's now 83.3 and 80.2 respectively. So, far more people, all living longer and all needing to be fed, housed and so on, placing a huge stress on the Earth's finite resources.

But humans are nothing if not innovative, and in trying to address these growing demands, technology has played a huge role, advancing in leaps and bounds. Consider life today without computers, mobile phones, the Internet or gaming consoles. On the telly front, ITV started broadcasting in 1955 bringing the total number of channels available to two, broadcasting just for a few hours a day, and only in black and white.

The number of cars on our roads has rocketed with dramatic effect. Our lungs have to combat the polluted air produced by all this traffic, not to mention the impact of the school run. Then there's international travel. In 1955, overseas travel was only affordable to the very rich; I saw a newspaper article suggesting that flying the Qantas "Kangaroo Route" from Perth to London and back in 1955 cost more than £18,000 in today's money, and that was in economy. The same journey today can be completed in a fraction of the time, and for less than £900, so now a large majority of Brits think nothing of hopping abroad for a break, often to faraway exotic places where we are always likely to encounter the familiar in the form of a McDonald's or Starbucks.

During the 50s and 60s the American and Russian governments saw the space race as a way to prove the superiority of their ideologies, Capitalism vs. Communism. From rockets it progressed to satellites, then monkeys and dogs were sent into space. Russia achieved the first manned spaceflight and the pinnacle was "one giant leap for mankind" as the Americans landed on the moon in 1969. Fifty years on, we take for granted space stations orbiting the earth, commercial spaceflight is in its infancy and we are seriously considering a manned visit to Mars.

Conflict still features permanently in our world despite lessons learnt from the two World Wars, the First optimistically named "the war to end all wars". In my lifetime there has been a never-ending stream of wars fought around the world in places as varied as Korea, Vietnam, Kenya, Cuba, Bosnia, The Falklands, Afghanistan, Iraq, Sudan, Cambodia, Rwanda, Yemen and, now, Ukraine. Human beings really can't live in peace. Between1969 and 1999, during The Troubles in Northern Ireland, violence came to mainland Britain, and numerous IRA bombings were carried out bringing new tensions, as ordinary people going about their lives became painfully aware of the risk of being blown to bits at any time. More recently, and related to conflicts in the Middle East, we have seen the evolution of international terrorism which can strike just about anywhere. The world has become a far more dangerous place.

So, a lot has changed, and I decided to write about it. But as it turned out, to use a phrase oft repeated in this tome, it's not that easy. I found a tendency to wander off-piste into a wider range of subjects than I had ever imagined, and my project developed a mind of its own, turning into a sort of rambling, vague social history of the period. I realised just how much had happened around me, almost without my noticing, and I felt I should try to explain to my kids just how easy it is to let things pass you by if you keep your head down too much. Whether I achieved this, or whether the book appeals to anyone other than family and friends remains to be seen.

At the core of the book are my own experiences; I realise that these may be of limited interest to anyone who doesn't know me, but that's not the point. If you were born within twenty years of me, and have lived at least part of that time in the UK, some of my experiences surely sound familiar. Growing up, you will have navigated the educational system, survived the Cold War threat of nuclear annihilation, discovered ways to earn a living, flown the nest, possibly found a partner and maybe had kids. You are likely to have watched and listened to some of the TV and radio shows I enjoyed, and possibly bought the same records and watched the same films. Like me, you may have had to earn pocket money when you were young, and the chances are you took holidays similar to mine and visited pubs and restaurants too.

Meanwhile, you will have witnessed the same momentous changes going on in the world around us. My aim is not to entertain you with my own story, but for it to unleash memories of your own. Some sections comprise little more than a list of names, but the subjects can be huge and, if you're like me, a name is all it takes to kick off the memories. I also live in hope that one or two younger types might flick through a few pages and come to understand a tiny bit more about what on earth us Oldies are going on about.

Before going further, I need to throw in a disclaimer. Don't assume that anything in this book is true. As a starting point, I've relied on my own memory which, to say the least, can struggle at times; as they say, nostalgia isn't what it used to be. To gather more detail, I then made numerous forays into the unregulated wilds of the Internet, a source not always renowned for its factual reliability. Painstaking verification has not been a key feature of this work, so if any of the 'facts' herein are of interest, please don't take them as gospel truth without further verification. With this in mind, I decided to leave out the names of all my friends and family in order not to cause offence by making them party to what might be imaginary events. Besides, as a kind of social history of the world around me, these names are not important in the greater scheme of things.

That said, most of the characters should be recognisable to those in the know. Henceforth, leading players appear under the monikers Wifey, Son, Daughter, Mum, Dad, Big Brother and Little Brother; I'm sure they'll be impressed. And I have even adopted a nom de plume; it's not about me it's about our world. Also, bearing in mind that a reasonably fast reader with serious masochistic tendencies could probably go cover-to-cover in a couple of sittings, and that the contents span more than sixty-seven years, it goes without saying that an awful lot has been missed out.

One final explanation. Through all the stages of my life, music has been a welcome companion, and my memories are often accompanied by songs around at the time. Occasionally, where my narrative has triggered a particular musical memory, I have added it as a soundtrack. Seemed like a good idea at the time.

There you are then. If you're bored already, you won't hurt my feelings should you just close the book and get on with your life, but if a brief nostalgic ramble appeals, then read on. The range of topics is quite impressive if I say so myself, but while a phenomenal amount has changed in the period covered, many issues facing us remain the same, hence the choice of title. I make no apology for a number of longer chapters where I have truly wallowed in nostalgia, although admittedly some, in particular those on television, music and cinema, could probably benefit from a prune. Feel free to skip anything; I can assure you that your quality of life won't suffer as a result. So, with no further ado, let's finally get started. Please join me on my journey; for us Oldies perchance the exercise will stir up a few memories, while for the youngsters maybe, just maybe, you'll learn something and understand better how we arrived at where we are today. Onwards and upwards.

2.

Setting the Scene

I was born in 1955, the year when the first McDonalds opened in California and the Children and Young Persons (Harmful Publications) Act came into effect in the UK with the intention, believe it or not, of protecting children from horror comics. I was brought up in a small house just a short walk from the Thames, living there for the next thirty-three years, on and off, with my parents and, for a fair bit of the time, with one or both of my two brothers, one three years older and one three years younger. Mum's family moved down from Sheffield in the 30s, while Dad had lived in the same town all his life, saying more than once that he couldn't think of anything he wanted that wasn't there. The town was a sleepy, leafy suburb where very little happened; it's undergone significant change in the last sixty-seven years although some would say very little still happens there.

Walking towards the river meant passing close to a large old run-down house, a country estate requisitioned by the government at the start of World War I to house troops before, in 1915, it was converted into a military hospital caring for a large number of New Zealander war casualties; many roads and buildings in the area were subsequently named in their honour to acknowledge the sacrifices they made. In 1965, the estate was sold for housing development. But of course, I was oblivious to all this, my concern was conkers. The house had the best collection of horse chestnut trees in the area, and we knew that after a good autumn storm the wind and rain would have brought down the conkers in their hundreds, so it was always a race to get there and find the best ones for the conker fights to come. These trips were exciting adventures; I remember it as always being gloomy or even dark when we went, and we knew we weren't supposed to be there. The place was rundown, spooky and intimidating and there were rumours that it was haunted. Still, it was worth it to get the best conkers. In those days conker fights were commonplace in the playground, obviously that was before the lethal nature of the pastime was recognised; we lived dangerously but survived, even though we played with no protective clothing or equipment.

An old disused film studio, home to 1950's TV series 'The Adventures of Robin Hood', was just down the road nestled in an expanse of trees. It was demolished to make way for a modern shopping centre in the 60s, ushering in the retail revolution and our first supermarket, Safeway. Before then, shops were generally small and, mostly, family run places. I do remember a Sainsbury's in the High Street though, but that bore no resemblance to shops of the same name today, it was more of a delicatessen, and my memory as a young child is of a gloomy place, with strong smells arising from various meats and cheeses on display; I would probably love it now, but not then.

In the last few years of his life, Dad delighted in regularly telling people what a lively baby I had been, "wouldn't sit still for a minute" he would say. He particularly liked to explain how, when I was left outside in my pram, I would rock violently back and forth trying to get the pram to move; apparently one time I even ripped out all the pram lining. He had fond memories of a Canadian builder who was so concerned at this behaviour that he would regularly use bricks as chocks to stop me rolling away, although Dad claimed that the brakes on the pram were efficient and always engaged.

But pause a moment to consider the significance of this little vignette; it seems that it was normal practice then to leave a baby outside for hours, strapped into a pram, alone, braving the elements, while mother got on with the housework and passers-by intervened to keep the baby safe. That was the way things worked then, but just imagine the social media outflow that such behaviour would generate today; comments on bad mothering, oozing with self-righteous, venomous bile and probably culminating in a visit from the Police or Social Services. Things, as they say, have definitely changed. And yet I have to say that, while our lives have been subject to huge transformations over the past sixty-seven years, a surprising amount remains the same, or similar,-and history does seem to have a habit of repeating itself. On with the story.

3.

Fresh Air and Exercise

"Youngsters today don't appreciate the benefit of fresh air and exercise", a mantra regularly espoused by more aging members of the population. But is that fair? The road I was brought up in bordered on a park, an absolute haven for any child with pent up energy to burn. Known to us simply as The Woods, it comprised three distinct large, grassed areas ideal for football, cricket and generally running about. There were a large number of trees, some very old, characterful and impressive, and all crying out to be climbed up or hidden in; and running through this great outdoor playground was some form of drainage ditch that seemed to serve no purpose other than to tempt children to cross it without getting stuck in the mud or getting a 'booty'.

An added novelty was a house backing onto The Woods that we knew was definitely owned by a witch. The whole area was the responsibility of a groundsman called the Old Geezer whose sole aim in life was to stop children enjoying themselves, but he wasn't always there, and we managed to keep out of his way most of the time when he was.. Hidden away among the trees stood a green wooden hut where the Archery Club stored their gear; this was suitable for hiding on top of, under or behind, and as we grew older, we became aware that visitors unknown would occasionally store dubious reading material under it. This was not actually that big a deal, as the type of material we're talking about would be freely available at newsstands by 1970, courtesy of The Sun tabloid. Times change.

At the town end of The Woods stood the Civil Defence hut. What went on in there was of no interest to us, but it had a sloping paved path which then encircled the building creating a perfect roller-skating track; scene of a few unfortunate accidents with at least one pair of my glasses coming a cropper. Finally, there was a fenced off area where the local Cricket and Hockey clubs were based, the only part of The Woods that we didn't consider 'ours'.

In those far off days, when it was normal to leave babies unattended in the street, it should come as no surprise that feral children roamed The Woods unsupervised from an early age; pretty much once they were able to walk. True, I did have an older brother to keep an eye on me, but I think I was probably a regular attendee from age three or four at the latest.

Unless the weather was atrocious, we would congregate on non-school days or after school and just play; we couldn't keep away. Providing we had enough kids, a football or cricket match would be on, and these could last hours, with occasional breaks to do something else. We were restricted a bit with gear though; cricket balls were expensive so not many people had one, and playing cricket with a tennis ball was never the same; it didn't help that the kid with the best ball would often decide to go home once he was bowled out. Footballs tended to puncture and weren't always available when a kickabout was fancied.

Time was a concept we had trouble grasping; we might go home if we were bored or hungry, but often mums would have to come and get us, standing on the edge of The Woods and calling out into the wilderness for whoever was due to go home; often a game changer if the kid summoned was the one with the bat or ball.

One particularly popular game was Wolf, a large-scale version of hide-and-seek where we could hide anywhere in The Woods. Once found, the prey would join forces with the hunter to find the rest. With so many good places to hide, including some very large trees that were virtually impenetrable when in full leaf, plus the added benefit that the hunted did not need to stay static but could keep on the move, games often lasted a long time. Winners were those who had not been found by the time boredom set in and the hunter accepted defeat by calling "Allee Allee In".

Another favourite was Monkey, covering a smaller area but no less energetic. All players started in the home tree; when the game began the catcher had to stay in the home tree counting to ten while his prey dropped to the floor and climbed other trees in the vicinity. Count over, the catcher would climb down and chase one of the others up their tree. Having touched his prey with his hand, a frantic race would be on as both scrambled down, back to the home tree and up to the designated 'safe' branch, the result deciding whether the prey was safe or caught. In the meantime, the other participants could make their way back to the safety of the home tree, but by climbing down from their trees they would become vulnerable if spotted by the catcher.

Health and Safety advocates observing us would have suffered a coronary as, to say the least, we were not exactly cautious in our play. Personally, I had numerous cuts and bruises and managed to wind myself more than once falling from trees. Grazes and grass burns were

13

commonplace, as were strained muscles and the like, but with the exception of one friend who, much to his mother's annoyance, made a habit of breaking his left arm, I can remember no other serious injuries. I did once need stitches in my head when, aged about six, I was too slow to avoid a tin can full of stones thrown at me by my best friend; but that doesn't count as we were playing in his garden at the time, so surely his parents. were to blame. As human animals we were young cubs pushing the boundaries to prepare us for the outside world. As they say, "what doesn't kill you makes you stronger".

Particularly relevant in the current climate, I wonder whether this lifestyle close to Nature may have helped develop robust immune systems. Many years later, a friend from university was talking of his experiences taking tourists by boat to view wildlife on the Galapagos Islands. The Ecuador government encouraged people to cull goats that had overrun the place since being introduced to the islands in 1920; apparently the meat was quite edible, if an acquired taste, and so the boats would land on an island to stock up with free, freshly slaughtered goat for their voyage.

This was generally enjoyed, or at least accepted, by most tourists with the exception of the Americans who, after their first goat meal, would remain close or confined to their cabin for the next few days as their bodies adjusted to the new diet. The suggestion was that they were so used to food having been pasteurised, homogenised and generally zapped to eradicate all possible microbes that their immune systems needed time to adapt to even harmless alien critters. Possibly a lesson there?

We also tended to use our bikes a lot. These were nowhere near the splendid machines darting everywhere today, but they did the job and we would travel miles on them. When I was about seven, Big Brother and his friends decided to ride to Bentalls in Kingston, where Chelsea footballers were holding a promotional meet-and-greet and kicking a ball around with the kids. Of course, being football mad, though not particularly a Chelsea fan, Big Brother had to go, and if he was going, there was no way I was staying behind.

No adult supervision of course, we had to make our own way. It would have been about seven miles each way, not a great distance but to a seven-year-old on a bike with small wheels, and of course no gears, it was a marathon. We made it, but it took a long time and is obviously an experience still burnt into my brain. Some five years later, three friends and I spent a week youth hosteling on the Isle of Wight, involving a trip of over 50 miles to Portsmouth along the old A3, a ride that we never saw as anything other than 'normal', although I admit that by then I did have a full-sized bike with the luxury of five gears.

In 1962, the film 'Mutiny on the Bounty' was released, resulting in significant changes to the way our lives ran. Until then our play had been somewhat disorganised; democratic mob rule generally dictating what games were played and, where it was necessary to decide specific roles in games, this would be achieved civilly using the time-honoured democratic methods of 'Who's Got the Cleanest Shoes' or 'Hot Potato'. Things were about to change.

Big Brother and a few of his friends went to see the film; I was deemed too young. They were so impressed by what they saw that they returned to The Woods for deep discussions on our need for change and organisation. I'm not sure how long these conflabs lasted, after all they could only have been about ten or eleven years old with short attention spans, but the agreement was that we kids needed to be organised along the lines of a naval ship. But first we needed a name. Bounty sounded good but had already been taken, so after much deliberation, and maintaining a confectionary theme, we became The Mars Bar Gang.

Next, we needed a home. We already had a favourite tree that we got into by climbing from an adjacent smaller one, so this would become our base; the larger tree was the Mars Bar and the smaller one The Milky Way. Finally, some structure. We would be organised along naval lines; as architects of the scheme, Big Brother and two of his friends were designated admirals of course. Various other ranks were dished out, I remember there being captains and midshipmen, and rank would dictate how high up the tree you were allowed to climb, a restriction put on hold when we played Monkey. At the bottom of the pecking order were two cabin boys who were only allowed in the lowest branches. I was one, by dint of being youngest, and my cousin the other, because she was a girl; she had the honour of being the only girl ever allowed to join the gang although, to be honest, she was probably tougher than most of the boys.

In order to join, it was necessary to undergo a series of, frankly quite unnerving, initiation tests. The Death Drop involved shinning what seemed miles up a particular tree, before hanging from a specific branch and dropping to the ground. I was so terrified that I hung for ages, watched by a rather bored Big Brother, until my arms could take it no longer and I plummeted earthward. But the euphoria felt on picking myself up from the ground, still alive, was incredible. In another test, the aspirant would join the end of a column of members queuing at the door to the Witch's garden; set in an old ivy-covered brick garden wall it definitely had a sinister air to it. One at a time, and painfully slowly, the gang would knock loudly and call out something like "Old Witch", then run away, so by the time the new kid got his turn the lady would be on her way, accompanied by her two barking dogs. Who knew what spell she would cast if she caught you? In retrospect I realise how horrible we were, both to this lady and the Old Geezer, harmless Oldies just going about life; there's no excuse, but it seemed the thing to do at the time. Actually, it didn't happen that much, and I truly hope they just saw us as annoying little buggers who were a bit of a nuisance.

Looking back, we were surprisingly compliant in accepting this new regime. In truth we probably were happy that someone else would make the key decisions such as what game to play next. We were a flock of sheep welcoming a border collie and the new setup didn't affect things that much; it was more a benign dictatorship. In later life I recognised the advanced thinking behind the organisation, in particular the use of promotions and demotions to encourage people to stay in line and not rock the boat.

Many years on I read William Golding's novel 'Lord of the Flies'. Written in 1954, this tells the story of a group of young boys marooned on an uninhabited tropical island. Initially they develop rules and a system of organisation, but with no external civilising influences i.e. adults, the situation rapidly deteriorates into violence and chaos. Who knows what sinister direction the Mars Bar would have taken had it not been for the mums calling us home for tea each night?

This high level of physical activity continued in schools where outdoor play was mandatory, except in the worst weather, and children of all abilities were

17

encouraged, some would say coerced, into taking part in sporting activities. At senior school, even bad weather was no excuse as we would splosh around a muddy cross-country course; not something I enjoyed, but it gave kids less bulky than myself and with greater stamina the chance to shine, and many perversely loved the pastime.

Unfortunately, state schools today are often unable to offer their pupils the same level of activity due to a number of factors; with a more crowded curriculum, reduced staffing levels and staff needing to spend far more time on administrative tasks than in our era, there is less time for sport during the school day, and fewer staff to support extra-curricular activities. Add to that the way that school playing fields have been sold off to raise cash, and the picture for sport in schools seems grim; I found a depressingly large number of articles on the subject and covering many years, like the 2019 report from the GMB union criticising the government for approving the sale of 215 school playing fields in England since 2010 during a time when childhood obesity has been recognised as a major issue. Presumably, that number is far greater today.

One final comment on encouraging outdoor unsupervised play. I understand how a steady flow of horrific news stories of paedophile attacks on children causes parents to be understandably protective and loath to let their kids out. We were regularly warned not to talk to, accept sweets from or go anywhere with, someone we didn't know, and there were always stories of strange people who would steal babies. We wouldn't usually go into The Woods alone. The threat was there then, and I have no idea the extent to which it has actually increased; either way, parents are far more cautious today. But caring too much can in itself be counterproductive, and I think many kids today lack the early-life experiences, risks and challenges that we faced, and which made us streetwise, increased our self-confidence and fostered independence in preparation for the adult world. That's my view and doubtless many will think it rubbish.

So, as some Oldies would have it, do the kids today not appreciate the benefit of fresh air and exercise? Are they different to us? First, I have to say that we didn't actually have a lot of options that seemed better than going to The Woods; the numbers turning out in the cold for a kickabout would probably have been considerably lower had Xbox been an alternative. Also, we had the green space on our doorstep, a luxury denied to many of today's kids; and many parents were happier then for their children to be out doing who knows what. Finally, schools now play a much smaller part in encouraging physical activity than they did. Maybe today's kids are no different; possibly they'd enjoy fresh air and exercise as much as we did, if only they had more encouragement, had access to more safe open spaces and got to breathe fresh air.

4.

Food, Glorious Food

Since coming down from the trees, us humans have proven ourselves highly resourceful in keeping fed. First, we foraged for tasty roots, leaves and fruit before discovering, at the expense of other animals sharing the planet, that not only could we kill them, but also some were nice to eat; double whammy. Other innovations followed as we discovered cooking meat made it tastier, and we could do things like crush wheat to make flour for bread. Change came along, but usually at a very slow pace; until recently that is.

In just six decades, we seem to have changed just about every aspect of eating. What, where, when and how we eat, together with how we source our food, have been subject to change almost beyond recognition. An army of scientists study the effect food has on our bodies, while others attempt to get optimal use from limited resources, including controversial subjects like genetically modifying food to increase crops or withstand pests and disease. Industries have grown up around instructing us on how and what to cook; miracle foods and supplements abound with diets claiming to achieve the perfect body; and all this is supported by a plethora of TV programmes instructing us how to do things better or telling "the truth" behind the food we eat; all this in turn generates countless books written by all types of 'celebrities'.

In my childhood all meals were cooked at home. Mum wasn't a keen or adventurous cook, but she always kept us well fed, no mean feat with three energetic young boys to keep going. We had a small fridge for things like milk, moo juice to us, which we seemed to drink by the gallon, but most food was kept in the pantry; a cool, ventilated, brick-built cupboard in the corner of the kitchen. The fridge had an icebox that I don't think ever held anything other than ice cubes, frozen peas, occasionally a pack of fish fingers and the rare block of ice cream. It was a short walk to the shops where all provisions were bought fresh on an as-needed basis. Nothing was wasted; there were no use by dates, so food was only thrown if it looked or smelled wrong. I remember an old grinder used to mince every bit of meat left from a Sunday joint to be magically turned into a cottage pie later in the week.

Our three meals a day were breakfast, dinner and tea, lunch or supper being for the posh people. Tea was the main cooked meal of the day, except for Sundays when we, along with a large part of the population, sat down to Sunday lunch, generally a roast. Through necessity, most food was sourced locally, with availability restricted by growing seasons. Salad was only available in summer months, apples and pears through autumn and winter and until stores ran out or rotted, root crops for stews became available as the days shortened; you get the picture.

A whole host of foods that we now take for granted were unheard of, or else "exotic" and too expensive for the average person. As a rare treat we might have a fruit cocktail or perhaps some peaches, but these would invariably be tinned, never fresh. Mangoes, kiwi fruits, nectarines, melons, all were either too exotic for us or even unheard of; bananas and grapes had been available in the UK for ages, but I can't remember them being commonplace in our household; peppers and aubergines never crossed the threshold; the list goes on and on.

The faithful spud provided carbohydrates in all our cooked meals. Boiled, mashed, roasted, chipped; it was the ultimate in versatility. Rice as a main course came much later, although we had been brought up on rice pudding, and I can't remember Mum ever cooking pasta or noodles. We didn't use spices, recognised a very short list of herbs; mint, sage and parsley to be precise, and garlic was that funny stuff popular with the French. Other than salt and pepper, little else was added to flavour food except the occasional sauce; brown, tomato, Worcestershire or salad cream.

Of course, all this is only based on memories from a small area of south-east England; anywhere more than fifty miles away would have seemed like a foreign country to us, and diets may well have been completely different. Haggis anyone?

As people started to travel further afield, so they came across new foods that would slowly make their way back into our kitchens. In 1971, after my 'O' levels, I travelled through Europe with three school friends. In Switzerland we uncovered two exciting new delicacies, muesli and yoghurt.

In my early years, the main competition to fresh food came in tins; baked beans, spaghetti (straight only, no hoops until 1969), fruit, Spam, corned beef and the like. I can't remember any frozen offerings other than fish fingers, the British version of which was introduced in 1955 by Birds Eye whose head office was nearby, so I suppose fish fingers and I have much in common. As technology advanced, and domestic freezers became more common, food companies saw the commercial opportunities; enter the ready meal. Products such as Findus Crispy Pancakes were launched specifically for these new kitchen gadgets while the likes of Viennetta and Arctic Roll joined Birdseye Fish Fingers on the shopping list.

The appeal of ready meals was also driven by other factors. Working days were becoming longer and more women were going out to work, although preparing the family meal was still considered mother's job, so finding time to prepare and cook fresh food became more of a challenge. Food companies latched onto this need for convenience in food preparation, and there was no stopping them as the market continually evolved to meet consumer demands. 1977 saw the launch in the UK of the ultimate convenience food, Golden Wonder's Pot Noodle; just add boiling water and bingo, dinner's ready. How else could the student population have survived?

Marks and Spencer launched its ready-made Chicken Kiev in 1979, ushering in a new age of chilled, rather than frozen food, thus giving the consumer the option of fresher prepared meals. Demand continued to rise, boosted further by technology; in the 80s, microwaves became a common fixture in the home, drastically reducing cooking times. Changing lifestyles and effective advertising continues to drive the demand for convenience foods ever upwards. Food companies accused of producing junk food now go to great lengths to produce food that they claim is healthy, with ranges low in fat, salt, sugar and so on. There are meals for vegetarians and consumers with specific dietary needs. According to figures from market research company Kantar Worldpanel, the British now buy around 3.5 million ready meals a day.

Advertising has played a huge part in the development of this market. Remember the 60s when Cadbury launched Smash instant mashed potato? The response was underwhelming until 1974 when the Smash Martians arrived on our TV screens and sales rocketed; if you don't know them, they can be found on YouTube. The power of advertising has now reached the point where the government is continually changing policy as to what can be advertised, and when, in an attempt to reduce the demand for junk food.

Eating out was considered a luxury; a small number of restaurants catered for the relatively rich, but for anyone else who fancied a bite to eat, options were limited. I remember two local fish and chip shops and a few pubs that served cooked meals, but generally their menus comprised crisps, possibly a sandwich or pickled eggs. There was a coffee bar over the Sweet Shop, I have no idea when it came or went, but in the sixties it had a reputation as a den of iniquity, frequented by beatniks who were weird enough to prefer coffee to tea. Then there was the greasy spoon café, a bikers' haunt, and at some point we got our own burger joint, a Wimpy, where we often gathered in my early teens.

There were doubtless other eateries, but I can't remember them. As kids, a great treat was to be taken to The Kings Head on the Hampton Court side of Kingston Bridge for a meal of chicken and chips. To our delight, the landlord would come over and regale us with outrageous tales while encouraging us to eat with our hands like Henry VIII; not an approach of which Mum really approved.

By the late 60s things were moving on fast; pubs expanded their food offerings with more exciting options like the ubiquitous chicken in the basket, and our first steak house chain, Bernie Inns, was expanding. The height of food chic was now prawn cocktail followed by steak and chips, all finished off with Black Forest gateau. If this wasn't sufficiently stylish, you could throw in a bottle of Blue Nun Liebfraumilch.

Since those days, the number of pubs serving food, and the variety of food on offer, has grown hugely. The Bernie Inns success story generated competition, first from Beefeater and then Harvester. A step change came with the Licensing Act 1988 which allowed pubs to open all day, giving a big boost to the industry and also launching the all-day Sunday roast revolution, carveries and all, that remains so popular today. Gastro pubs took off in the 90s and in 2001, for the first time, a pub was awarded a Michelin star. Times have changed, although personally I am not so sure about this. I like my pubs to be pubs; they sell beer, and while there is room for good food alongside good beer, when the quality of the wine list is more important than that of the ale, things have gone too far.

Google Maps suggests that around my old hometown there are now over 40 restaurants and pubs selling food of some sort where once there was just a few. Compared to my youth, the range of food on offer is mind-boggling; along with traditional British fare you can now get Thai, Tapas, Indian, Argentine, Chinese, Italian, burgers and more. Truly cosmopolitan.

The volume and variety of food now available to us would have been impossible without major technological advances and it is now economically viable to transport fresh food from around the world; in 1955 most of our food was produced domestically, yet we now import around 50%. But all this variety doesn't come without cost. Transporting food releases carbon dioxide and other greenhouse gases into the atmosphere, adding to pollution, and it has been suggested that food transported by plane can generate 100 times more emissions than other modes of transport, so relying on home produce makes more sense. Except… it's not that easy. For example, importing tomatoes from Spain in the winter creates a smaller carbon footprint than heating a British greenhouse to grow our own.

Local food production is not without cost to our environment either. Generally speaking, British farming is intensive and highly mechanised, placing much of our flora and fauna under threat, or rendering it already extinct. As land use is intensified, not only are natural habitats like hedgerows and marshland destroyed, but also wetlands are drained, and the use of agrochemicals is increased. Our wildlife simply cannot survive if we poison or take away its food and destroy its habitats. But farmers aren't out to deliberately destroy our environment, this is just collateral damage from their drive for greater productivity and profit. Reversals can be achieved by, for example, banning the use of specific chemicals, and British farmers now use about a third less pesticides than they did in 1983; or through government schemes encouraging farmers to leave areas of their farms wild, but I fear we are fighting a losing battle.

While food is essential to our existence, both how it is produced and the way it is sourced can create risks to our wellbeing. To make food last longer, taste better or look more attractive, producers are continually adding magic ingredients that are not necessarily good for us. A host of food scientists spend their time analysing this or that additive before dire warnings hit the front pages advising us on things to avoid. Unfortunately, no sooner does one bunch come out with a story than others publish information rubbishing the original theory or taking us down another road. Remember when, having been warned of the evils of sugar, many consumers turned to products containing aspartame instead, only to be told that 'research suggests' aspartame might be carcinogenic; so which do you prefer to risk, diabetes or cancer?

The list of what may be harmful to us seems endless and advice is continually changing. Another example: parents who followed advice and dutifully fed their children low fat everything, subsequently found their kids suffered from illnesses arising from calcium deficiencies. So what's the answer? Frankly, I haven't a clue, but something I heard on TV might be worth considering; someone said, "ask yourself if this is something your grandparents ate, if the answer is 'yes' it's probably good for you". Hearing that suggestion, many people will go off on one, explaining all the deficiencies of the old days, but I don't think it's too far off the mark. Our grandparents ate less and had a diet dictated by the seasons and a different lifestyle; maybe that's the way forward.

If you're the worrying kind, not only are you having sleepless nights over what is and isn't good for you, but also there is the continual risk that your food can somehow become contaminated. In my lifetime there have been a number of scares, including the discovery that the level of mercury, which can cause serious health issues for humans, tends to be high in tuna; the suggestion in 1988 by junior Health Minister Edwina Currie, that most of the egg production in UK was infected with salmonella; the spread of bovine spongiform encephalopathy or Mad Cow disease; various foot and mouth outbreaks; and a scandal in 2013 when frozen beefburgers sold in several British and Irish supermarkets were found to contain horse DNA. This final issue highlighted the problems of tracing ingredients within a global supply chain, when a study carried out by University of Surrey scientists concluded that ingredients for one Burger King hamburger could be sourced from some 200 different suppliers located around the world, making it very hard to identify the origin of any problem.

Not only has food itself changed, but in recent years it has also given birth to a whole array of peripheral activities. Gone are the days when Fanny Craddock, dressed in twinset and pearls, was the only television personality to provide cookery instruction, TV cookery shows presented by innumerable 'celebrities', covering all aspects of cookery and all tastes, are now available for viewing at just about any time of day or night. While educational, presenters try to entertain and be 'characters', and of course a number of the programmes are competitions for added appeal; Great British Bake Off anyone? There are programmes that show us the factories and farms where our food is mass-produced and explain what actually goes into the food we eat, and if that isn't enough a whole variety of programmes advise us on how to eat better and get fitter. And of course all these programmes produce books and Internet sites for further consumption. Phew.

Though not, strictly speaking, food, I can't finish this chapter without a brief reference to an important indulgence of my childhood years, sweets. There were two sweetshops within easy walking distance of home and we would regularly be sent on errands to the nearest, the Sweet Shop, mainly to buy cigarettes and matches for the parents; my, how times have changed. On these trips we were unlikely to be buying sweets for ourselves, but that wouldn't stop us staring longingly at the cornucopia of confectionery delights on display. Young customers were catered for with the Penny Tray, a variety of sweets that you could buy in low volume. For one old penny, you could get four blackjacks or four fruit salads, a penny chew or a liquorice stick. There were Flying Saucers made from rice paper and filled with sherbet, and foam shrimps. Four aniseed balls cost a penny, as did a single gobstopper. Bubble gum was popular with the kids, though not with the parents who seemed not to appreciate the effort needed to remove it from clothes and furniture.

Another sign of the times; you could buy a 10 pack of sweet cigarettes, white with a red end, to pretend you were smoking. In the same vein, there was Spanish Gold sweet tobacco, and chocolate smoker's outfits, comprising moulded chocolate in the shape of cigars, pipes and the like, were popular at Christmas time.

When we did have cash, it would often take ages to decide what to buy, but the people in the sweetshop understood our dilemma and would wait patiently. If you were feeling slightly more extravagant you might splash out on a packet of sweets; Spangles and Polos both came in a variety of flavours, then there were Fruit Gums and Fruit Pastilles. Love Hearts were popular but, of course, the messages would always be a source of mockery for us boys. We were impressed when we first came across Pez sweets; lozenges that could be bought in packs of twelve, the best part being that you loaded them into a plastic dispenser and popped one out when needed. It got even more exciting when they started making the dispensers topped with heads of characters such as Santa Claus, Popeye, Mickey Mouse and Donald Duck. We're talking high-end merchandise here, but we all had to have one.

A real treat would be to buy a quarter pound of sweets from one or more of the many big glass jars behind the counter. You may have only bought two ounces if you were short of cash, but either was an event. Again, it would take ages to decide what to buy, but eventually the merchandise would be carefully weighed out on the shop scales as you eagerly watched on, hoping they might throw in one or two extras because they liked you. The sweets were then tipped into a white paper bag; square for the larger portion, triangular and cone-shaped for the smaller. The top would be screwed up to stop any fallout and, having handed over your pennies, you left excitedly nursing your purchase. There was always plenty of choice, but I particularly remember humbugs, rhubarb and custard, sherbet lemons, toffees of various flavours, barley sugars, Everton mints, pineapple chunks, tea cakes, sour apples and pear drops. Even now, come Christmas or my birthday, Daughter will regularly address the present issue with bags of old-fashioned sweets, and I'm happy.

On occasion we would find ourselves desperate for sweets but with no cash; that didn't stop us. At the time, if you bought a bottle of fizzy stuff from one of the sweetshops you paid three old pence deposit for the bottle, to be refunded on its return. We could never understand such profligacy but, after consuming their refreshing beverage, people would often just throw the bottles into a large patch of stinging nettles and brambles in The Woods; we simply had to recover them and bingo, we had assets. We weren't always successful and tended to suffer a multitude of scratches and stings, but that was a small price to pay. As another source of income, we also believed that if we took a grey squirrel tail to the police station, we would receive a two-shilling bounty, nearer £2 in today's money. This isn't quite as mad as it sounds; apparently there was such a scheme, introduced in an attempt to control the number of grey squirrels at the time, but it was stopped in 1957 so we would have been disappointed had we ever managed to get one.

If you look hard enough today you can still find virtually all the sweets we adored in our childhood, but as suppliers are few and far between, I assume there is limited demand and that tastes have changed with the kids preferring newer creations.

So, food-wise are things better now than they were then? I believe that in my youth our diets were probably healthier, food production had far less impact on the environment and, through necessity, far more people knew how to cook, which I consider a good thing. In many ways things seem far worse today. The way in which we farm the land and source our food is causing significant environmental impact, and what we eat is largely dictated by aggressive marketing, resulting in a dependency on ready-made meals, full of who-knows-what, causing untold damage not only to the health of the consumer, but also to their environment. Much of the population consider themselves unable to cook, which increases this dependency and takes away the chance to eat healthier while saving money. And yet... I cannot pretend that we would not have loved to have access to the variety of food now readily available today.

5.

Celebrating the Gogglebox

Technology has been the driving force behind many changes that society has undergone in my lifetime. While many innovations have been short-lived one, television, seems always to have been there. My life has never been controlled by TV schedules, and I assumed that this chapter would be just a short recognition of the Box before getting on with the main story; how wrong I was. No sooner did I start than I found myself wallowing in nostalgia, the result being one of the longest chapters of the book. So, join me in a brief trawl through our televisual past; but if that sounds boring just move on to the next chapter and, like a good soap, you'll find you haven't really missed anything.

Television broadcasting in the UK started in 1932 but it was the Queen's coronation in 1953, the first time such an event could be watched live, that it really took off; some 20.4 million people watched on, although there were only 2.7 million television sets at the time. The Broadcasters' Audience Research Board says that now, around 26.7 million UK households have a TV set and only 1.6 million don't. Around one million households have 5 or more!

Excitingly new, the 1952 viewing experience was considerably different to that of today, with viewers gathering around and squinting to interpret grainy, black and white pictures on a very small screen; the Bush TV22, an inexpensive and popular television at the time, had a 9-inch screen.

My childhood memories are of a black and white TV, screen size probably around 20 inches, with a tuning knob that manually clicked around to find the station required. The design showed some foresight though; the dial had about a dozen different settings although there were only two stations available at the time; the BBC and Independent Television, ITV, the UK's first commercial television station, launched in 1955. A third station came in 1964 with the launch of BBC2, aimed at more highbrow audiences. There then followed a wait of eighteen years before Channel 4 arrived on the scene.

The viewing box itself has evolved considerably from those days. Valve technology replaced by solid state; the introduction of colour transmission in 1967; digital broadcasts replacing analogue which, with various types of flat screen replacing Cathode Ray technology, brought ever higher picture quality and the ability to produce larger screens, with 43 inch now a fairly average size and screens of 59 to 65 inches commonplace. And how did we ever manage without a remote control?

All this development means that the very identity of the television set has become blurred as people may now use the same device to play games, view photos, listen to music and browse the Internet as well as 'watch TV'. But it's not only the viewing box that's changed. The only way we could receive TV signals was through an aerial; programmes were financed either through license fees or advertising on commercial stations; the broadcasters were in charge of what you could see and when. But that all changed with the arrival of Sky.

Following the UK launch of SkyTV in February 1989, sales remained lacklustre until, in 1992, it bought exclusive rights to broadcast the FA Premier League. This had a huge impact, not only on the landscape of UK TV broadcasting but also on the fortunes of top clubs and players and encouraged Sky to move into other sports including cricket, rugby and tennis.

Introducing digital transmission in 1998, Sky Digital offered 140 channels with basic interactive services leading to further innovations such as recording on hard drives and the ability to pause programme viewing. Their programmes have evolved from an uninspiring start to encompass internationally acknowledged offerings such as 'The Simpsons', 'Stargate', '24', 'Game of Thrones', 'Atlanta', 'Boardwalk Empire' and 'Mad Men'. Personally, I am ambivalent about Sky; I dislike the fact that sporting events once available to anyone with a TV license were suddenly restricted to those who can afford to pay, but I accept that the superior quality of at least some of our viewing and the huge increase in viewing options is a direct result of Sky's success. According to Wikipedia, UK viewers can now access, via a variety of distribution media, more than 480 channels as well as on-demand content.

So, since 1955 there have been huge technical changes in the world of TV, but what about the audience and their tastes? Established by Royal Charter in 1927 as a public service broadcaster, the BBC enjoyed a monopoly position in both radio and television; its role was to inform, educate and entertain the public. Television broadcasting started in 1932, with the emphasis very much on informing and educating. It was the 50s before entertainment became a major role, and the British viewer was hooked; with growing popularity and limited choice, audience figures reached a level that modern day broadcasters can only dream of; 'The Morecambe and Wise Christmas Show', for example, would attract huge audiences, 28 million viewers in 1977. The largest television audience recorded in the UK was the 1966 World Cup final, viewed by some 32.3 million.

In my early days, with only two stations and very limited broadcasting hours, television was not the first port of call if I had time to kill and the weather kept me indoors. Still, I would have watched it most days. My first experiences of TV almost exclusively involved puppet shows. The aim of 'Watch With Mother', which started in 1950, was to provide education and entertainment specifically for very small children. Broadcast every weekday at around 4 o'clock, there were five different titles, one for each day of the week.

Monday's offering was 'Picture Book', with stories of various characters and their adventures like The Jolly Jack Tars sailing to Bottle Island in search of the Talking Horse. Tuesday was 'Andy Pandy' and on Wednesday the 'Flowerpot Men', Bill and Ben took to the screen with episodes usually involving some mischief and, as the two stars were identical the main question at the end was always "Was it Bill or was it Ben?" I didn't really care, but obviously it stuck as even today, when trying to establish fault, people of a certain age can be heard saying "was it Bill or was it Ben?" But perhaps the most famous aspect of the show was their language, Oddle Poddle, that would become a part of youth culture for years to come as in the joke; Bill and Ben walked into a pub, Bill said "oddle pop tooky rap", to which Ben replies "I'll get these Bill, you're drunk".

35

Thursday was 'Rag, Tag and Bobtail' about a hedgehog, a mouse and a rabbit, and the week ended with 'The Woodentops', a type of sociology lecture for the young; Daddy Woodentop was always busy doing men's work in the field or workshop while Mummy Woodentop stayed in the kitchen, sometimes aided by Mrs Scrubbit. There were also the Woodentop twins and a few animals including Spotty Dog, with his strange mechanical walk. Old folk today can occasionally still be seen imitating this, when not talking Oddle Poddle of course.

That was the toddler slot; offerings for slightly older children were available albeit still in the puppet world. I was particularly fond of 'Four Feather Falls', the adventures of Sheriff Tex Tucker whose four magic feathers gave his dog and his horse the power of speech, and made his guns swivel and fire automatically whenever he was in danger. Tex would thwart dastardly crimes by villains like Pedro and Fernando the Mexican bandits, Big Bad Ben and Red Scalp, the renegade indian chief involved in gun-running for enemy tribes. All exciting stuff and by current standards, not very politically correct.

Other stars included Lenny The Lion, a large wide-eyed ventriloquist's puppet who couldn't roll his 'r's and regularly put his paw to his head sighing "Aw, don't embawass me!" Glove puppet Sooty never actually said anything, he just squeaked and communicated through his operator Harry Corbett, played the xylophone or did magic with oofle dust and spells of "Izzy wizzy, let's get busy". Enid Blyton's Noddy, was one of the first puppet shows on the new ITV in 1955.

I rather liked two slightly quirky shows, although none of the others could really be called normal. 'Torchy, The Battery Boy' commuted between earth and Topsy-

Turvy Land, and 'The Adventures of Twizzle'. The latter starred a character created from a broom. Both were about mistreated toys, a seemingly common theme, and they were created by Gerry Anderson who went on to create 'Supercar', 'Stingray', 'Thunderbirds', 'Captain Scarlet' and the like using Supermarionation, the electronic system that made the puppets move in a more realistic way, supposedly.

But I was growing up, and by the age of about five found real life stuff more appealing; I would sit glued to the exploits of heroes like Robin Hood, made at the local studio, William Tell, Zorro and The Lone Ranger to name but four; swashbuckling yarns where good always prevailed and baddies were larger than life.

"It's Friday. It's five o'clock. It's Crackerjack!" So began possibly the UK's most popular children's' television ever. Broadcast live from 1955, 'Crackerjack!' included music and comedy acts and competitive games for teams of children; Crackerjack pencils were given out on the show and owning one really boosted your street cred. 'Blue Peter' came to our screens slightly later in 1958, catering for an audience of five to eight-year-olds who were growing out of 'Watch with Mother' but considered too young for 'Crackerjack'.

Every Saturday afternoon Dad's family would gather around Nan's house. There would be chat, possibly a beer, sandwiches, orange squash and biscuits for the kids. Grandstand would be on the television, and Pop would check the football results to see if he had won a fortune on the pools. Then, in November 1963, something humungous happened; Doctor Who burst on the scene. The first episode was creepy, but nothing compared to the second, when the Daleks arrived to exterminate the world.

People often talk of where they were when they heard of important events like Kennedy's assassination; folk my age know exactly where they were when earthlings got their first view of the Daleks, we were cowering behind the sofa. They were terrifying but irresistible, and Saturday afternoons would never be the same.

I got my first taste of grown up television in the 60s. It was inevitable that action stuff like 'Danger Man', 'The Saint', 'The Avengers', 'Callan' and 'Z Cars' had the highest appeal. A steady flow of US programmes made their way to our shores too; 'The Man From Uncle', a flashy, high budget production compared to those of the BBC, was one of my favourites.

Westerns were popular and had been for years before I was born. We had already cut our teeth on 'The Lone Ranger', marvelling as our hero, masked like Zoro, and his pal Tonto travelled the Wild West righting wrongs. The theme music was 'March of the Swiss Soldiers' from the William Tell Overture, slightly confusing to youngsters recognising it as, less surprisingly, also being the theme from ITV drama 'William Tell'.

Westerns appealed to all ages. On Saturday at Nan's, a little after our weekly dose of 'Doctor Who', we would turn over to 'the other side' and watch 'Bonanza'; exploits of the Cartwright family in the Ponderosa ranch. To this day, mention cowboys in a pub full of Oldies and chances are someone will sing the Bonanza theme tune, point skyward and yell "burning map". There were other good westerns like 'Gunsmoke' and 'Laramie'; 'Rawhide' introduced Clint Eastwood to the world in the role of drover Rowdy Yates and had yet another unforgettable theme tune "....Ride 'em in, cut 'em out, cut 'em out, ride 'em in, rawhide......Yah". They don't make them like they used to.

Science fiction dramas had their appeal too. In the 1950s and early 60s, dealing with threats from hostile extra-terrestrial aliens was all in a day's work for Professor Quatermass who would also take an occasional pop at how science can be hijacked by the military and governments. US import 'The Invaders', which started with a deep voice warning "The Aliens are coming!" arrived in 1967. I suspect that, post-Covid, there will be a host of programmes similar to 70s series 'Survivors', the premise of which being that, following the accidental release of a deadly virus and its rapid spread through growing international travel, most of the human race were wiped out leaving a few to face the problems of surviving without clean water, electricity or other modern amenities.

Soap operas are defined by Wikipedia as 'radio or television serials dealing especially with domestic situations and frequently characterised by melodrama and sentimentality.' British audiences lap them up. In their early years shows like 'Coronation Street', 'Emmerdale Farm' and 'Eastenders' revolved around minor day-to-day problems that we could all identify with, but as time passed they have evolved into high drama with storylines including murders, assaults, drug taking, racism, incest; you name it and the soaps will have a story about it, often getting criticism for including sensitive subjects before the watershed, a concept introduced in 1964 to restrict the time when harmful or offensive material can be broadcast.

Numerous soaps have covered specific walks of life. 'Emergency Ward 10', 'Dr Finlay's Casebook', 'Casualty' and others for the medical world. 'Eldorado' concerned the exploits of expats in a Spanish resort while the trials and tribulations of running a motel provided the theme for 'Crossroads'. The police have had their share with offerings such as 'The Bill' and 'Heartbeat' with its added twist of 60s nostalgia, while life in a comprehensive school was the idea behind 'Waterloo Road'. If all this home-grown stuff isn't enough, we also imported foreign offerings such as 'Neighbours' and 'Home and Away'.

Personally, I've always been a little bemused by these programmes. Early Corrie, in black and white of course, baffled my young brain with the likes of hairnet-wearing Ena Sharples supping stout in the snug bar while gossiping about her neighbours in a strange accent; and for a while, some twenty-five years later, I was happy to watch the antics of Dirty Den et al in 'Eastenders', but the appeal soon waned. Still, I admit I am in the minority, as the popularity of soaps remains resilient through changing times, with 'East Enders' and 'Coronation Street' dominating UK viewing figures.

Comedy has played a big part in TV's popularity, and like everything else this has changed considerably over the years. Sitcoms, a sort of small-scale soap played for laughs, took off in 1956 with 'Hancock's Half Hour', originally a radio show; a number of classics still command significant audiences today, decades after they were first aired. Sitcoms have been produced in a hugely diverse range of settings and to varying degrees often include references to, and comment on, more serious social topics.

The 60s brought programmes such as 'Dad's Army', poking fun at the wartime Home Guard as Captain Mainwairing, Corporal Jones et al valiantly trained in preparation to repel the Hun in the event of invasion; 'The Rag Trade', based in the machine shop of a clothing factory, satirised the growing strength of the trades unions with shop steward Reg Varney calling a strike at the drop of a hat with the words "Everybody out!"

'Steptoe and Son' was first broadcast in 1962; to me it just provided 30 minutes of light entertainment, so I was a little surprised to find an article on the BFI website describing it as one of the most famous and influential programmes ever broadcast on British television. The show had a huge audience, and apparently when it was due to go out on election night in 1966, Harold Wilson asked the BBC to reschedule it for fear that Labour voters would stay in to watch it rather than vote. Apparently, Steptoe broke down the boundaries between comedy and tragedy while tackling British attitudes to class, sex and race, and its themes of disappointment, failure and embarrassment remain relevant to this day. Well, I can only admit that for many years I watched the show just for laughs, totally unaware that I was witnessing such cultural profundity.

As with Steptoe, the significance of 'Till Death Us Do Part' went over my head in the early years. At the heart of the show, Alf Garnett ranted against everything he hated, which was just about everything; he had no time for foreigners, socialists, women, scroungers and so on. Writer Johnny Speight and actor Warren Mitchell apparently loathed his character; their aim was to air his views in a way that held them up to ridicule so that nobody could take them seriously. But things are never that simple, and it transpired that many of the audience tuned in for the very reason that they shared Alf's views and he was their hero. Tricky.

Sitcoms continued evolving through the 70s. In 2000 a BFI poll of television industry professionals and critics suggested 'Fawlty Towers' was Britain's greatest TV show of the 20th Century; not bad considering there were only twelve episodes. Remember Manuel's Siberian hamster or the phrases "don't mention the war" and "I know nothing"?

Inspiration for sitcoms was unbounded. There's nothing funny about prison, yet 'Porridge' is a classic; the escapades of Fletcher reluctantly guiding naïve first-timer Godber safely through his incarceration were tempered with occasional more sobering incidents or quotes causing even Fletch to become a little depressed and philosophical at times. The winning formula behind 'The Fall and Rise of Reginald Perrin' was another sensitive subject as it tracked Reggie's mid-life crisis, nervous breakdown and eventual return; his increasing frustration with the rat-race of meaningless office life and tedious commuting struck a chord with many of us at the time.

'Citizen Smith' concerned the antics of urban guerrilla 'Wolfie' Smith, attempting to emulate his hero, Che Guevarra, by bringing true socialism to Britain through his revolutionary group, the Tooting Popular Front, and environmental awareness was behind 'The Good Life' as it gently ridiculed the suburban middle-class and their response to one of their own stocking their garden with chickens, goats and the like while aspiring to self-sufficiency in conservative Surbiton.

'Rising Damp', a comedy around three tenants of a dingy northern bedsit and their miserly, opinionated and bigoted landlord Rigsby, took a novel approach to racism with student Philip, a British African from Croydon, as the social and intellectual superior of the four. He claimed to be an African prince, son of a tribal chief, and while Rigsby regularly dished out racist barbs he put them down with merely a deep sigh, raised eyebrow or "Oh dear Rigsby". His superiority was never in doubt, as when he advised gullible Rigsby, desperate to earn the attentions of lovelorn spinster Miss Jones, that to win the love of a woman, men from his tribe would burn wood of the love tree outside her door. He then gave Rigsby a piece of his broken wardrobe, claiming it was from the love tree; Miss Jones was not impressed.

Tuesday 8th September 1981 saw the birth of a national treasure as the first episode of 'Only Fools and Horses' was aired and Derek Edward Trotter, Del Boy, purveyor of hooky merchandise from the back of his yellow Robin Reliant, arrived on the scene. For twenty-two years we lapped up seven series and numerous Christmas specials concerning the life and times of this dodgy market trader from Peckham, together with his family and friends including Rodney, Grandad, Uncle Albert and his Nag's Head drinking buddies Trigger, Boycie and Denzil plus many more. Del's views on the local constabulary were reflected in regular references to Roy Slater who always grassed on his mates at school before going on to join the police; and his unique version of French, and ability to twist the English language, are legend.

Del wasn't the only one with the great lines though; remember Trigger explaining how he received a council award for using the same broom for twenty years even though it had had 17 new heads and 14 new handles? Or when Boycie, on a visit to Del's flat in Nelson Mandela House, apologised for not staying long but explained that he was worried about his beloved Mercedes parked outside, saying that, on this estate, if a Jumbo jet flew too low over the estate, the residents would probably pinch its wheels.

Another classic from this era is the timeless 'Yes Minister/Prime Minister', brilliantly mocking the friction between MPs and the civil service who both think they run the country. Produced between 1980 and 1988 topics raised at the time are still relevant today: the need for new hospitals, arms sales, corruption, fears of an encroaching Big Brother society, university funding and the politics of oil are just some of the subjects covered. The air of hypocrisy and cynicism sounds so current as when, in answer to Bernard's suggestion that citizens of a democracy have a right to know, Sir Humphrey explains that, to the contrary, they have a right to be ignorant and thus not be complicit in questionable actions taken by their government.

Combining comedy with tragedy, the final episode of 'Blackadder' ended with an incredibly poignant scene where the main characters leave the trenches to attack the enemy. The picture is frozen as presumably they are all going to their death.

Sitcoms covering just about every topic imaginable continued to roll out through the 80s and 90s. 'The Young Ones' reflected on the trials and tribulations of a motley trio of students while 'Red Dwarf' was set on the mining spaceship of the same name, and saw Dave Lister emerge from three million years of suspended animation to find himself the only remaining human whose only company was the ship's computer, Holly, a hologram of former bunkmate Rimmer and Cat, a cool dude evolved from Lister's pregnant cat over the previous three million years.

'The New Statesman' concerned the shenanigans of ruthless Conservative MP Alan B'stard. It seemed a bit over the top at times, but following recent events within our government, culminating in the defenestration of Liz Truss, maybe it wasn't so far from the truth. There was 'Absolutely Fabulous', and 'Father Ted' took a pot at religion, something done more gently in 'The Vicar of

Dibley', while the trials and tribulations of growing old provided subject matter for 'Last of the Summer Wine', and 'One Foot In The Grave'.

The list of popular British sitcoms seems endless and yet we still found time to import a considerable number from America. Shows I remember from my childhood include 'Bilko', 'The Munsters', 'The Beverley Hillbillies', 'The Addams Family' and 'Bewitched'. In my teenage and early adult years there was 'Mash' and 'Cheers'; the 90s brought us 'Frasier' and 'Friends' and into the new millennium we have had the likes of 'The Big Bang Theory', 'Scrubs', 'Two and a Half Men', and 'How I met Your Mother'. The message remains that the British love of sitcoms seems insatiable and while subjects may change with the times, many are ageless.

But sitcoms are only a part of a huge range of comedy programmes. In the 60s and 70s shows comprising a variety of sketches were popular; these tended to be fronted by comedians who, with their infectious catchphrases, became household names: Tommy Cooper, "Not like that. Like that!"; Bruce Forsyth, "Nice to see you, to see you nice!"; Frankie Howerd, "Titter ye not!"; Dick Emmery, "Ooh you are awful…but I like you!" and Ken Dodd, "How tickled I am!", to name but a few. The most popular was without doubt duo Morecambe and Wise whose Christmas Show was watched by half the population each Christmas night from 1969 to 1977. Famous guests lined up to appear, often as the butt of the duo's jokes, and to this day both weekly shows and Christmas specials are repeated regularly.

There were also more surreal offerings. In 1963, radio show 'The Goons' was reinvented as a rather bizarre television puppet show, 'The Telegoons', bringing to TV

Spike Milligan, Harry Secombe and Peter Sellars. 'Do Not Adjust Your Set' was a curious children's show, soon adopted by adults; I was twelve or thirteen at the time and remember the adventures of a young David Jason and his battle of wits with the evil Mrs. Black, aided in his quest by the Mrs. Black Detector, an inverted black umbrella. There were odd animations by Terry Gilliam and bizarre sketches acted out by the likes of Eric Idle, Terry Jones, and Michael Palin who, in October 1969, were main players in the launch of 'Monty Python's Flying Circus' the television phenomenon that, through four series over five years, would change the face of comedy on British television.

I was 14 when Python arrived, and can clearly remember sitting in front of the Box completely flummoxed by what was going on. Dad would loudly air his opinion, questioning how this rubbish could possibly be called comedy before suddenly, at the drop of a hat, we would all be convulsed with laughter, hardly able to breathe for minutes. We were often eating at the time, and offerings like the Dead Parrot sketch and the Flying Sheep sketch genuinely caused serious risk of choking. To this day, I can't fathom how a sketch performed by a highbrow group of Oxbridge graduates, playing a bunch of boozy Australian philosophers, all bar one called Bruce, while singing of the drinking habits of renowned philosophers, managed to achieve such widespread appeal.

First broadcast in the UK in September 1976, 'The Muppets' were an instant success. Kermit and crew were on at 7 o'clock every Friday night and the likes of Miss Piggie and the Swedish Chef would be quoted ad nauseum later down the pub. Their influence lives on; just the other day I was talking with a friend when he commented, "we must be getting old, we're sounding like Statler and Wardorf".

But the BBC's original role was mainly to inform and educate the public, and over the years we have been spoilt with a huge variety of factual programmes. Independent channels have tended to follow suit, although to a lesser degree as their success criteria tend to be based on viewing figures ahead of subject matter.

The main stations all have news programmes, essential adult viewing for many, broadcast a few times a day with schedules set in stone. The advent of 24-hour news and the plethora of channels now available means that viewers can tune into significant events around the world and watch them unwind in real time; although political or local bias and censorship might mean the view given is somewhat distorted.

We have also had excellent current affairs documentary series such as 'This World', 'Dispatches', 'World in Action' and 'This Week', but when it comes to consistently good investigative reporting, the king of them all must be 'Panorama'. This BBC programme was first broadcast before I was even born, and continues to this day covering a huge range of subjects both home and abroad from political skullduggery to drug dealing, from the contaminated blood scandal to racism; the list is long. 'Panorama' is also remembered for a lighter story when, on April 1st 1957, they covered harvesting of spaghetti from the Italian spaghetti tree. At the time pasta was a novelty, and a surprisingly large number of people fell for the hoax.

More often than not, the first reason viewers turn to the TV is for entertainment and to escape from the drudgery of modern life, soaps notwithstanding. But educational programmes can also be popular. In my youth

I thoroughly enjoyed Tomorrow's World with its predictions of how the future would evolve. Some proved fairly accurate, but others were way off; by now cars should be rare as we all travel by jetpack. But producers soon realised that attracting audiences to a more serious or 'educational' programme needed something special. Showing stunning pictures of things not seen before is a start, but the real key is the presenter. They have learnt, as I did at school, that full audience attention is best achieved through a teacher who can perform rather than just churn out the facts; programmes need to be fronted by people who can gain a rapport with the audience, and there have been quite a few.

As a nation of animal lovers, the British were bound to fall for wildlife programmes and, thanks mainly to David Attenborough, this area of British TV has thrived. As a child I loved his 'Zoo Quest' and Johnny Morris's 'Animal Magic', but it was Attenborough's 'Life on Earth', first broadcast in 1979, that was the real game changer. Creative use of new technology and improved film stock meant viewers could see wildlife, some never before filmed, in their natural habitats, and all with hitherto unimaginable picture quality.

Like so many others, I sat mesmerised as Attenborough interacted with a friendly mountain gorilla family in Rwanda; throw in a low key, comfortable and informative commentary style and we had a new celebrity. There followed 'The Living Planet' and 'The Trials of Life' (remember amazing shots of killer whales hunting sealions?) completing a trilogy that set the standard for wildlife programmes to follow.

Attenborough went on to produce documentaries covering not only all major groups of animals on earth but also plants, all the while pushing technical barriers; low-light and infrared cameras used to reveal the behaviour of nocturnal mammals, macro photography recording for the first time the life of very small creatures, time-lapse photography to record the development of plants, advanced underwater photography, broadcasting using 4K picture quality and so on.

At the age of 96 Sir David, rightfully knighted in 1985, has not been idle; he has been a key player in raising awareness of environmental issues and the way humans are wrecking the world. For years, scientists have warned of the devastating impact of plastics on the environment, but interest rocketed globally after graphic examples were shown in detail on the BBC documentary 'Blue Planet II', presented and narrated by Attenborough.

Where Attenborough led others followed. In the 70s and early 80s, 'Bellamy on Botany', 'Bellamy's Britain' and 'Bellamy's Backyard Safari' were popular as David Bellamy attracted audiences on the subjects of botany, ecology and environmentalism. His enthusiasm and eccentric behaviour, as when surfacing from a river, head covered in weed, to explain the deposition of silt, captivated audiences.

For the past sixteen years we have avidly tuned into 'Springwatch', growing into 'Autumnwatch' and 'Winterwatch', to observe real-time events in the lives of animals around Britain. Once again, advances in technology have made these programmes possible, not only in the way images are captured in hitherto inaccessible places, but also in the way they are transmitted; viewers can now access the cameras over the Internet 24 hours a day, even when the programme is off air.

Since 1957, BBC's 'The Sky at Night' has been required viewing not only for astronomers, but for anyone interested in worlds outside of our own. The timing of the programme was fortuitous, as just a few months after its first transmission the Russians launched Sputnik, the world's first artificial satellite, marking the start of the space age and firing the starting pistol for the Russia vs America space race that would in turn give birth to many of the technical advances we take for granted today, like non-stick frying pans. Presented by Patrick Moore, monocle and all, from 1957 until his death in 2012 the show's popularity is, at least in part, down to his huge knowledge and obvious enthusiasm for the subject, plus his skill at explaining complex ideas in an easily understandable way. He holds the record as the longest running host of the same TV programme ever.

Astronomy on TV was given a boost with the arrival of Brian Cox, another hugely impressive presenter with an engaging smile and the ability to impart fascinating nuggets of information in easily digestible chunks in a way that totally captivates his audience. His BBC television series, 'Wonders of the Solar System', followed by 'Wonders of the Universe' and 'Wonders of Life', gained large audiences making this Lancashire physicist a household name. Since 2011, with comedian Dara O Briain and various assorted celebrities he has presented 'Stargazing Live', a sort of astronomic version of 'Springwatch', that has further grabbed the attention of a whole range of new viewers.

A large number of programmes have brought 'academic' subjects to our front rooms. I particularly like those of a historical bent, and through 1973 sat glued to all twenty-six episodes of the ground-breaking series 'The

50

World at War' which covered many varied aspects of the war from the perspective of both military and civilian participants from all sides. Judging by the current number of programmes on offer, interest in history seems to be growing with programmes hosted by a long list of presenters like Neil Oliver, Andrew Marr, Dan Snow, Mary Beard, Simon Schama, Lucy Worsley, Tony Robinson and many more. Keep it up team.

More modern developments have seen a surge in programmes around the domestic scene, crafts, home improvements, gardening and the like. Our list of television celebrities now includes numerous chefs, gardeners, home designers, crafting experts, builders and so on. Variations on the theme of talent shows abound with the likes of 'X Factor', 'Strictly Come Dancing' and 'The Great British Bakeoff' all of which I can understand, if not particularly enjoy. But I remain puzzled by the appeal of 'reality' shows where millions of people tune in regularly to watch a bunch of uninteresting people doing uninteresting things. Still, they are incredibly popular so I suppose I must be missing the point.

When I started this exercise I had to ask myself 'why?' Why waste my time looking back over things that, in the greater scheme of things were, frankly, pretty trivial. I would definitely have put television in that category; I've never considered myself a great fan and feel sorry for the people whose lives are dominated by TV. Yet looking back has been a real eye-opener; the subject is huge, and I have only scratched the surface. I took television for granted, a source of entertainment when needed, nothing more; yet I must have watched an awful lot of it, and never thought of the impact it might have on our society.

We live in a democracy where free thought and free speech are taken for granted, but messages received through television programmes, whether overt or more subliminal, can seriously affect audience views and opinions. Over the years, the BBC has regularly been accused of political bias, the government has occasionally taken steps to stop broadcasts, and controversies regularly arise over topics such as sex, violence, religion and race regarding not only what can and should be shown when, but also how if at all, views can be expressed. To some, free speech should only be allowed provided it doesn't offend anyone, yet someone always seems to be offended.

Looking back I realise the power that television has to shape minds and opinions, not only through factual programmes but also in 'entertainment'. This issue is still with us and may be more of a concern now as audiences have the option to focus on channels promoting particular messages and ideologies.

But let's bring this ramble to a conclusion; is television better or worse today than in my youth? The technology behind what was once the simple television set has advanced in leaps and bounds and in many ways is unrecognisable from where we started; we can now watch an enormous variety of programmes, old and new, from all over the world, 24 hours a day, through a huge variety of channels. From that perspective the world of television is far superior to that of my day. However, commercial concerns are now the main driver for most broadcasting and I think that in many ways this has devalued the quality of today's programmes when compared to those of the past. All a matter of taste of course and probably, dependent upon your age, a draw I think.

6.

Memories of Primary School

My memory may have blurred with passing years, but for me I think school was generally enjoyable. School life started at the age of four, when Mum would take me on the back seat of her bike to a kindergarten, a mile or two from home. I went on weekday mornings, staying Wednesday afternoons to develop my latent artistic talents that the headmistress had identified and felt should be encouraged; to this day those talents have remained dormant. I wore school uniform and can remember being a sunflower in a school show.

Aged five, it was time for infants' school, a bit further away and involving more travel. Mum, Little Brother in hand, would walk me through the wilderness at the edge of the Studio to a bus stop where I, with a number of other kids, caught the bus to school, about four stops up the road. It was only a short trip, but in today's world it seems strange that a bunch of five- and six-year-olds would be sent off, unaccompanied, on public transport for this daily excursion. Perhaps not quite so exciting though when you realise the bus driver knew where to stop, right outside the school, and the conductor would have made sure we all got off.

I did have a bit of a scare one day though, travelling later than usual after a dentist visit. Mum put me on the bus and waved me off but failed to tell me that I needed to press the bell for the bus to stop, it only stopped on request during the day. To my horror, as I was preparing to get off, we sailed straight past. Having explained my mistake to the conductor, he let me off at the next stop from where I walked, rather nervously I imagine, back the way we had come. It was probably only a few hundred yards, but it would still have been quite a relief to see the school buildings come into view. No problems at the end of day though as Mum was always waiting outside the school to take me home on the back of her bike.

To this day, one particular event from my infant school years leaves me with an unanswered moral dilemma. "Lying is wrong", I was always told, a message I have passed on to my kids. "Nothing good comes from lying". My dilemma is this: during an arithmetic lesson, I had a headache and felt a little unwell, Teacher oozed sympathy and placed me in a large chair in the headmistress's study with a blanket over my knees and a few Quality Street, a Christmas luxury in our house, for comfort; I'd found Heaven.

So, when we came to arithmetic again, I decided to feel unwell once more, and bingo, more sweets. Then one day, having pulled this stunt a number of times, I was sent home with a letter for my parents; my many headaches had not gone unnoted, and it was suggested my eyes should be tested. Imagine my shock when the optician found a problem with my eyes and prescribed glasses! Trust me, that is not what a lively six-year-old boy wants to hear. So, I definitely paid the price for my lying.

But it doesn't stop there; aged around thirteen it transpired that my eyesight had been corrected by my glasses and I no longer needed to wear them. Had I not lied at the age of six I would probably soon have been wearing glasses permanently; so perhaps my lying had saved my sight. That's my dilemma.

As an aside to this event, a comment on one way that teaching has changed. While my glasses were being made, the headmistress, who was aware that I wasn't exactly looking forward to wearing them, decided she would make me feel better by making light of the issue. In a full school assembly, she had me stand up while she told all the other kids that I would be wearing glasses, that this was not a bad thing, and so on. But then, with me still standing and feeling a bit of a wally, she put her glasses on me to show what I would look like. That might have been OK had they not been of a design that Dame Edna Everage would have approved, and all the kids immediately burst into laughter. It was totally humiliating, and so perhaps that was part of my punishment for lying.

At seven I followed Big Brother into junior school. This felt a little like home from home as my grandparents on Dad's side were caretakers there, and we would regularly prowl round the school when visiting at weekends or in the holidays.

Another example of how things have changed since those days. I got into a scrap in the playground with one of my fellow pupils and we were duly sent to the headmaster for punishment that, in those days, ranged from a stern reprimand to a hefty few smacks with a plimsole on the palm of the hand. He talked to us both about the disagreement before suggesting that there was only one way to resolve our differences, the boxing ring of course; we were probably ten at the time.

So, after school a 'ring' was constructed using PE benches, and with most of the class looking on and the headmaster as referee, we gloved up and slugged it out.

Well not really; I was always pretty good at grappling, but no boxer; on the receiving end of a quick jab to the nose I kind of lost interest. My point is this; can you imagine the response such an approach would generate today?

One particularly strong memory is of a school trip to St Paul's Cathedral. Such outings were rare and to be relished, and my memory concerns lunch, packed in my trusty duffle bag; I don't remember what sandwiches I had, but definitely a currant bun, boiled egg and a bottle of Tizer, a treat indeed as this would usually have been shared among the whole family. The trip involved travel by coach 20 or so miles to London through strange and alien lands, but my main memory concerns events later on.

We wandered, a little bored I imagine, around the cathedral before climbing the 257 steps to the Whispering Gallery. This was more like it; looking down on all the people below, thinking they probably didn't even know we were up there. I leant over to get a better view and then… let go of my bag; it plummeted earthwards and hit the ground with a crash of breaking glass. Oops! By the time I had made my way back down the 257 steps to where my bag had landed there was a, not particularly smiley, man in a black cassock mopping the floor. Obviously, my main concern at the time was my lunch, but to this day, it makes me shudder to think what would have happened had the bag, with full glass bottle, landed on someone's head.

It was at junior school that I discovered my love for swimming, even though I couldn't actually do it. There was a small outdoor pool, unheated and probably no more than 15 yards long, where we had swimming lessons in the summer term. 'Wallowing' would probably be a more accurate description than 'swimming', as I had very little success as far as actually moving forward was concerned.

My highpoint was during my last summer at the school when I took part in the annual swimming gala and managed to complete the whole length. Swimming sessions were the highlight of each summer though, together with being able to wear multi-colour summer shirts, light cotton shorts and sandals; without realising it I was becoming a beach bum.

Theme music for this period of my life is 'With The Beatles', my first album, comprising 14 tracks with a total running time of 33 minutes and 2 seconds. At the time, my usual practice was to run home for lunch, bolt down my food and then rush back to play with my friends, but for a while my routine changed, as I took time eating while listening to a few tracks. Of course, that didn't last long, contemplating the universe was trumped by play every time.

After four years you moved on from junior school, either to a secondary modern or grammar school depending on how you fared at the Eleven Plus. I passed, but thought little of it until some of my friends suddenly became less friendly, calling me a snob because I was off to grammar school. This came as a bit of an eye-opener; until that point, I had been happily enjoying life, bowling along thinking that, apart from the occasional minor disagreement, everyone was happy and equal and getting on fine. I had a lot to learn, but not just yet. As I recall they soon got over it, and in no time school, and more importantly play, continued as before.

I can't leave junior school without a final memory; after all it was 1966. By the time of the World Cup final, school holidays would have started but the build-up was memorable. Unlike Big Brother, I hadn't really gotten into following football, but I soon became an expert, at least in the important stuff, the World Cup Willy merchandise, although that word was probably not in use then; all those badges, pencils and various paraphernalia. And, of course, we went around continually singing how World Cup Willie was favourite for the cup. The final is Britain's most watched TV broadcast ever; the population was 54.5 million, only 15 million homes had a TV set, yet more than 32.3 million of us looked on. Heady times indeed, and here we are fifty-six years later still waiting for a follow up.

Now, fast forward to the early 90s and I was back, this time as a parent. Had things changed? The first thing of note was the school run. As kids, we got to school on foot, by bike or bus, then train for senior school; this helped develop our independence. All that has changed now, with the school run clogging roads, polluting the environment and possibly contributing to increased obesity in children. Of course, for some the school run is unavoidable, school may be too far to walk or cycle, and public transport may not be an option; still, I think that for an awful lot of children there are healthier options and there is no excuse.

As a parent I witnessed little difference in the way the kids behaved. There was still the drama and emotion of friendships made and broken; the politics of playground disputes; bestest friends; teachers loved and teachers loathed; the occasional excitement of a school event attended by parents; and the pinnacle, a day trip on a coach, it didn't matter to where. Actually, they had it better than us on this last point, with the added adventure of staying away overnight for one trip.

It was at this time that technology started to get its hooks into the kids. We were in no rush to help them leap into the world of electronic gaming, but eventually succumbed as they came home from school full of talk about this or that game that their classmates all had, so in the end we somewhat reluctantly bought a Sega Master System with games like Sonic the Hedgehog and Castle of Illusion with Mickey Mouse. That was it; we did our best to be good parents, limiting the amount of time spent on machines and making sure games were 'appropriate', but the floodgates were open. There followed a variety of different platforms like Nintendo and Sony PlayStation, and if that wasn't enough, we had portable machines such as Gameboy and the likes of Tamagotchi, the appeal of which I never could fathom. There was no way back.

While the raw material for schools, the kids, was much the same as in my day the setup had changed dramatically as a result of The Education Reform Act of 1988. This not only brought in a national curriculum dictating what subjects had to be taught at all schools, it also introduced National Curriculum assessments, SATs, for all children, with results published to provide an indication as to how schools were doing. For the first time parents were given the chance to choose the school they wanted for their children.

All very laudable I am sure, but as with so many government policies, the Law of Unintended Consequences kicked in. Not surprisingly, parents chose to send their kids to the schools scoring highest, so some were hugely oversubscribed while others were shunned. We had direct experience of this; children from our area all went to a good local junior school and we assumed that was where Daughter would go, but when her time came, she was refused a place because kids from outside the area, but with siblings already attending the school, were given priority. The idiocy of this process unfolds as parents shun a local school in favour of something 'better' further afield while, usually unhappy, outsiders are bussed in to fill the spaces. Attention is then focused on raising standards at the 'bad' school which, after a while, is turned around. But by the time this is achieved, the school has been filled with 'outsiders' whose siblings are given priority over locals wishing to attend, and who are then denied places and bussed further afield.

It is easy to criticise the way local authorities implement government policy but impossible to see a solution that is fair to all. Personally, I think the answer is a system whereby parents have much less choice and instead take responsibility for increasing standards in their own local schools. But that isn't going to happen.

The aim of these changes was great and the idea was simple; to give parents an objective measure both of how their children are progressing and how different schools are performing but, as is so often the case with government initiatives, the result has not been exactly as hoped for, and there are many tales of parents being unfairly treated while others play the system, and of shenanigans at schools trying to improve their rating to attract high quality pupils and staff. The system also generates considerable administration overheads for teachers, using valuable time that could be better spent with the kids.

For some parents, education seems to have become a competitive sport. This might simply arise from a desire to help their children achieve their best in a world where competition for 'good' jobs is fierce, and the gulf between rich and poor is immense, but others seem to view their child's progress as a direct reflection of their own status and success, causing them to go to any length to be seen as 'winners', giving little thought to the child's welfare and happiness. I distinctly remember attending a parents' session at my kids' infant school. It was my first experience of such events and I had intended to keep quiet, listen and learn. Then one of the parents asked whether the school could send home copies of teaching material so that they could go through the lessons with their children in the evening. I was stunned and said so, as far as I was concerned, a day's schooling was sufficient for any five-year old, and when they came home I wanted my kids to relax, play and learn informally about the world around them. Looking expectantly around the group for support, it slowly dawned on me that I was the only one with this view. As Dad would regularly say, "perhaps I'm mad".

Parental attitudes notwithstanding, there were many things I did like about my children's early school. I was surprised to find my daughter's class had a lad with Down's Syndrome; I don't think that would have happened in my day. He participated in all activities and the kids all wanted him as their friend; I am sure it did both him and the other kids good as he was able to live a more normal life while they came to understand some of the challenges faced by others.

Sadly, since my childhood schools have become far less open places with security now a major factor. In March 1996, in Dunblane, a gunman entered a primary school and killed sixteen children and their teacher before shooting himself. With our own kids in similar schools, it was impossible not to picture the same thing happening to them, and I can't describe my emotions. At the time, both Andy and Jamie Murray were pupils at the Dunblane school and knew the assailant; imagine the effect this would have had both on them and their parents. Other such incidents around the country, together with the increased risk of indiscriminate terrorist attacks, a fear of paedophiles, drug dealing and other illegal activity straying onto school grounds, means security is now a prime concern within our academic institutions. It seems so sad that where in my day the main disaster we prepared for was a fire, now it is necessary for staff and pupils to practice procedures for lockdown in the event of a threat of violence on or near the premises.

There have also been major changes arising from increased levels of immigration in recent years. The effects have been huge in some city areas where teachers can face the problem of teaching numerous pupils who have little or no knowledge of the English language; or arguments can arise over clashes between British and immigrant culture, particularly since the introduction of faith schools. But as this has not had an impact on my life or the area in which I live, it is not an issue that I will dwell on here.

In conclusion, there seems to be no difference between the kids fed into the schooling system today and those of sixty years ago. They start happy, innocent and full of optimism, and the teachers are probably just as caring as before. But the system has changed considerably into a production line for homogeneous young adults, with some parents piling on the pressure to win; there seems limited scope for play, for dealing with kids' individual needs or with anyone who doesn't quite fit the mould. One outcome of this approach, I believe, is that some kids are forced to grow up early and are robbed of their childhood, though ironically, I also believe that kids left more to their own devices in the old days became independent and truly 'grown up' much earlier than those of today. Just my opinion, but all things considered I would say things were better then.

7.

Remember, Remember the Fifth of November

We didn't call it Guy Fawkes Night, to us it was always Firework Night, we were far more interested in pyrotechnic wonders than the antics of a 400-year-old Catholic activist. Local toy and sweet shops sold individual fireworks, and for weeks before the actual day we would horde our pocket money and buy an occasional rocket, pack of bangers or Roman candle. Anything with a plastic spike was likely to be exciting, but Catherine wheels were generally avoided as, however easily they moved before lighting, they seemed to freeze once ignited, and the gunpowder just fizzed in a circle. On Friday nights, Dad always stopped on his way home from work to buy a bag of sweets that we would carefully share out between the three of us, but for the weeks running up to Firework Night this ritual changed, and he would bring home fireworks instead.

Although not particularly interested in Guy Fawkes himself, we were happy to use him as a source of income, and about a week or so before the actual night we would build our Guy; knotting pyjama legs and sleeves before stuffing them full of newspaper, then crafting a head from an old stocking or some such; we just had to make and tie on a mask and bingo, we had our Guy. With a 'Penny for the Guy' notice attached, it only remained to transport him to the High Street, not always that easy as our craftwork was often none too robust, and then wait for people to donate to our firework fund.

Despite being a keen gardener, ours was about the only Dad willing to have his garden wrecked, so every Firework Night festivities would be at our house. The vegetable patch would be sacrificed to a large bonfire painstakingly built up over days, if not weeks and, come the great day, we would be indoors impatiently watching darkness fall, while waiting for Dad to get home from work. This is obviously selective memory, but the weather always seemed to be right; cold but not too cold, clear and a certain smell in the air. Local kids would come, some with their parents, bringing whatever fireworks they had; Mum would dish out cups of tea or coffee for the grownups, Dad would light the fire, a pile of potatoes would be thrown on to cook and the fireworks would begin.

There tended to be quite a pile of fireworks and the show would go on for some time; except, that is, for one night. As a fire precaution, all the fireworks were placed in a dustbin with the lid firmly closed; but not long after the festivities began, a rocket shot up vertically and did its stuff before falling back onto our roof, sliding down and dropping into the bin, the lid of which had been left off in the excitement. Unfortunately, the stick was still glowing, and before anyone responded, the whole lot went off. Although the shortest of our firework displays, this has to be the most impressive. No damage was done, and nobody was hurt but we all stood there a bit dazed, before Dad jumped in the car and drove to the Sweet Shop to buy their last few remaining fireworks and we enjoyed a slightly muted end to the celebrations.

As a kid, this had been a really important day in my calendar, and I was determined that any child of mine would have the same fun, whether they liked it or not. Around the time we got married, we discovered the annual fireworks display at a local rugby club and, as soon as the kids were old enough, decided to take them along for some excitement. I hurried home from work, we bundled the kids up in thick coats and wooly hats, got them in the car and headed off to the display. They were quite excited. We arrived just as things were about to start, found a parking space and began unloading the pushchair; the kids were more excited. A big rocket went off and they stood mesmerised looking skyward, before.....BANG!!!. They were terrified. Both burst into tears and continued crying until we had repacked the car and were on our way home. We stopped to buy sparklers and a few bangless fireworks and had our own, somewhat subdued, display in the garden.

But we were determined that, like it or not, they would enjoy Firework Nights to come, and over the years hosted our own events inviting their friends, together with families. One year we decided to do it big time and invited a bunch of families. I had a large pile of wood for burning, we got in some drink, got the spuds ready for the fire and Wifey cooked up a pot of sausage and bean casserole. Party time. It had rained a lot during the week before though, come the day, the sky was reasonably clear, but the wood was wet and didn't want to burn; I was still trying as guests turned up and lingered in the garden. A couple of the Dads offered to help and set about lighting fireworks while I continued with the fire. Then the rain started; and got worse. Undaunted, the Dads went about lighting fireworks while the Mums and children went inside to watch through the windows. Shortly after, I looked to the house and nobody was watching; by now they were playing games or some such, and it was just the Dads, drenched through, having all the fun. But we were made of stern stuff and set off all the fireworks before finally retiring, drenched, indoors by which time the fire had taken hold and it continued to burn throughout the night.

We soon came to the conclusion that doing it ourselves was too much effort, particularly as the kids weren't that bothered; by now they were OK with fireworks but not particularly keen, so from then on we just went to the local display.

Today, fireworks are common throughout the year and displays are held weeks before and after the actual night. In my time it was very rare to see fireworks other than on November 5th, making the event a special treat, even if the fireworks themselves were generally less impressive. It was more of an adventure than it is today, and I think we had it better.

8.

Yo-Ho-Ho and a Merry Christmas

If you stop to think about it, the whole Christmas thing has become, well, a little strange to be honest. Around half the UK population is allegedly Christian, although according to faith surveys I saw on the Internet no more than 5% attend church regularly; and regardless of faith, only 28% answered 'Yes' to the statement 'I believe in either God or a higher spiritual power'; so whichever way you look at it, the number of people who believe in the original event is fairly small; yet the impact is huge.

Any figure for the amount we spend on Christmas is going to be suspect, but consider the following from two sites that should be fairly reliable: the Office for National Statistics say there are 27.6 million households in the UK, and the Bank of England says that, on average, in December monthly household expenditure increases by £800, suggesting that in the UK we spend in the region of £22billion extra in the Christmas month; that's a lot of money. All this expenditure requires tons of planning, running around, time and energy, while leading to serious financial problems for many. Anxiety, depression, marriage breakdowns and even murders and suicides are often blamed on the pressures of Christmas; yo-ho-ho. Now let me stop right there and say no, this is not the Grinch speaking; I have always enjoyed Christmas, I just think things may have got just a tiny bit out of hand.

As a kid with two brothers, Christmas truly was magical. The buildup started much later than these days, there was probably no sign of Christmas in the shops before December. At some point Mum would bring out her Brian Mills shopping catalogue and we would point out the things we liked; a few weeks before Christmas we would all take a trip to Bentalls in Kingston, a very up-market shop to us, where we'd queue to see Santa, tell him what we were hoping for, promise to be good and then walk out beaming, clasping our first Christmas gift. After a further stroll around various boring shops, of which Kingston had many, we would head home, but not before stopping for chicken and chips at The Kings Head. The buildup had truly begun.

The buzz would continue everywhere. At junior school, a cardboard box wrapped in red tissue paper was the Christmas post box; we could post cards to our friends here, and later in the day they would be delivered around the school. It was like Valentine's Day when we were older, wonderful for those who got cards and sad for those who didn't.

We made paper chains and various decorations to hang in the classroom, sang carols, and prepared for the Nativity play. Mum was a dab hand at making a shepherd's headdress from an old tea towel, or a crown that any Wise Man would be proud of, created from cardboard with fruit gums as jewels. I recall playing King Herod in one particular Nativity performance; I needed to look stern while reading a scroll, so I'd been instructed along the lines of "…pretend to stroke your beard to look thoughtful". We didn't have a scroll, so used a paint-by-numbers picture of a cat donated by some kind person. All went well building up to this dramatic moment; I thoughtfully stroked my pretend beard and frowned, but then people in the audience sniggered! Manfully I went on slowly unrolling and pretending to read my scroll. "That's not a scroll, it's a cat" came a loud whisper from nearby, and the moment was lost.

Dad was a member of two Working Man's Clubs in the area, which was great for us as, in the lead up to Christmas, both had parties for the kids; these were large-scale affairs with loads of children, organised party games with prizes, singing, tons of food and drink and, most exciting of all, a film projector. At some point we would all sit on the floor and watch old cartoons, which I now realise was a great tactic to give the adults a breather; at the end a great time was rounded off by a present from Santa.

I would have been about five when Big Brother let me into a secret. We were playing upstairs and crept into my parents' room where he opened the wardrobe to reveal a pile of presents for us kids. Well! For years to come we had an early warning of at least some of our presents, yet somehow it was still a few years before I stopped fully believing in Santa.

Sleep didn't come easy on Christmas Eve, particularly as I shared a room with Big Brother, and we would keep on nattering before eventually dozing off, only to wake a few hours later. We each had one of Mum's old stockings on the bed, no pillowcases for us, and would wake to find them stuffed with goodies; comics, pencils, colouring books, puzzle books, sweets a few Walnuts and the obligatory Satsuma. Waking in the dark to such wonders was enough on its own, but then we'd wake the house and go downstairs for the presents. Even then we had lots of presents though they wouldn't have been expensive; Airfix models, toy guns, a football and the like. Everything would be unwrapped and played with hours before sunrise while the folks looked on bleary eyed and smiling.

Christmas Day was always spent at home. Playing. Dozing. Eating. Watching TV. 'Billy Smarts Christmas Circus' was on each year along with the Queen's speech, a bit of religion with carol concerts and, until 1965, the last year football matches were played on Christmas Day, the football results. Christmas TV evolved through the 60s with new 'traditions' like Christmas Top of the Pops, when all the year's Number 1s were played; 1968 saw the first Morecambe and Wise Christmas Show. Boxing Day was always my Nan's day; we would walk round to her house and gather with all Dad's family for fun, food and frolics. Lovely jubbly. Then a tired walk home in the dark and cold, and so to bed. That was it. Christmas over. Everything was closed on Christmas Day and Boxing Day, but after that most adults were back to work and the kids were bored.

In my teens I had a Saturday job in a clothes shop. Schools broke up only a few days before Christmas, but I would work those days for the extra money. Even then we had Christmas songs to drive us mad; 'It's the Most Wonderful Time of the Year' by Andy Williams or Dean Martin's 'Let It Snow, Let It Snow, Let It Snow' were soon joined by the likes of Slade, Wizzard, Mud et al to complete the torment. My theme tune for this time of year has to be 'Fairytale of New York'. When it was released in 1988, I thought it was brilliant, though for a while nobody else seemed to agree; but now it has achieved the recognition it deserves. It's not a super nice, tinsel-wrapped version of Christmas, but a more gritty, booze-sodden version with an uplifting end when the drunk responds to his lover's complaints by saying how he has kept her dreams with his own; suddenly the argument has stopped and, despite everything, the future just might be OK. I like that.

For many years, all our Christmas shopping was done locally. Mum and Dad might have had presents hidden in their wardrobe for weeks, but we'd leave things much later. A day or two before Christmas, both brothers and I would go to the pub for a quick pint before heading out to shop. We all went our separate ways, circling the town and occasionally our paths would cross; "Got anything yet?" "One present bought, two ideas. You?" "Nothing yet." As time passed panic levels rose, but we were men, thriving under pressure, and soon we were all back in the pub for a celebratory beer; job done. Years later, during my first Christmas with my wife-to-be, I drove home from her flat on Christmas morning and, passing through Whitechapel, was amazed to see all the shops open; perhaps I'd started my shopping too soon?

As us kids got older, Dad decided it was alright for him to join my uncle, father to the only girl ever to be in the Mars Bar Gang, for a pre-Christmas dinner pint. A new tradition started one year when he came home with unexpected company; one of the guys at the pub was going home to open a tin of beans or some such for his Christmas Dinner, but Dad wasn't having any of that and invited him back. Mum was a bit surprised but, to her credit, adapted quickly, laying another place at the table while Dad introduced us to our guest. From that day on, Mum would never know how many she was catering for, but she would always manage.

Over the years the format of Christmases at home evolved. Nan and Pop retired and moved to a small flat so the Boxing Day gathering became more compact. And as time passed my brothers and I would join Dad at the pub in what somehow seemed a particularly special bonding session. Mum was quite happy staying at home in peace cooking the dinner, but we were under strict instructions to be home on time. We would down the last pint at speed and hurry home from the pub, leaving Dad with a full glass complaining that he'd been stitched up again; but we'd usually wait for him to catch up.

At some point Mum decided to join us; lunch would be left ticking over and we started to eat a little later. The walk home passed by the house of some musical neighbours, all of whom were sociable regulars at the pub, and one Christmas day they lured us in for a drink, just the one of course. Mum went home to finish the cooking and us menfolk stayed awhile; another new tradition was born. Then one year Mum decided to stay with us; we all had a thoroughly enjoyable time but stayed a little longer than we should have. To say the turkey was overcooked was an understatement; the skin was rock solid, and the meat had to be scooped out of the legs. Beware the evils of drink.

Around this time, another Christmas tradition took hold of the family, the Boxing Day football match. Every Boxing Day our old school football club held a tournament, under-25's vs over-25's, comprising three teams of each. Kickoff at 10:00 meant arriving by 09:30 to put up the nets, while still suffering from the effects of overeating, overdrinking and undersleeping. Throw in some nasty winter weather, and this was the time we would wonder whether it was really worth it. But after a short spell of fresh air, with blood reluctantly pumping through the veins, the world seemed rosier, and three short matches later we could retire to the bar knowing we'd earned a pint. This was a great social event too; Mum and Dad often came along, as did family and friends of many of the other players. The highlight was the Christmas raffle for which we'd been press-ganged into selling tickets for weeks; this was the main fundraiser of the year and would go on for ages. Then home for feet up and a relax.

I spent Christmas 1980 in the southern hemisphere, and that was a strange experience. I was invited to Christmas lunch with an ex-pat family and their friends. Outside, the sun was burning down, and the beach was packed, but that didn't stop us tucking into roast turkey with all the trimmings, and Christmas pud. To get all the right ingredients for the day must have taken meticulous planning and not insignificant expenditure, but my hosts obviously considered this reminder of home to be essential.

Little Brother was first to marry and move out; Big Brother and I were harder to get rid of, leaving home before returning a few times until finally buying our own flats. I married next, then Big Brother followed suit, and we all now have children of our own. Time passes, and three of the kids have since married; throw in two grandchildren and the logistics of catering for such large numbers while factoring in time with in-laws means the extended family Christmas is now almost impossible.

But for me the seismic shift started in 1988, our first Christmas with Daughter; a bit of an anticlimax really as she was only a couple of months old and had no idea what was going on, although that didn't stop us and all the family buying her presents. Little changed regarding who we saw and where we met, except it became much harder as we now needed a car full of support gear and had to work our timetable around feeding time. Son came along shortly after, and for years to come Christmas would be for the children, with adults a mere sideshow, a situation Big Brother found hard to cope with. "Children should be seen and not heard" was his mantra, and he couldn't understand when Little Brother and I chose not to dally at the pub, instead leaving promptly for Christmas lunch; we knew what a pain kids could be if they weren't fed on time. It was more than ten years before he came to understand this inconvenient truth, for by then he had a baby daughter to worry about whereas our kids were now older and more patient. While he regularly checked his watch, a smile would pass between Little Brother and I; "What rush brother? Tarry awhile and partake in another foaming ale. Thy child can wait." And of course, sheer bravado would cause him to stay a little longer. But we'd had our fun, savoured the moment and headed home.

Once again Christmas was magical. The kids would write their lists and post them out through the letterbox for the elves to collect. I would ask Wifey which presents on their lists we were going to buy, to which she would inevitably reply "all of them of course". She would get just as excited as the kids with buildup starting earlier and earlier each year, while I still had to traipse up to Town and work. I was Scrooge, insisting that we only bought some from the lists, although I knew full well that by Christmas they'd have the lot. At least by resisting, I could reduce the risk of buying additional stuff; although of course I would then spot things I wanted to buy as well; they were totally spoiled. Come Christmas Eve, there would be a glass of port, mince pie and carrot by the fireplace; all gone bar a few crumbs the next day.

One year as they were beginning to suspect that, just maybe, Santa might not be real, we had to up the deception levels; the kids would leave notes for Santa by the fireplace just in case the elves hadn't done their job right, so that year I put my hand and foot in the fireplace and left sooty fingerprints on the lists and a footprint as evidence causing some excitement when they noticed. A few years later, a friend explained his trick; he would strategically place a wrapped present in his roof gutter and just wait until one of his kids spotted it, proof that Santa had been on the roof. Brilliant; I wish I'd thought of it.

The kids would leave empty pillowcases on their beds; each one of a pair so we were able to fill matching ones in advance; unlike devious Big Brother I don't think they ever looked for the presents in advance although I have never actually asked them. I would make the switch and wait for them to wake. This would usually happen early; history was repeating itself.

The problem as we saw it was that, no sooner had we opened our presents, than we would be heading off for Christmas lunch somewhere before the kids had time to play with the new stuff. So, after a few years we decided to stay at home for Christmas, as I had done as a child, to give them more time to play. Seemed a good idea at the time, but we soon realised that the kids didn't want our company; they wanted grandparents, uncles, aunties and cousins, so that approach was dead in the water.

The kids were about eight or nine when crunch time came, as they sat us down saying there was something they wanted to know; playground chat suggested Santa didn't exist and parents provided all the presents; was this true? Awkward. We wanted to keep the magic going, but didn't want them mocked at school as the only kids who believed;

so it went something like this: "Is it important? If you believe, that's all that matters." "That's not an answer. Does he exist?" "Well, isn't it better to believe, just to get the presents?" "Still not an answer, does he exist?" I have to admit they were good. "Well suppose he exists, but only if you believe in him?" "You still haven't answered the question." It went on like this for a while until I finally looked at Wifey and we caved. "OK, so maybe he doesn't exist. Yes it's us. Guilty as charged my lud." There was a pause, they looked knowingly at each other, then burst into tears. "Why did you tell us?" You can't win.

Things change. The kids got older and inevitably the magic wore off, at least for now. We soon came to the point where we had to wake them up and drag them out of bed for a quick unwrapping session before heading off to join one branch of the family or another, unless we were hosting. Christmas Eve for Son meant a late boozy night with his mates and a long walk home, so he would often be less than lively company on Christmas Day, but we still managed to enjoy ourselves. He's married now and so has to include his wife's family in his Christmas plans, the wheel turns.

As I said at the start, I enjoy Christmas, but for different reasons than when I was younger. As a kid, it was the excitement around all sorts of treats; true the presents were a big part but also events at school, parties at the Working Man's Clubs and getting together with the family all added to the fun. As a teenager and young adult, the social side was far more important. Then, as a dad myself, it was all for the kids, just tuning into their excitement. Time passed, the kids got older, and it became a holiday from work and a chance to relax and socialise. Recently retired and with no need for a holiday from work, it just leaves relaxation and socialising; I think I can manage that.

From a personal viewpoint Christmas today is not as good as it was in my youth. The dominance of commercialism and the extended timeframe of the Christmas period creates an atmosphere nowhere near that of the old days, not to mention the stress caused, which I don't think was such a problem then. But the kids still seem to have a pretty good time, so perhaps this is just the Grinch speaking after all.

9.

The Shifting Sands of History

When I first came up with the idea for this book, I had in mind a relatively short list of things that had changed during my lifetime and then, not surprising really, the list grew. One particular new entry did come as a bit of a surprise though, history.

During my early school years, vast swathes of the world map were coloured either red or dark pink depicting parts of the British Empire or British Commonwealth. We learnt of the heroic deeds performed by the likes of Drake and Raleigh as they outwitted the dastardly Spaniards; of Rorke's Drift where 150 British soldiers repelled an attack by thousands of Zulus; of Admiral Nelson, Gordon of Khartoum, the Duke of Wellington and countless other examples of the British spirit; a stiff upper lip, honesty, courage under fire and the instinct to 'do the right thing'. More recently we had won two World Wars through the dedication of our armed forces and stoic grit shown by the civilians at home. Stirring stuff indeed and the inspiration for countless movies.

But not only does the victor receive the spoils of war, they also get to write history, and in so doing may sometimes be a little economic with the truth. Digging into the past people have realised that the goodie/baddie split might just have been a little oversimplified, or even based on downright lies, and around the world historians have been digging further in an effort to understand what really happened in their neck of the woods. Napoleon expressed a rather jaundiced view of history when he said "History is a set of lies that people have agreed upon".

I worked for a number of years with an Israeli friend and we would often chat about our early lives and the joys of growing up; how we had enjoyed similar things yet at the same time had some completely different experiences, me in Surrey and him on a kibbutz. We were around the same age but it was hard to imagine him younger, bespectacled and soft-spoken, completing his national service as a tank driver in the Israel Defence Force, careering around the desert defending his homeland. To me, growing up in a land surrounded by enemies, many of whom want you wiped from the face of the earth, was impossible to imagine.

An advocate for peace with the neighbours, he talked of how hard it was for Israelis to reconcile the fact that a key player in any peace negotiation was leader of the Palestine Liberation Organisation, Yasser Arafat, whose name had been used to terrify kids for years; "if you do that Yasser Arafat will get you!" they were told. Then, as now, Palestine often made the news and I wanted to understand the subject better, so I asked him to recommend objective authors who might enlighten me. "It's not that easy" he said, or words to that effect, as 'truth' often depends on perspective; one man's terrorist is another man's freedom fighter. Such profundity over a lunchtime sandwich.

These conversations came to mind recently when I heard a radio article about ongoing arguments in Lebanon concerning the format of the school history curriculum for the period of the Lebanese Civil War that ran from 1975 to 1990. The problem, it seems, is that a number of the people who were active in the war, or at least their close friends and relatives, are alive today and will not accept versions that show their side in a bad light; the argument goes on.

Challenges facing the revisionists in their quest for 'the truth' are magnified the further back they look, filtering through vast amounts of conflicting evidence all of which is subject to personal perspectives at the time. Consider one larger than life character, Winston Churchill. He topped the charts in a BBC audience poll for the programme 100 Greatest Britons, yet many think him a villain. Considered by many as the man responsible for us winning the war, Churchill comes with baggage, not exactly surprising bearing in mind both his upbringing and career.

An aristocrat born during the reign of Victoria, he was a great believer in the Empire, served in the army in various theatres of war and filled a variety of government posts during a long and active political career. As President of the Board of Trade, he was responsible for introducing a number of significant social changes; the 1908 Mines Act restricted the working day in all mines to 8 hours; the first British minimum wage system was implemented across a number of industries as part of the Trades Boards Act of 1909 and the Labour Exchanges Act of 1909 set up offices to help the unemployed find employment. He was also a strong advocate for the People's Budget; introduced to Parliament by Chancellor David Lloyd George in 1909 this bill introduced radical social welfare programmes such as pensions for the over 70s and free school meals, to be funded by unprecedented levels of taxes on the wealthy.

On the flip side, Churchill is remembered by some as the man who deployed troops to control striking miners during the Tonypandy riots of 1910, whose failure to act during the Bengal Famine of 1943 significantly added to the death toll of around three million Indians, and who authorised the area bombing of German cities causing the deaths of tens of thousands of German civilians. Labeled a racist by some, he expressed inflammatory views on Muslims, yet his supporters claim many of his words were taken out of context and point out that his cabinet set aside £100,000 for the construction of a mosque in London in 1940; Churchill allegedly had a fascination with Islam, holidayed in Istanbul, played polo in India with Muslims and at one point his family thought it possible he could convert. He expressed views that could be seen as anti-Semitic yet at the same time was a strong advocate for the creation of a Jewish state, Israel. The list of contradictory views and actions goes on.

When my kids were learning history at school, great stress was put on identifying the source of any information, trying to ascertain whether it was genuine, reliable and unbiased. I can't remember this emphasis in my time at school, but it's a pretty obvious first step if you are genuinely trying to get to the truth, particularly in current times when not only can stories be easily made up and widely circulated over the Internet, but also where "fake news!" is the first defence of politicians who fear they have been rumbled.

We are lucky enough to live in a democracy where freedom of thought and speech is still considered sacrosanct, although many would question that. Our history is not dictated to us, and nobody stops us questioning it, but having done so what next?

I have always assumed myself to be of Anglo-Saxon stock, British. Yet the further I look back the more vague that idea becomes. At junior school I learned about the Roman, Viking and French invasions but not that 'the Romans' comprised a variety of nationalities and that William the conqueror was actually of Viking descent. I was also taught that 1066 was the last time we were invaded, with no mention of the fact that when William of Orange was 'invited' to become king in the place of Catholic James, he arrived with an army of 14,000 Dutch soldiers; surely an invasion even if there was no resistance.

With so many outsiders free to roam and procreate over the years our genuine personal history becomes less reliable. And if that doesn't sufficiently blur the picture of who we are, then think back to prehistoric times when Britain was probably left uninhabited between ice ages as various peoples wandered in and stayed a while before wandering south again as temperatures fell. Further back still, scientists believe all human ancestry can be tracked back to the same source, the Great Rift Valley, where around 200,000 years ago some of the locals started a walkabout that would eventually cover the world; so we may all be related, and African to boot.

My point is, to use a phrase that I hate because it is so often used as an excuse not to take responsibility, "we are where we are". Learning about and understanding history is essential if we are to avoid repeating mistakes made in the past, but attempting to rewrite it by retrospectively applying modern day standards and experience is not the answer; neither is seeking to expunge those bits we don't like. Churchill was neither a 'good' person nor a 'bad' person and without doubt some of his actions would not have been acceptable today; but he was a man of his time, and had he not been there, Hitler would probably have prevailed, with all the implications that thought carries for the rest of the world.

So, what conclusions have I drawn from these ramblings? I think that the kids today are lucky in that they perhaps have access to more 'truth' than we did. But this is a double-edged sword. An understanding of history is essential if we are to avoid repeating the mistakes of the past, but attempting to avenge past events or delete the bits we don't like is not the way forward. We are where we are.

10.

Life in Secondary School

Dad had a pretty basic pre-War education and viewed school as a necessary evil, a prison sentence to be escaped at the earliest possible chance to join the grownup world of work. Mum, too, had a fairly limited education. Dad regularly told us "it was your mother who was keen on you boys going to grammar school, I thought it would be a waste of time". Yet another thing for which I am eternally indebted to Mum.

Moving on was a huge step. No longer was I the biggest kid in the school, walking in and coming home for lunch, short trousers, short-sleeved shirts and sandals in the summer. Now it was up early, a bike ride to the station followed by a twenty-minute train trip and a short walk at the other end. I was a new boy, one of the youngsters in a school full of what looked like adults. Long trousers, blazer, cap and tie were compulsory. School lunches were a totally new experience that took some getting used to. Teachers seemed threatening. All in all, a bit daunting.

My first sight of the school had been a year earlier when I went with Mum and Dad to see Big Brother perform in the school play; a version of Hamlet. I have vague memories of being in awe of the whole setup, but doubt I had a clue about what was going on; Mum smiled proudly, and Dad fell asleep. Presumably Little Brother was too young and stayed at home.

Not surprisingly, memories of my first day are much clearer. We were allocated classes and met our teacher; I can't remember his name but presumably, like all first form teachers, he earned the role by being relatively young and sensitive. Then assembly. Six hundred boys standing in lines in the school hall, policed by the most frightening individuals, prowling, scowling and yelling at anyone who spoke or played up. It was terrifying. Particularly menacing were the two teachers running the show; the short and balding deputy head who also ran the Latin department, and his associate, the head of Geography, taller with bristling eyebrows and a terrifying frown. Their purpose was to tame the audience and instil timidity ahead of the arrival of the main act, the headmaster, who welcomed the new boys before getting on with school business. Quite an introduction, as all three strutted their stuff in flowing academic gowns adding to the effect.

Throughout my first year these characters retained their fearful aura, but from the second year on, as I met them as teachers, I discovered that they were just dedicated, keen on their subject and determined to get the best from the boys, even when they encountered resistance, which doesn't mean they weren't terrifying on those days when I had been a trifle slack with my homework. In retrospect, I realise that a number had fought in the War which, partly at least, may explain their focus on discipline; not a bad thing really.

It definitely helped that I was following Big Brother into the school. By now he was a hardened veteran of the fourth year and knew the ropes. Our paths didn't cross that often, but he was there with advice and support when needed, and his friends knew me. It did no harm having older contacts, and I would like to think that, three years down the line, when Little Brother came to the school to complete the family hat-trick, that I provided a similar level of support.

Sport was encouraged; we had two PE periods a week and one of Games. In good weather PE was held in the school playground and involved various amounts of running around and exercising, which we didn't particularly enjoy, but invariably ending with a game of football that we did. Playing the real thing on grass unfortunately required a bit of a hike; our games field was a fifteen-minute walk away from the school. True, the stroll wasn't unpleasant in good weather, but on a cold wet winter day we could do without it. Games lessons were two periods long, 80 minutes in total; we'd walk down through our break period and walk back in time for the second lunch sitting or, if they were in the afternoon, would head home afterwards. Of course, the fields were on the opposite side of school to the station, so following an afternoon Games lesson or an after-school training session, we had a twenty minute walk back to catch our train, passing the school as we went. Again, not so much fun on a cold, wet winter's day.

If the weather turned really bad, we instead had the pleasure of cross-country. At least we could do this from the school building without the walk first. Still, while it may be character building, splashing through muddy ditches and scraggly undergrowth was definitely not my idea of fun.

In the Upper Sixth I had the opportunity to renew my acting career and build on my successful nativity performances in primary school, King Herod being the highpoint. The school play was to be The Royal Hunt of the Sun by Peter Shaffer, one of our English Literature 'A'

Level books, based on the relationship between Spanish conquistador Francisco Pizarro and Atahualpa, son of the Sun God and king of the Incas. Our English master suggested I might audition for the role of Atahualpa, an invitation I respectfully declined. The right move I feel as the role, including a rather impressive dance around the stage, would not really have been 'me'. In the end the guy who took it was remarkably good, and I could only watch in awe, glad that it wasn't me, as he sprung around energetically, dressed in little more than a loincloth.

The star had in fact made his name a year or two earlier at the school public speaking competition. This was a remarkably tedious event for most of us, but attendance was compulsory, and we had to listen to a variety of boys who thought they had something to say, possibly with a career in politics in mind. Most tried to impress, rambling on about intellectual or political subjects, but not he. "Good afternoon", he began, "I would like to talk to you today about smiling".

There followed a brilliant discourse regarding how people didn't smile enough and that, when they did, this merely caused suspicion in others. He went on with a few humorous examples and ended with suggestions as to how we could go about improving the situation. Brilliant. Went down a storm with the whole audience, and he won hands down.

School dinners were an experience. Meals were cooked on the premises using fresh ingredients, all under the control of a formidable lady whose name I forget. The kitchen was run with military precision and boys tended to treat the dinner ladies with more fear and respect than they did the teachers.

The dining hall was laid out with tables and benches, sitting boys in groups of sixteen. Each unit had a sixth form head of table and at least two fourth form waiters who would usually be wearing old blazers with various unpleasant food stains for what could be a messy job. There were two sittings, and boys would sit wherever there was a space, although places could be held for people, or you might be encouraged to move on elsewhere if your face didn't fit.

The duty teacher would decide the order in which the tables would eat and, on his command, table waiters retrieved a pile of plates and containers of food that the head of table would then dish out, with any remaining food distributed at his whim; so for hungry schoolboys it paid to be friendly with him or the waiters. In the early days my fourth-year network really paid dividends.

I ate, and on the whole enjoyed, school dinners for three years before deciding that it took too much of my valuable break time, and I resorted to taking in sandwiches, giving me extra time for a game of football, a wander around the town or later, as we considered ourselves more sophisticated, a game of Bridge.

Town strolls were often fun, and sometimes character-building as was the case when three of us once visited a menswear shop which had in the window a horrible, flowery matching shirt and tie set; remember those? My friend said he needed to go into the shop for something, and I duly followed behind like a lamb to the slaughter. "Can I help you gentlemen?" asked the aging shop assistant. "Yes please," answered my friend with a smile, "my friend wants to buy that nice shirt and tie in the window." They watched, still smiling, as I burbled on making up questions about sizes and colours before coming up with some excuse and leaving the shop saying I would think about it. Another time, we feigned interest in the newly launched Polaroid colour cameras and returned to school with a variety of lovely pictures of our group.

I tended to drift through lower school, and when called upon to make a choice went for subjects that I found easy or enjoyable, dropping the more challenging sciences. For 'A' Levels I chose Economics and Maths, which I thought would be 'useful' in planning a career, and English Lit because I enjoyed reading.

As I coasted through school in my own little bubble a number of things were going on outside, but I'm afraid I wasn't taking that much notice. A lot happened in 1968. In April, Martin Luther King was assassinated in Memphis. May saw the start of seven weeks of civil unrest in France where students protesting against the Vietnam War, capitalism, consumerism and the like were soon joined by a whole variety of people with a host of different grievances; apparently at one point many considered civil war a genuine possibility, but in the end life got back to normal; as we say in England, c'est la vie. In August the USSR invaded Czechoslovakia to halt the spread of liberalism growing there.

In 1969, the Apollo 11 lunar module, the Eagle, landed on the moon and Neil Armstrong and Buzz Aldrin went for that first lunar stroll; two catchphrases were coined to be used for generations to come, "The Eagle has landed" and "That's one small step for man, one giant leap for mankind" (apparently Neil Armstrong meant to say "for **a** man", which would have been more logical but he fluffed his lines in the excitement of the moment). I had been with friends down to the coast for the day, and can remember on my return, standing mesmerised watching a grainy yet hugely impressive black and white live transmission of the event.

Meanwhile the Vietnam War went on, as did anti-war demos worldwide. We were shocked when, in May 1970, we heard of the Kent State Massacre where Ohio National Guardsmen killed four unarmed student protestors and wounded nine others. I did take more notice of events at home when, in February 1972, the IRA detonated their first bomb on the mainland at an army base in Aldershot killing seven civilian staff. The sad fact is that, while I was a supposedly intelligent young man fast approaching adulthood, I didn't really have a clue as to what was going on outside my own little world.

My musical tastes developed hugely during the senior school years, ranging from the Four Tops through James Taylor to Led Zeppelin. Theme music for this period is the Leonard Cohen album 'Songs From a Room'. As a moody teenager, I would sit in the dark listening and thinking, not understanding half the lyrics, and yet somehow after a few tracks I always felt better; something still true to this day. Dad slated Cohen's music as tuneless groaning until a few years ago when he came across film of a live concert on BBC4. The next day he admitted that he had been wrong, a rare event indeed! He'd found the performance moving and poetic and said it nearly made him cry. How I enjoyed hearing that.

During sixth form, many of my school friends were preparing for university. They had brothers, sisters or friends telling them about university life, and would often spend weekends visiting this or that 'uni' to return to school on Monday with tales of rock concerts, late night parties and debauchery. This had little appeal to me, partly because I never really believed my classmates' claims of what they'd been up to. Besides I didn't socialise with these friends much after school, choosing instead to return to home territory and all it had to offer. None of my home friends or family had been to university and my general instinct was that it probably wasn't for me.

But as time passed, I began to reconsider. True, university would be full of incredibly intelligent people, and I would have to work hard just to keep up, but if, as my teachers promised, I came out the other end with a 'good job' the sacrifice would be worth it. So, I started rethinking my future. First, what subject? Teachers said University was a place to study new and interesting subjects, not just continuing something we found easy at school; but I couldn't think of anything of interest. Economics was relatively easy, and it seemed to offer a good first step to that 'good job'. It is rather sad that in later life there are numerous subjects far more interesting that I wish I'd studied and pursued as a career. Why is it that just about every significant choice you have to make when growing up comes before you are ready to make it? Anyway, Economics on its own sounded far too academic, I needed something more practical; Economics and Business Studies sounded just the thing. Decision one made.

Next question, where to locate for three years of hard study? Obviously a key decision that could have a huge impact on my life, but luckily there wasn't too large a choice to confuse me as only five or six universities offered Economics and Business Studies at the time; I later found that a whole variety of places did similar courses with slightly different names, but had I known that then it would just have confused me further. There seemed little point in visiting for an interview as I thought you couldn't learn much in a flying visit; all options probably had similar facilities and it would take more than one day to understand the strengths and weaknesses of each. Besides I would be there to study, so nothing else really mattered. After further deep thought I decided the most important thing was to be by the seaside. Only one university fitted all my criteria, so the decision was made. Job done

I started revising for my 'A' levels a little later than planned, then got distracted by reading The Lord of the Rings. I had avoided this cult offering up until then; talking about little people with hairy feet and names like Frodo Baggins, wizards and a cloak of invisibility would certainly have damaged my street cred back home. But someone lent me the book and one sunny afternoon, sitting in the garden trying hard to concentrate on revising, I succumbed. I turned to the book for a short well-earned break only to be immediately hooked and did nothing else until I had finished it; not good for my revision as it ran to some 1200 pages. I can only guess at the effect this had on my underwhelming 'A' levels results, but I managed to scrape through with the necessary grades.

Some twenty-five years later, and I was back in the wonderland that is secondary education, this time with our kids. From my perspective, the biggest change over the years was the end of state grammar schools. The system had worked well for me and, while I might have been guilty of the occasional smugness and feeling of superiority, if I thought about it at all I probably assumed that it also worked well for those who didn't pass the Eleven Plus. After all, the government could be trusted to put us all where we should be and treat us all fairly, couldn't they?

I now realise that with a few exceptions, at the early age of eleven, anyone not sent to grammar school would have found it very hard to stray from their pre-ordained route to get the 'A' levels required for university in order to move into vocational and more lucrative careers as doctors, lawyers, financiers and the like. Grammar schools received a higher level of funding and were predominantly attended by middle class pupils, while the majority of working-class students went to secondary modern schools. While many of the latter might have baulked at the idea of attending a grammar school anyway, remember my primary schoolmates denouncing me as a snob, it seems unfair that so many doors were closed to so many at such an early stage in their lives. Labour's comprehensive system aimed to address this by offering a broader variety of options and giving similar opportunities for all with the formal abolition of grammar schools in 1976, although a small number remain.

Since my time at school, the leaving age for full-time education has been raised twice, first to 17 in 2013 then again in 2015 to 18, with cynics suggesting a major driver of this being to reduce unemployment figures. My kids both attended a very good local comprehensive and I can see a number of improvements on the old setup. For a start, the variety of topics available for study is impressive. The subjects required for a move into academia are there, but so too are far more practical subjects that can help prepare a pupil to face the outside world. Design and Technology, Computer Science, Drama and Sport to name a few. My teachers would have been mystified by the idea of studying sport. Such variety is only possible as a result of the school being much larger than mine, with over 1500 pupils compared to 600.

Comprehensive schools are all mixed, as were secondary moderns while grammar schools tended to be single sex, although Wifey did attend a co-ed grammar in

London. There were various arguments for keeping the sexes apart, some reasonable, others less so. My kids' dining hall was like a café or restaurant compared to ours which bore more resemblance to a spartan military mess hall; they were luckier than many state school kids in having a relatively new indoor gym and access to good quality council playing fields adjacent to the school.

There are now more opportunities for overseas travel both educational, such as History trips to WWI sites, and fun, like the annual ski trip. I was envious when Son was offered the chance of three weeks in jungle and island locations, assisting environmental scientists while at the same time learning to dive and generally having a true adventure. And I was sad that he turned the offer down, before realising that I was projecting my views on him and that, for a sixteen-year-old with limited interest in science, spending three weeks of his summer holidays without his mates, locked away with a bunch of boring old scientists, might not have held that much appeal.

By the time my kids started secondary school there was considerably more news being broadcast 24 hours a day, and they were probably by default much more attuned to what was going on. Like me though, I suspect they were oblivious to much of the world around them, although some major events were unavoidable. The Good Friday Agreement had been signed and the threat of IRA bombs was no more, but in 2001 the horrendous 9/11 attack in the USA heralded a chain of events that would lead to, among many things, the return of terrorism to the streets of Britain. On Boxing Day 2004, the Indian Ocean tsunami killed around 230,000 people in 14 countries. Returning to school after the holidays, Son and his mates came up with the idea of a lunchtime school concert to raise funds. With staff support they held the concert, charging pupils £1 entrance fee and raising over £600. His sister created a video of the event, and I still can't listen to 'Sweet Child of Mine' without thinking of it, smiling and feeling rather proud. 2005 saw protestors in France taking to the streets, torching cars and public buildings. Some things never change.

Sounding once again like an old timer, one thing that has definitely changed is discipline. I admit that my old headmaster's tendency to hurl a wooden blackboard rubber at a pupil in order to gain their attention may be a little over the top, but teachers today live under perpetual threat of suspension if they are accused of saying or doing just about anything that the pupils don't like. And the chances are that parents will usually side with their children, parental attitudes having changed significantly since my day when teachers, like doctors, were treated with respect by parents, and left to get on with the job; if you were punished, parents assumed that you had misbehaved and deserved it. No more. If a child is punished, their teacher is likely to receive verbal or even physical abuse from a parent determined that their dear child has been wrongfully treated.

Teachers are expected to get the best from children while their parents often abdicate responsibility, yet woe betide if they suggest the kid is lazy, disruptive or ignorant. Of course, this is not the case with all parents, at the other end of the spectrum are the ambitious ones.

One day, while Daughter was being shown around a university, I was taking tea and sandwiches with a number of parents and a couple of lecturers who were trying hard to sell the benefits of their institution. One of the lecturers asked if we had any questions, and a dad started a conversation along the following lines: "Yes, how do I find out how my son is doing?" "I'm sorry, I don't quite understand." "How do I find out if my son is doing the necessary work or misbehaving?" "Um, I'm afraid it has nothing to do with you." "I beg your pardon?" "The university has a contract with the student who, at eighteen, is a responsible adult. It has nothing to do with the parent."

I had intended keeping quiet but, of course, that was impossible; so I said how I was in total agreement, that uni years were when kids learnt a bit about life, and that parents had to cut them some slack and allow them to get on with it. I looked around expecting support from other parents before realising, once again, that I was on my own. Funny old world.

So, when it comes to secondary school education, do the kids today have it better than in my time? I think I would have preferred state grammar schools to have remained to cater for the truly academic kids, but the system definitely needed overhauling with regards choices and opportunities for those more practically inclined; there are plenty of highly intelligent people who just don't like schoolwork. And schools do now provide a far broader range of options than in the past, so in many ways education is better preparing them for the world of work in the twenty-first century.

I do, however, feel that schools have become so large that kids can become lost in them, almost anonymous input to 'education factories' that aim to churn out homogenous mini-adults; furthermore the extent to which teachers' hands are tied with regards discipline means that, while the kids might get away with more than we did, they are not necessarily as well prepared as they could be for the outside world of work.

11.

The Changing Face of Sport

Some 250,000 years ago, give or take, homo sapiens came down from the trees and began wandering the earth. We've evolved considerably since then, a process that, with the aid of technology, has accelerated markedly in the last few hundred years to the point where we take for granted space travel, nuclear fuel, organ transplants and the like, which is pretty mind-blowing. It's no surprise that such an advanced species needs a break some time, and we've come up with a suitably refined solution on which an inordinate amount of time and money is now focussed; playing games. Nothing trivial though, we're talking sport.

Arguably, the thing to have brought about the biggest changes in sport is television. Technical developments have driven the demand for more and better quality coverage, to the point that it is possible to view just about any sport, anywhere in the world, at a price. Sport has become a highly profitable business, at least to some, and this has brought huge changes since I was young.

Sport played a major part in my formative years. I loved playing anything, although had little interest in spectating. At first it was football in the winter and cricket in the summer, with a little athletics come school Sports Day. Then, at the age of 10, I discovered swimming, probably the only sport I was any good at. While the course of my adult life was largely dictated by my education, the type of person I became was also significantly affected by my love of swimming.

Like so many key things in life, my introduction to swimming was almost accidental. Aged 10, I loved to swim but for the unfortunate fact mentioned earlier, that I couldn't actually do it. I was totally happy floundering around in the water, but that's all it was, just floundering, so I wasn't particularly bothered when a new swimming pool opened in town, after all we had the Woods. Then friends talked of a swimming club being formed with trials for anyone who wished to join; sounded good to me, but unfortunately I was ill on the day of the trials and had to stay at home. Apparently loads of kids lined up at the deep end, dived in and swam the length, observed by various senior members of the club; anyone managing the length successfully was signed up and grouped on the basis of age and ability; those that failed were tactfully turned down.

A week or two later, now over my bug, I went along for a belated trial. I was the only hopeful by then, and everyone else was splashing away in their training groups. The club coach said he would watch and assess me, so I dived in manfully and headed for the shallow end thirty-six and two third long yards away, but I soon ran out of breath and sadly held on to the side.

Looking up, I realised the coach was in conversation with one of his assistants rather than watching me so, after a quick breather, I let go and continued on my way, stopping again a short while later, to see he was talking to someone else. This happened at least once more before I finally touched the end, breathlessly hauled myself out and went to see whether I was in or out.

"Did you do the length?" he asked. "Yes". "Without stopping?" Pause, then "Yes." "Well, you're in then." And that was it. Once again, my moral compass was spinning; had I been wrong to lie? But heck, I was only 10, and I so much wanted to join.

Luckily the beginners' class only involved swimming widths in the shallow end, I took to it like a duck to water, so to speak, doubling the distance swum each week, and in no time I was winning races and never looked back; not actually true, as backstroke became my main competitive stroke.

Swimming was soon the main thing in my life, and for years to come there would hardly be a day when I didn't go to the pool. Compared to what kids go through in sport today, our two training sessions a week were hardly arduous, but I probably achieved greater fitness from general swimming and playing daft games of endurance and pursuit during public sessions. Taking a running dive off the top board, swimming the length of the pool underwater and jumping out of the pool to hide in a storeroom or changing cubicle probably did me as much good as a structured training session; and was far more fun. Ah the pointless joys of youth.

My growing interest in aquatic sports wasn't really shared by the rest of the family. Both brothers are competent swimmers but neither really had any interest, football and cricket being far more important. Big Brother joined the swimming club from the beginning but didn't stay too long, although he did manage one major achievement before moving on. Probably around 1968, he won the Men's Open Freestyle Handicap, only one length, but the winner received the most handsome trophy the club had, a large silver cup inlaid with various fish; I went on to win trophies but all paled into insignificance compared to that beauty.

But swimming gave me far more than just exercise. True, concentration and dedication was called for, but not that much as, on the whole, I was enjoying myself. Competing was exhilarating, and while I honestly believed that taking part was more important than winning, losing was considerably less enjoyable. While primarily a solo sport, I was now a member of a team and enjoyed the camaraderie, particularly at competitions. Outside the pool my social life evolved around a group of team members that was pretty much classless. We covered both private and state schools, secondary modern and grammar; our homes varied from expensive private roads through to council estates and our family incomes ranged from the dole to that of high paid multinational executives; yet unless I was missing something, none of that mattered much.

Football has also played quite a part in my life, mainly playing rather than spectating, and at a lowly level at that. It was always a fun thing to me. As kids we were forever kicking a ball around. I recall a photo taken with Big Brother and a friend when I was little more than four; we were on our way to The Woods at the time, all in football kit of sorts, with one of us clutching a heavy old, laced leather football. We're wearing thick home-knitted sweaters, football shorts below our knees, striped socks and the most amazing boots; brown leather, high enough to protect the ankles, big round toecaps and leather studs nailed to the soles; quite a contrast to the essential team shirts and expensive lightweight boots of today.

The recent announcement of Ian St John's death reminded me of the 1965 FA cup between Liverpool and Leeds. In those days, northern clubs playing in the final often stayed at a hotel near us for a few days' pre-match preparation, and the local kids would go up there to catch a glimpse of the stars. The 1965 Christmas album of Charles Buchan Football Monthly featured a picture of eager fans gathered round St John to get his autograph; in prime position is Big Brother and, although the picture is black and white, he is obviously sporting Liverpool colours, which is surprising as he was, and still is, a Wolves supporter.

My favourite memory of school football comes from my final year at senior school. I was in the Second XI, enjoying a stellar run of victories although the First team members just mocked, claiming our success was down to the poor quality of the opposition. One Saturday, neither team had a game, so we held a match between ourselves.

The Firsts had all the stars and turned up ready to show us how real football was played but, sadly for them, we hadn't read the script; we played for fun, functioned well as a team and duly trounced them 3-0; I can still remember the Geography master responsible for us, jumping up and down on the sideline as the PE master who ran the Firsts prowled and scowled, muttering to himself. The victory was further rubbed in on Monday when the headmaster read the result out to the school assembly.

At eighteen I joined the old school football club, following Big Brother and soon to be joined by Little Brother. They would both spend most of their time in the First or Second XI while, with the exception of a couple of seasons in the Seconds, I languished in the Thirds, Fourths and Fifths. We competed in the London Old Boys League, allegedly the largest league in the world and, in the days before the M25 and satnavs, away matches often meant long tortuous drives meandering through London. At some point, Big Brother became a fan of musicals, particularly 'Oklahoma'. As First XI team captain he spread the joy and, while cruising down the A3 towards an away game with a carload of hefty footballers, he would have them all singing along to the cassette; I still remember puzzled looks from opposition teams gathered in our clubhouse for a convivial post-match pint as the First XI would burst into a rendition of 'Oh What a Beautiful Morning' or 'The Surrey With The Fringe on Top'.

Until the demise of grammar schools, playing in the London Old Boys League was restricted to anyone who had attended or taught at one of the competing schools. My swimming chum with the car met neither of these requirements and couldn't kick a ball, but that didn't stop him becoming club chairman after the league was opened to non-grammar boys; and a jolly good job he did too.

I played my last game for the club in my late thirties although occasionally return for a beer to see how things are going. But a decade or so later I was tempted to dust off my boots and turn out for a bunch comprising touchline companions from Son's Sunday team. We played occasional games in a small league of similar minded Dads, and for another ten years or so I would occasionally stroll around the pitch marveling at the speed and silky skills I had retained. Well, I can dream. In fact, one of my teammates summed it up nicely when, having been substituted off, he stood breathlessly watching the game before saying "it seems so much faster when you're out there".

Back in the day, televised matches were rare, with grainy distant black-and-white pictures. Even if filmed in colour, TV transmission was only in monochrome, so England's iconic red shirts from the 1966 World Cup were only seen in shades of grey. No close-ups; no video replays; virtually no post-match analysis. Since 1966, agreement has never really been reached as to whether Geoff Hurst's second goal did or did not cross the line; imagine the goal-line technology and different camera angles available if this were to occur today. That said, the introduction of VAR has not been without controversy; perhaps people still see what they want to see.

Even back then, television had a significant influence on the timing of the World Cup. The 1966 tournament schedule ran from Monday 11 July to 30 July; considerably later than the norm in order cater for other BBC outside broadcast commitments like Wimbledon and the Open Golf Championship.

In those days, the Football League comprised four groups imaginatively called First, Second, Third and Fourth divisions. Then, in 1992, the First Division teams resigned en masse to form the Premier League, giving them access to lucrative TV contracts with Sky; the cash started flowing and it has since become a truly multinational business; twelve of the twenty Premiership clubs currently have overseas owners, ten have non-British managers, and with Premier League teams allowed to register up to 17 non-home grown players in their 25-man squads, over 60% of players are now foreign.

Football has morphed from national pastime to huge international business. Consider the cash up for grabs for broadcasting rights alone; in the 2018/19 season Liverpool received the largest payment related to broadcasting rights, some £152m. Then there are sponsorship opportunities; apparently Manchester United's shirt deal with Chevrolet for the 2019/20 season was worth £64m. That's on top of ticket sales, merchandising, hospitality and so on.

Much of this cash end up in the players' pockets. In 1955, the average weekly wage for a footballer was £8, about £210 today, compared with £11 for that of a factory worker; only after much lobbying by the Professional Footballers Association was the Football League's £20 maximum weekly wage cap finally scrapped in 1961. Fast-forward to today, and apparently some 27 Premier League players receive annual salaries exceeding £10 million, with nearly one hundred on salaries of £5 million or more; the highest paid being Cristiano Ronaldo at nearly £27 million.

We used to watch football standing up. A small number of seats would be available for the more affluent, but for the full experience you just had to be on your feet. There was no real control on the numbers in attendance and during the 70s hooliganism became a major problem, with terraces the scene of large-scale punch-ups. Then came the Hillsborough disaster. At an FA Cup semi-final match between Liverpool and Nottingham Forest, 96 fans died and a further 766 were injured as a direct result of overcrowding. In the aftermath, one outcome was the introduction of a law requiring football grounds to become all-seated; a requirement that holds today for the Premier League and for Championship clubs who have been in the league for more than three seasons.

Women's football dates back to the 1800s; It was particularly popular during WWI, there being a shortage of players for the men's game. Then, in 1921, the FA suddenly banned it in all their grounds citing various reasons, although it was generally believed that they didn't like the distraction from the men's game. The ban was only lifted in 1969. Today the amount, quality and media coverage of women's football is at a level we would never have imagined as kids.

Golf is another sport whose image has changed in my lifetime. Golf clubs were solely bastions of the rich, and rich men to boot; their hallowed grounds were off limits to the poorer types who would only be allowed past the gates if they came to serve food or carry the master's clubs. My first best friend, the one who threw the can of stones at my head, was Jewish, and Dad told me how he would often see my friend's dad going out into The Woods in order to hit a few practice shots on the green because then, in the early 60s, Jews weren't allowed to join golf clubs.

Thankfully, things have changed; while many clubs continue to keep what they see as the riff-raff at bay, golf has become a considerably more inclusive sport; Dad often joked that you could never find a plumber on a Friday afternoon as they were all out on the golf course. Major tournaments can now all be watched live on TV, and the number of courses has ballooned, there now being some 2270 in England alone

The changing face of the Olympic Games perhaps illustrates best the way sport has evolved in my time. My earliest Olympic memories are of Tokyo in 1964; I was nine and can remember celebrating the news of Mary Rand's long jump gold medal. Our first female athlete to win gold, Mary also broke the world record and won two other medals. But all this was going on in Japan nine hours ahead of us, the event was during our nighttime, and we had to wait for breakfast radio to fill us in on the results. Such a contrast to current day when satellite broadcasts mean you can stay up all night to watch the thing live.

Costs of staging the Games were already rocketing in 1964 and they've gone ever upward. Average sports-related costs for the Summer Games since 1960 are allegedly $5.2 billion. To meet these spiraling costs, the IOC chose to sell off marketing rights to the Games and, hey presto, like some kind of Frankenstein's monster, they changed almost beyond recognition from a celebration of human endeavor, achievement and sportsmanship through amateur sport, into a huge commercial juggernaut.

The first sponsored Games were those in Los Angeles in 1984. Back then, any commercial relationship with a company led to an athlete being banned, but in1986 the IOC allowed a select number of professional athletes to participate, and by the turn of the century the presence of professional competitors became commonplace. Despite the high level of commercial support generated, the 2004 Athens Olympics cost a staggering $9 billion and probably contributed big-time to the Greek financial crisis.

But occasional glimmers of the amateur past shine through as when, at the Sydney Games in 2000, Eric Moussambani Malonga or "Eric the Eel", a swimmer from Equatorial Guinea, won his 100m freestyle heat after the other competitors were disqualified for false starts; his winning time was the slowest ever, 1minute 52.72, the Gold ultimately being won with a time of 48.3 secs.

Since the first modern Games held in Athens in 1896, only five sporting disciplines have featured in all subsequent Games, namely Athletics, Cycling, Fencing, Gymnastics and Swimming. Many sports have come and gone; more traditional sports like Tennis, Golf and Rugby have returned in recent years, while others have raised a few conservative eyebrows, as when Beach Volleyball events were introduced in Atlanta in 1996 or when Surfing and Skateboarding were included in the postponed Tokyo

Games. Paris 2024 is to include breaking, or breakdancing to us less hip types.

It is inevitable that in proceedings as prestigious, expensive and far-reaching as the Olympics, politics will raise its head. Ten days before the start of the 1968 Mexico Games, police opened fire on students protesting that their government had given priority to hosting the Games rather than feeding the poor; more than 200 protestors were killed. During a medal ceremony at the same games, two US athletes each raised a black-gloved hand in salute; a gesture of support for the Black Power movement that was witnessed around the world.

In 1980, the USA and 65 other countries, boycotted the Moscow Olympics in response to the Soviet invasion of Afghanistan; so naturally, the Russians, East Germans and twelve other Eastern Bloc countries chose to boycott the 1984 Games in LA; Iran and Libya boycotted those Games for other reasons. On a smaller scale, North Korea and their ally Cuba boycotted the 1988 Seoul Games.

In 1992 a 32-year ban on South Africa was lifted following the abolition of apartheid and South Africa was welcomed back into the Olympic fold.

It also goes without saying that, in an event with so much money and prestige at stake, the temptation to cheat can be strong, and the Olympics have not been without their share of controversy. By far the biggest concern is the illegal use of performance-enhancing drugs, a problem that's been around since the modern Games began. In 1989 an Australian Senate committee report into the 1980 Moscow Games concluded that any gold medal winner was probably on at least one banned substance, and that this was likely to be the case with the majority of other medal winners. The challenge was indeed daunting as, particularly in some communist countries where athletes' lives were run by the state, doping was seen as a legitimate means to improve performances. In 1999, the World Anti-Doping Agency (WADA) came into being with the aim of standardising a global approach to drug abuse in sport; but it remains an uphill struggle with regular high-level scandals as the cheats develop new ways to circumvent the rules.

There have been countless other accusations of cheating. At the Munich 1972 gold medal basketball game, after the US appeared to win the game by 1 point, the final three seconds were replayed, not once but three times, before the Russians scored and were declared winners. Or Montreal 1976, when a Russian competitor in the pentathlon was disqualified after it transpired his epée had been doctored so that touches were scored despite their being no actual contact made with his opponent. At the 1988 Seoul Games a South Korean boxer beat a US opponent despite the latter landing 86 punches to 32. It is regularly said that taking part is more important than winning, but it seems some would disagree.

The Paralympics is a sporting event that's flourished in my lifetime. The concept originated with a sports competition held in England in 1948 for British World War II veterans with spinal cord injuries. A similar event was held four years later, this time including athletes from the Netherlands, before evolving further until, in 1960, Rome hosted the first Olympic-style Games for disabled athletes. Since 1988 the Paralympics have been held a couple of weeks after the Olympics closing ceremony at the same venues used by the non-disabled athletes and is now an integral part of the package.

This previously low-key event grabbed the public attention big-time in London 2012 by way of an effective publicity campaign and significant prime-time coverage on TV, in particular Channel 4. "Humbled" was a word regularly used as people discussed the performances of athletes who had shown such grit and determination in overcoming their disabilities. Athletes like David Weir and Tanni Grey-Thompson powering around the track in their wheelchairs and swimmer Ellie Simmonds who, four years earlier aged just thirteen, had already won the public's affection and two gold medals at the Rio Games. 'Blade Runner' Oscar Pistorius who, despite losing both legs, competed successfully at the highest level against non-disabled athletes, although unfortunately he would later gain global notoriety for shooting dead his girlfriend. Since 2012 the Royal Mail has honoured British Paralympic gold medalists the same as non-disabled gold medalists by painting gold a postbox in their hometown.

The Winter Olympics used to be held in the same year as the Summer games but, since 1994, they have been held on a four-year cycle, two years after the summer equivalent. In my youth they didn't grab the public attention to the same extent as the summer events, probably as most of the population had never skied, and because far fewer British athletes participated. We did however celebrate three figure skating gold medals through the efforts of John Curry, Robin Cousins and Torvill & Dean, whose performance of the Bolero at the 1984 Sarajevo Games gained the highest ever score achieved in a figure skating programme and was probably viewed by most of the British population either live or in news bulletins.

Among my fondest memories of the Winter Olympics are the exploits of "Eddie the Eagle" at the Calgary Games in 1988. A failed downhill skier, Eddie turned to ski jumping and was the first British competitor in the event since 1928. He of course came last, but that wasn't the point. Calgary was also when the Jamaican bobsleigh team, inspiration for the Hollywood film 'Cool Runnings', first came on the scene.

In recent years, as more and more Brits have taken to the slopes, the Winter Olympics have gained in popularity. We can boast a slightly wider range of medals including Amy Williams' and Lizzy Yarnold's Gold medals for the skeleton in 2010 and 2014 respectively. Even hitherto unknown events like Curling have grabbed our attention; I recall the 2002 Salt Lake City Games, watching late into the night, cheering on Rhona Martin and her team of Scottish ladies as they took Gold from the Swiss favourites.

The Winter Olympics also has its fair share of controversy and, following the Sochi Games of 2014, evidence came to light showing how huge state-run drug abuse was rife, leading to a four-year Olympics ban for all Russian athletes.

Perhaps that's enough on the changing face of sport; but are things better or worse today? In one area I think that things are definitely worse: that of role models. Young professional athletes can only spend so much time training and competing before, like hyperactive kids, they get bored and need entertaining. Many have no financial worries and some, Premier League footballers in particular, have more cash than they know what to do with. Not surprisingly, in their search for entertainment there can be some misbehaviour and the tabloids are always there to report on their misdemeanours, whether related to drink, drugs, sex or anything else that will sell papers.

In my youth, most sportsmen earned 'normal' wages with little spare cash for excesses; of course, they were worshipped by their fans and open to temptation, but when they succumbed their escapades were far less likely to be reported in the press. Bobby Moore was accused of stealing a gold bracelet in Colombia before the 1970 World Cup finals, although he was ultimately proven innocent; Georgie Best's hedonistic lifestyle often earned more press coverage than his brilliant footballing skills and yes, Lester Piggott definitely evaded the taxman, culminating in a short stay at her majesty's pleasure; but these were rare events and soon forgotten. Youngsters need someone to look up to and, with the exception of a few like Marcus Rashford who recently made a name for himself standing up to the government in support of the poor, good role models for youngsters seem few and far between.

It is hard to think of a sport that has not been affected by money one way or another. Cash often trumps loyalty to fans and home clubs, as stars worshipped by their followers leave to chase the money. The cost of tickets continually escalates, and priority is frequently given to corporate entertainment over real fans.

As more sports are televised, their appeal may increase, and as professional participants have more time and financial incentive to improve their game, the quality of performances, records broken and the like go up. But all this costs money, and many fans have been priced out of watching live major professional sporting events; meanwhile equipment endorsed by the stars becomes must-haves for kids, regardless of cost.

Sports stars are in a position to bring a great deal of pleasure to their fans so I can't begrudge them making a good living from their skills, but there are definitely times when I feel things have gone too far and I pine for the good old days when, in my mind at least, sport was mostly amateur, played for fun and sportsmanship generally trumped a 'win at any cost' attitude. So, call me old-fashioned, but I think that despite all the improvements brought about by injections of cash, the world of sport was better in my day.

12.

If Music be the Food of Love Play on

"If you don't like music, you've no soul", a view regularly expressed by Dad, and one with which I heartily concur. He never played an instrument but loved to listen and given the chance, to dance. Opera and classical weren't really his thing, he was more a fan of crooners Frank Sinatra, Nat King Cole and Bing Crosby; of band music by James Last and Bert Kaempfert or jazz by the likes of Louis Armstrong and many more. As kids we were treated to such classics as 'My Old Man's a Dustman' by Lonnie Donegan and Tommy Steele's 'Little White Bull'. They don't write them like they used to!

Our record player was a source of wonder to me. Only vinyls of course, with the option of three speeds, 45 rpm for singles and $33^{1/3}$ rpm for LPs, or albums to you. A third option, 78rpm, was only for very old records of which we had none, but this could be used to play our records at speed and was an occasional source of merriment. Up to ten singles, never LPs, could be stacked on a central spindle and the machine worked through the pile dropping a new one onto the turntable as the previous record finished. Magic.

The record player was usually on the landing, convenient for Saturday nights, which at some point became bath and music night. To begin with, my brothers and I, aged around 2, 5 and 8, all somehow managed to fit in the bath with Dad while pretending to paddle down the Orinoco or some such river, all to the accompaniment of Frank Sinatra, Tommy Steele et al. As we grew, bathtime became less communal but always to music. The mix was eclectic to say the least, 'I'm The King of the Swingers' from Jungle Book becoming a favourite. Later, as Big Brother spread his wings and prepared for Saturday nights out, the music changed, not always to Dad's taste, to include artists like Otis Redding, Geno Washington and The Ram Jam Band, Bob Dylan and Leonard Cohen.

In December 1965, courtesy of my cousin, the only girl ever in the Mars Bar gang, and her hairdresser auntie, I saw the Beatles live at Hammersmith in 'Another Beatles Christmas Show'. John Lennon lived in a mansion not far from us at the time, and one day as auntie was doing the hair of a nice young lady, Cynthia Lennon I assume, she told how her husband was in the Beatles and offered free tickets to their upcoming show. Auntie was given three and I was invited along; quite an adventure for cuz and me, including a bus ride all the way to Hammersmith, although I'm not sure what Auntie made of the whole do. One of the support acts was The Yardbirds featuring Eric Clapton so, at such a tender age not only were we witnessing the early days of the most influential pop band ever, but also one of the most famous guitarists of a generation, even if I had no idea on either count.

Reading details of the event today, it sounds more like a family variety show. The two daily performances included a pantomime sketch featuring The Beatles dressed as Antarctic explorers searching for the Abominable Snowman; what more can I say? Tickets were 15 shillings or 1 pound (roughly £15/£20 today). What I do remember is being totally bemused, sitting in the balcony looking down on thousands of screaming girls; what on earth was going on?

Singles then cost 6s 8d and LPs were 1 pound and twelve shillings; equating to around £6 and £30 today, which is hard to believe, although I suppose they were very rare purchases. Each side of an LP usually had about six or seven tracks and would play for up to twenty minutes. My earliest memory of buying a record is the Beatles single 'I want to Hold Your Hand'.

Television coverage of our music was limited and we relied heavily on radio. Particularly popular, were battery-powered transistor radios the size of a cigarette packet; with a single earphone I would listen under the bedcovers into the night. Rebels as we were, the main source of listening were pirate radio stations like Radio Caroline, an unlicensed outfit transmitting from a boat anchored outside British waters. Another, Radio Luxembourg, was not a 'pirate' although their nightly English language broadcast wasn't covered by British radio licenses so technically it was illegal to tune in. Here for the first time, we heard of Keynsham in Somerset, "spelt K-E-Y-N-S-H-A-M", home of Horace Batchelor's Famous Infra-Draw Method for winning the football pools. In 1967, in an attempt to meet obvious growing demand, the government responded with BBC's Radio 1 with a first broadcast hosted by Tony Blackburn, himself a Radio Caroline veteran.

On TV we had the BBC's 'Jukebox Jury', presented by David Jacobs. A jury of four celebrities listened to new releases, discussed their merits and gave each a score from 1 to 5; "I'll give it five", delivered with a strong Brummie accent, became a catchphrase nationwide after regular use by one of the judges. The ITV had 'Ready Steady Go!' ("The weekend starts here!"), and in January 1964, along came BBC's 'Top of The Pops', not to be missed by schoolkids for generations to come. I loved it then, but as my tastes matured it lost its cool, though I now realise how radical TOTP could be; from the start there were corrupting influences like The Rolling Stones, but the list of undesirables is long, including Alice Cooper and The Sex Pistols who were pre-recorded for fear they would start a riot. They also gave the outside, or grownup, world a first look at David Bowie in his Ziggy Stardust persona and androgynous Boy George, and they were definitely not amused; I imagine it brought on a few coronaries as the Oldies rushed spluttering to put pen to paper complaining to Points of View about how their license fees were being wasted on such depraved rubbish. The show was at the heart of British youth culture for many years and finding a recording artist who hasn't been on it is quite a challenge.

Other shows came and went, but in 1971 the ultimate arrived, 'The Old Grey Whistle Test'. Compulsory viewing for discerning music fans, it was on late and aimed at an audience old enough not to need permission to stay up. It was dedicated to albums, not singles, or as we rather pompously thought at the time, 'real music'. Tuesday nights would never be the same.

Early shows were broadcast from a tiny continuity studio with a budget to match. The first show had a budget of just £500, and on being informed he would receive £15 for an interview recorded in New York, John Lennon reputedly asked to be paid in chocolate biscuits. Most artists performed live in the studio, although overseas bands would occasionally be represented by promotional films or collections of archive clips. The music was varied to say the least and introduced mainly by 'Whispering Bob' Harris. It was commissioned by David Attenborough, and by BBC standards, was pretty anarchic; apparently the air in the studio was often heavy with pungent fumes and the noise level was extreme, but housed well away from the mainstream they were able to get away with it. Attenborough does tell, however, of being regularly hauled up to explain to his bosses why the programme had overrun yet again; by law, broadcasting was to stop by around 11:30 I think but, for example, when Lynyrd Skynyrd played 'Freebird' and just kept playing, it would have been rude to pull the plug. Those were the days.

"If you remember the Sixties you weren't there" is a phrase often used in reference to the growing use of recreational drugs, presumably responsible for a lot of the song lyrics of the time: I mean, what other explanation is there for the Beatles singing about the escapades of a semolina pilchard? This was the era of the hippy movement, a time of Cultural Revolution when many kids challenged what they saw as the failed norms of society; some dropped out, moving into hippy communes and following a counterculture advocating political decentralisation, sharing, peace and love; all assisted by a hefty dose of LSD and other psychedelic pharmaceuticals, although Grateful Dead guitarist Bob Weir apparently said "….it was not about drugs. It was about exploration, finding new ways of expression, being aware of one's existence." Hmmm.

The 60s saw the advent of the outdoor music festival so loved today. In the US, events like the Monterey Pop Festival in 1967 built up to the pinnacle, Woodstock, attended by some 400,000 fans, in the Summer of Love 1969. But the Brits had their coup a few days later when, having turned down an invite to Woodstock virtually in his own backyard, music god Bob Dylan headlined the British version on the Isle of Wight instead. 1970 also saw Jimi Hendrix on the Isle of Wight, and the inaugural Glastonbury festival, now a recurring major event in the British music calendar.

I have never been to a festival, originally through lack of money although later purely due to laziness, but I do love live music when I make the effort. One of my favourite memories is of a mid-summer extravaganza at Wembley stadium in 1975 where Elton John was promoting his new album 'Captain Fantastic and the Brown Dirt Cowboy'. I was a fan of Elton's but, to be honest, not terribly impressed by the time he spent playing the new stuff. But… support included the Beachboys, who I had loved for years and a new band, The Eagles with Joe Walsh. The weather was glorious, not a cloud in the sky, and the music sublime.

Saturday 13th July 1985, Wembley. Another beautifully sunny day and Live Aid, a musical extravaganza arranged by Bob Geldof and Midge Ure to raise funds for the Ethiopian famine. Doubtless not everyone's motives were altruistic, but the event definitely raised global awareness of issues in Africa. There were publicity stunts like Phil Collins' supersonic dash by Concorde to perform both in London and New York, and supporting concerts were staged in numerous countries; coordinated television broadcasts through global satellite linkups meant an estimated 1.9 billion people allegedly saw the event; that's nearly 40% of the population of the world at the time; pretty impressive if true.

There have been countless discussions as to how much money was raised, where it actually ended up and the extent to which the famine victims benefited, but this event surely marks the point at which mass media was recognised as the most effective method of drawing attention to, and raising funds for, charitable causes. It was inspired by George Harrison's 1971 Concert for Bangladesh, the first time music was used to raise awareness and support for the starving.

Time passes, and in 2018 I saw the Beach Boys in the more refined setting of Hampton Court Palace where, incidentally I saw Bryan Ferry the year before. By 'The Beach Boys', I mean Mike Love plus a group of very talented young musicians who ably reproduced the harmonies required to provide a great night. I had tickets to see The Eagles in 2020 at the new Wembley Stadium, 45 years on, but that was cancelled thanks to Covid.

The problem that I have is that 'my' music is getting very old; I have never really been a fan of tribute bands, but this is what most of the old bands still touring have become with little resemblance to their original lineup. I saw Chris Rea in 2017 at the Hammersmith Apollo. He was recovering from a stroke, which obviously had an impact, but it was still great to hear him play. Shortly afterward, he was taken ill again, and presumably he is unlikely to return to the stage. Similarly, John Mayall's 85th anniversary tour was cancelled due to ill health.

One of the strangest, yet most enjoyable, musical experiences of my life was in 2004 when Wishbone Ash, a huge band in my later school years, performed at the village hall in the small Surrey village of Chiddingfold. One of the dads at Son's football club told me of the gig and we took the boys to introduce them to 'real music'. The lineup had significantly changed over the years, but there was Andy Powell and his Flying V blasting it out about 10 yards away from where I, and fans of various ages, stood mesmerised. Fantastic. And the boys' response? "Alright I suppose."

I realise now how my, admittedly limited, live music experiences have circled around a small number of venues. In the early seventies I saw Stevie Wonder live in Brixton, possibly at the Sundown Centre, which is now the Brixton Academy where I saw Rag 'n' Bone Man in 2017. In 2018, Stevie Wonder, was in Hyde Park with Eric Clapton, fifty-three years after my 1965 experience at Hammersmith Odeon, where Chris Rea had performed in 2017. Also playing in Hyde Park was Santana who I first saw in 2013 at Wembley Arena where I once worked as a steward in order to see Dire Straits. And so on. For me, it's a small world after all.

But if musical tastes and styles, together with our choice of venues, have evolved significantly over the past sixty-five years, the level of change is trivial compared to that brought about by technology. From the very instruments played and the way music is produced, through to the way it is distributed and consumed, a large part of the industry is unrecognisable to that of my youth.

Music was available through radio and, to a lesser degree, television, but to listen to music of our choice we had to buy the record and play it on a gramophone, or record player. Then, in 1963, Philips invented the compact cassette, a game changer. Cassettes and the machines they played on were smaller and more portable, and the advent of battery-operated machines made music accessible outdoors. This went further in the 70s as they became common in cars; car radios had been around a long time but the listener had no say in what they were listening to. We now not only had a new way of listening to music but, with a blank tape, could record our own. It's hard to express the new power this gave us: the hours spent holding a microphone close to the radio as it played our favourite song; desperately trying not to make a noise that would be picked up by the microphone, and hoping the DJ would keep his mouth shut to the end of the record. I took this to extremes in 1972 when I smuggled my cassette recorder into an America concert at The Royal Festival Hall and sat unmoving, microphone concealed in my sleeve, for the whole performance. The resulting bootleg recording was muffled and completely useless and I didn't really get to enjoy the performance either. There's a moral there.

Reel-to-reel tapes had been around for a while, although they were expensive and tended only to be owned by the more technically minded; but as stereo music centres became more commonplace their popularity increased. Music could now be copied directly via a wire, as opposed to a microphone, and played back through the stereo. We could make long uninterrupted recordings lasting hours, or shorter more portable ones on cassette. In 1973 I worked in a hi-fi shop and got for Dad a second-hand Akai reel-to-reel recorder. He loved it and was forever copying his old record collection to tape and creating a variety of playlists, definitely a man ahead of his time. As years passed, his needs changed and he went on to edit and copy those tapes to cassette, then finally, about 7 years ago, I copied the cassettes to CD for him; to my aging ear the sound quality was surprisingly good after so many reincarnations.

Chronologically, between the gramophone and compact cassettes came eight-track cassettes with tape in a loop that played continually, repeating ad infinitum until turned off. They were popular in the US, particularly in cars, where music was not seen as the luxury option it was in the UK, and in time a fair library of pre-recorded tapes became available; the format gathered a small foothold in the UK but was quickly overtaken by the cassette.

1979 saw the release of the Sony Walkman cassette player; we now had a genuinely portable means of listening to songs of our choice while on the move. This was truly revolutionary and took the world by storm.

Recording digital information on an optical transparent foil, initially developed as a means of storing computer data, became a commercial success in the early eighties with CDs offering much clearer recordings, welcomed by many but scorned by aficionados who prefer the 'real' sound of vinyl. I got my first CD player in 1984. At the time I read an article apologising that a prediction made a few years earlier, that once setup costs had been recovered CDs would be far cheaper than vinyl, had not come about. The author blamed greed for keeping prices at £10 but felt that, as costs fell further prices must surely fall dramatically too. Huh. Greed won out and prices only came down decades later in response to the success of streaming services.

Next came the mp3 file format and, in 2001, the iPod; suddenly audio files required 95% less storage space. A Sony Walkman with a C120 cassette held 120 minutes of music, say 30 to 40 tracks. My old iPod holds 8,000 tracks with plenty of room for more. Finally, the current norm, streaming; keeping music in hard format as discs or tapes, is so old hat when, for a small fee, any listener with access to the Internet has an almost unlimited range of music at their fingertips.

Technology has also hugely impacted the way musical acts evolve. There used to be no easy way for bands to achieve exposure other than through live performances, a hard apprenticeship. Kit would be bundled into the back of a van and driven the length and breadth of the country where the band would play to small, often disinterested or even hostile audiences in pubs and clubs, for fees barely covering the cost of food and fuel. While they weren't all to my taste, the few that made it must have had something special to offer in order to take the next step, a recording contract. They needed considerable dedication, and throughout the journey gained a hell of a lot of experience.

Today greater, even international, exposure can be achieved in next to no time courtesy of the Internet. This might well give more people a chance of fame, but that tends to be short-lived, possibly because of the fickle nature of fans, or maybe the artist's limited abilities are rapidly exposed; or sometimes they are just not prepared to cope with the life that instant fame brings.

Digital technology gives the ability not only to complete recording much faster, but also editing is far quicker and more sophisticated so that even mediocre acts can be made to sound good, one reason why I have developed a liking for live recordings. True, these can still be edited, but the fact that the live performance took place at all suggests a reasonable level of competence.

Artists can now create the sound of a musical instrument, band or even an orchestra, electronically at a relatively low cost at home without repairing to a studio. This not only adds to the flood of musical offerings available, but can also undermine the market value of all but the top musicians, recording engineers and the like. Where is it all going to end?

Covid has highlighted yet another way that things have changed. Traditionally, artists' and record companies' financial wellbeing was largely determined by record sales, but as music becomes more easily available and cheaper, this is no longer the case, and many artists depend more on ticket sales from a growing number of live performances to make a living. The ban on large gatherings during the recent lockdown has caused many artists and recording companies serious grief and the actual fallout will only be clear in years to come.

At sixteen I bought my first guitar. School music classes were uninspiring and recorder lessons held little appeal to a lumbering teenage lad, but I had friends who were keen musicians and wanted to join them. So when one of them was selling a lovely sunburst acoustic guitar for £25, a princely sum to me in those days, I desperately wanted it. My parents had little 'spare' cash, but I asked them to lend me the money and, presumably after considerable discussion, Mum said they would buy me the guitar on the proviso that it wasn't just a fad. What lovely parents!

They may however have reconsidered the wisdom of their move when, only a few weeks later, I was continually, slowly and very painfully, strumming a Bob Dylan song while they called for me to "stop playing that bloody guitar"; the joys of parenthood. I guess that's what you get when you leave your baby in his pram on his own to face the elements. I was never very good but so what?

I'd only been learning a short time before reluctantly agreeing to play bass at a school rock concert. My friends worked out some simple riffs that I was to follow slavishly while they did the hard bits and would catch up if I wandered off. We had a name of course; Mortimer Crowbar's Twenty Minute Boogie Blues Rock Band. Catchy huh? It was going to be Forty Minutes but we didn't manage to learn enough tunes in time. To be honest we

124

weren't exactly brilliant; I don't know the extent to which my performance contributed to this outcome, but I have never felt inclined to join a band since.

Instead, I've passed many an enjoyable hour solo on my acoustic, happily singing along in a voice that I like to think is not light years away from the actual notes being played, but I rarely sing if anyone else is around. I put this down to a traumatic event when I was about ten. In preparation for a carol concert, our class was rehearsing their song in the school hall; I loved singing and belted the words out with gusto. Unfortunately, as an early maturer my voice had already broken. Standing at the back of the hall our teacher, with a slight scowl on her face, started moving slowly towards us like a hunting beast before coming to a halt in front of me; "perhaps you could just mime," she said. I was devastated, and to this day am self-conscious about my voice.

It seems a lot more common these days for kids to play musical instruments; for a start they are cheaper and far more available. Also, with YouTube and other apps, it is now possible to access a huge variety of music and not only see the chords and notes required, but also to watch videos of how they are played. For us it was either scribbled notes from a friend, or buy books that not only cost as much as the actual music we were trying to copy, but weren't terribly easy to follow either.

It's still not easy for a beginner to get the coordination right and put everything together though, and I suspect only a small minority of kids continue after the first few months. I'm happy that both mine have gotten into their music; Daughter played violin at school and now piano, guitar and bass; after a brief early attempt at guitar Son moved to drums; he is a good drummer but has since also returned to guitar and bass, both of which he also plays well. Other than a few early lessons they are both pretty much self-taught and better than I ever was. They are also far more relaxed about performing in front of people, and I just love listening to them. Son now occasionally plays drums with a band formed by an old family friend; his tender years brings their average age down to around sixty and, momentarily, they considered calling themselves Old Play.

So, after much self-indulgent rambling, what conclusions have I come to? Have the changes I've witnessed been for the better? In my teenage years the technological advances to come were unimaginable; easy access to the huge range of music available today would have seemed a dream. And yet an infinite supply of music may come at a cost, as the listener can be overwhelmed, not really identifying with any of it. In the seventies we would gather somewhere, anywhere, to listen to music, LPs (never singles) clamped proudly under our arms or, for the hippier element, in their army surplus bags. Our albums proclaimed who we were, or at least were trying to be, and I think this is missing today.

I also think that the huge increase in quantity has been at the expense of quality; in my view a relatively small number of talented acts have emerged in recent years accompanied by a flood of mediocre or even terrible ones. As my kids and their friends learned guitar, it was the music of my era that they turned to far more than current stuff, which I think speaks volumes; how many of today's stars will be performing forty or fifty years on? Perhaps it's just me, but it seems that while music provides a permanent background to life today, little of it has much meaning to your average listener; then again perhaps it never did. So, with my more than slightly biased view, I have to say music was better in my day.

Postscript. Hard to imagine I know, but occasionally my family poke fun at my musical tastes or my tendency to stand transfixed by a particular riff, solo or line. But that's OK; I'm man enough to take it. I would however like to choose a piece of music that I particularly associate with each of them. For Daughter, Chris Rea's 'Wired to the Moon' will always remind me of the joy and terror we faced on first experiencing parenthood. I can never listen to 'Sweet Child of Mine' without a smile and a proud glow recalling Son's Tsunami performance. And for Wifey, Bob Seger's 'Always in my Heart' says it all.

13.

Oh the Lure of the Open Road!

There were between 3 and 4 million cars on the road in the UK the year I was born; by the end of 2019 that number had risen to 31.9 million. Throw in another 4 or 5 million lorries and trucks, 1.3 million motorbikes and 150 thousand buses and coaches and that's an awful lot of internal combustion engines spewing out vast amounts of noxious gases, not to mention noise.

Cars tend to be a 'man thing', with aging petrol heads lovingly polishing their classic motors before taking them for a nostalgic spin down memory lane. Of course, not all men treat their cars like pampered children. Big Brother had a Bentley for a while; being a keen gardener he would often get manure from the local stable and would think nothing of placing a tarpaulin in the boot before shovelling the manure in. For some reason I like that.

In 1955, Britain was the world's second largest motor vehicle producer behind the USA. More than 95% of the cars on our roads were made in the UK, an overwhelming majority being built by just five companies; Nuffield/BMC, Ford, Rootes, Standard-Triumph and Vauxhall; there were also some 60 smaller marques. Sadly, today less than 20 per cent of all new cars sold in the UK are assembled here.

The story of the Mini, launched in August 1959 as the Morris Mini Minor and the Austin Seven, reflects the fate of our car industry. The Mini was designed in response to a slump in demand for larger cars after the Suez Crisis led to increased prices and shortages of fuel; at just over 3 metres long and weighing in at a little over half a ton, the car was genuinely mini, yet that didn't stop it becoming a true British icon. In 1964, the Mini Cooper S won the Monte Carlo Rally, beating larger and more powerful rivals, a feat to be repeated in both 1965 and 1967; and who hasn't enjoyed Michael Caine's red, white and blue minis in the 1969 film 'The Italian Job'?

But alas, that age is history, the Mini brand is no longer British having been bought by BMW who introduced their first model in 2001. Bentley, Rolls-Royce, Aston Martin, Lotus and Morgan are all that remain today of the smaller British car makers and all, too, are now under foreign ownership. Personally, I was a fan of the Jensen Interceptor; remember them?

The MOT test was first introduced in 1960. Cars underwent a basic test on brakes, lights, steering and the like when they reached ten years old. Since then, the test has become vastly more stringent and costly. I first heard of the MOT Test when I was about twelve. The oldest member of our swimming club group would have been about eighteen at the time and, while the rest of us depended on bikes for transport, he had the luxury of a car. 'Luxury' might not be the exact word I'm looking for, the car in question was a matt beige-coloured 1953 Ford Prefect that had definitely seen better days. It included features like a block of wood raising the seat so the driver could see over the dashboard; if, as often happened, one of the rear passengers accidentally kicked the block, the seat would drop and mayhem would ensue, although we were lucky enough never to crash.

As this was our only form of group transport, we would often have to cram in more people than there were seats; eight would not be uncommon although this was luxury when you consider that, according to the Guinness Book of Records, 27 people once crammed into a classic mini. One day we were stopped by the Police, and a number of passengers got out with the driver to observe his interrogation, leaving three behind. At one point, a constable asked how many people there were in the car; "Three" came the answer. He seemed satisfied with that and soon after they drove off.

Once we used the car to tow a dinghy to the nearby gravel pit. It didn't have a towbar, but that problem was easily overcome, it was only a couple of miles drive so we simply tied it to the back and the boat owner stood on the bumper holding it in place. For some reason, the father of one of the swimmers forbade him to travel in this car, so we always had to drop him off a short walk from home.

But back to MOTs. As the car was due for a test, my friend took it in. Apparently, all was going well until the car was put on the ramps and raised for the tester to examine the underside. The car's ascent was suddenly cut short when the tester happened to notice the four G clamps my friend had added in order to hold the suspension together; back down went the car and the tester, obviously an understanding type, said "just get it off my forecourt and I'll pretend I never saw it".

The next thing I knew, my friend was driving a 1954 Wolsey 1550, a very smart car in its time, walnut dashboard, leather upholstery and a revolutionary manumatic gearbox. Needless to say, by then it wasn't quite so smart. I think these experiences set my expectations regarding motor transport.

Occasionally on a Saturday night, with nothing else to do, four or five of us would just get in the car and drive. A favourite haunt was what I now know are the Surrey Hills, but to us then it was just an area of unlit, winding narrow country lanes where you might suddenly come across a welcoming country pub. We particularly liked The Parrot in Forest Green, but as we generally had no idea where we were, we tended to refind it by accident; that was the fun.

We just drove, while holding deep intellectual conversations of course. Eventually we would come across a major road with signposts to names we recognised, usually somewhere near Dorking, and would wend our way home. In the summer we might leave the pub at closing time and head south to the coast, sleeping in the car ready for an early morning dip.

Aged 18, I bought my first car for the princely sum of £30; a matt grey, 1955 Morris Minor with split windscreen. Owned by a man in Dad's local, it hadn't been started for years, and as it had been parked under a tree it was coated in all sorts of gunk. But it was solid with no signs of rust and, amazingly, started first time. Cash changed hands, and I became a proud vehicle owner. I cleaned it up, painted the wings blue and drilled a hole for a long fibreglass aerial, just before hearing that the Montagu Motor Museum were looking to pay good money for a car such as mine in its original condition i.e. without blue wings and an aerial; another opportunity missed.

The car would be an unnecessary luxury at uni, so I knew I only had it for a year. I have one particularly fond memory of it standing proud in the car park at the prep school where I worked as a temporary PE teacher; alongside was a parent's 'shopping car', a brand-new shocking pink Lamborghini. They seemed so perfectly matched.

Cars those days were far more basic machines; no computers, and minimal electrics to worry about meant faults usually came down to problems with the distributor cap, spark plugs or fuel feed. Garages were too expensive and so we always tried to fix them ourselves. One time, I couldn't source a basic spare part, so Dad got a friend who worked at the local dental factory to make it for me. My talents were definitely limited, although I did become a dab hand at fixing exhaust pipes with some wire, a baked bean tin and a pot of Gun Gum.

There followed a variety of old cars, a few lasted a while but my general approach was to buy something very cheap with a full MOT, drive it for a year and then scrap it when the next MOT was due. There was a Renault 4 that started grey before we sprayed it bright orange, a black Vauxhall Viva, hand-painted complete with brush marks, an Austin 1100 and an MG 1300. I was particularly fond of my old BMW 2002; it was matt grey and a bit of a heap, but its looks belied the quality of the engine that managed to surprise a few boy racers. Dad gave me his old Cortina MkII estate, and I was driving an aging red VW Beetle by the time I met my wife-to-be. I think she must have been impressed.

We got married and moved into a house that needed a fair bit of work, meaning I had no time to mess around with old cars, so when the Beetle became temperamental it had to go. Wifey had her large, impressive, Opel Rekord and we decided I needed something newer and more reliable; so I bit the bullet and bought my first new car. For

132

the huge sum of £2,999 I bought a Citroen 2CV; a lovely pale pastel yellow, like custard. It had a 600cc engine with a top speed of 70½ MPH.

Of course, I was at the receiving end of much stick at the football club where the advertising execs preferred their Porsches, but nothing I couldn't handle. One bright spark did come up with a particularly good line though, when he said, "I never realised they made them new." But the car actually proved to be a useful investment, as long as we weren't in a hurry. Designed by the French for farmers to carry 50Kg loads across unploughed fields it was incredibly cheap to run and surprisingly practical as large items could be carried by simply removing the back seat and rolling back the roof for access. But it really proved itself in the winter, when its thin tyres and featherweight meant it could deal easily with snow-covered roads where larger, more expensive cars gave up.

It was only when I got my first company car that the 2CV had to go. Since then, we have had a number of cars, all of which have been new or nearly new. They have all been carefully selected, safer and more reliable than the old bangers I used to drive, and yet somehow, I've never felt the same attachment since.

Not surprisingly, laws concerning driving have changed a bit since 1955. By modern standards our approach to drink-driving was shamefully lax but, in our defence, earlier generations had generally believed that if you could walk a straight line, you were capable of driving. It has been an offence since 1930 to drive while under the influence of drink or drugs but it had been left to the police to make a subjective decision as to whether a driver was a risk to others. Until 1967, that is, when a legal drink-driving limit was first set and the breathalyser was introduced. Early models were pretty basic, much like blowing up a balloon. To his surprise, my car-owning friend from swimming club passed a number of tests using these; but that all changed in the early 80s when more refined electronic devices came on the scene, and he failed at his first attempt. A driving ban followed, and to this day he has a downer on the microchip which he blames for his downfall.

The 70 mph limit for motorways was introduced in 1967, the same year that seatbelts were first introduced in the UK, although wearing them was not compulsory until 1983 for front passengers and 1991 for those in rear seats.

Since 1955, from the outside at least, the basic design of cars has changed little; usually four wheels, seats, steering wheel, engine, brakes, lights and so on; but look a little closer and everything has been messed about with. Driven by environmental awareness, safety or commercial factors, innovation is the name of the day. Virtually all cars ran on leaded petrol until scientists realised the detrimental effect this was having on our health; unleaded petrol was introduced in the UK in 1972 becoming compulsory in 1986.

Diesel cars were very rare until the 90s and electric cars were inconceivable. Catalytic convertors now help make our air more breathable, and materials used to build cars are lighter, stronger and longer lasting than in the past. Virtually every car today has some form of onboard computer and electronic ignition is the norm. We have anti-lock braking, four-wheel-drive, remote keyless electronic locks, airbags, alloy wheels, sophisticated sound systems, cupholders, satellite navigation and much, much more.

But while all this innovation might have led to increased safety, greater comfort and reduced environmental impact, somehow it all seems rather soulless to me. No character. And I have a question. With all this space-age technology why, when it rains, do I still have to rely on a piece of rubber to wipe back and forth across my windscreen to enable me to see?

The roads have changed too. In 1955 Britain had no motorways; the Preston Bypass in Lancashire, our first section of dual carriageway 'motorway' opened in 1958 followed a year later by our first full-length motorway, the M1. When not grinding to a halt, motorways can get us places quickly, but does anyone like them?

I remember the M25, inspiration for Chris Rea's 'The Road to Hell', being opened by Margaret Thatcher in October 1986. Sometimes dubbed the largest car park in the world, it had been the subject of many conservation protests, but it at least helped us to get to away football matches without the need to traverse central London on a busy Saturday afternoon.

An interesting pub quiz fact, apparently in 2019 the total length of roads in the UK was estimated to be 247,100 miles of which 31,800 miles are major roads and 215,200 miles are minor roads.

But that's enough on motoring. To wrap up, I believe that with regards cars and driving we had it better in the old days. True, cars today are far more comfortable and safer, but we didn't exactly fret overmuch about safety, and it all seemed so much more fun then. Driving in London can now be incredibly expensive with the Congestion Charge and Ultra Low Emission Charge, and speed limits of 20mph are becoming common. Recently I saw an RAC report saying "...the dominance of the car as a mode of transport in the early years of the 21st Century is absolute and that policy makers must recognise this fact as they introduce measures to cut traffic and hence ease congestion and fight climate change." Sounds to me like more and more rules and regulations. Oh dear.

14.

On Travel and Holidays

In 1955 most Brits took their holidays in the UK. Flights were expensive and very much the province of the rich. Drive-on-drive-off ferries were in service and gaining in popularity, but for the majority the idea of an adventure that involved driving on the wrong side of the road, eating strange food with lots of garlic and communicating with people who spoke no English, was a step too far.

In my childhood, the summer holiday, a fortnight on the coast, was a major event to be looked forward to for months ahead. I suspect there were times when the money could have been spent on other things, but the holiday was sacrosanct. Despite usually being away in August I have many memories of rain, howling winds and grey crashing rollers, but that didn't put us off. Taking sweaters to the beach; making sandcastles in the rain; skin turning blue in freezing water; these were the characteristics of the real British summer holiday. And we loved them.

To start with, it was always somewhere glamorous on the south coast, like Hayling Island or Dymchurch. Dad drove estates then to carry all his work gear, so there was a fair bit of room, although it still was always a tight squeeze. Mum didn't like sitting in the front and Big Brother allegedly suffered from carsickness, so he always sat alongside Dad with the three of us in the back. Heading south, one landmark that proved we were in foreign territory and really on our way was The Jovial Sailor on the old A3 at Ripley, which seems funny now as it was only a few miles from home. Bury Hill sticks in my mind too; our cars were never particularly new and, whether to wind us up or because he was genuinely concerned, Dad always seemed worried that we would not make it over Bury Hill which had supposedly defeated a number of cars in his past.

To us kids, summer holiday meant playing in the sea, rockpooling, exotic seafood like winkles, donkey rides on the beach, Punch and Judy shows and a game of prize bingo or amusements on the pier if there was one. Cricket and football on the beach were compulsory, along with candyfloss, toffee apples and an occasional evening trip to the pub, sitting outside with Mum and Dad while nursing a bottle of Coke and a packet of crisps. Heaven. My memory is of holidays lasting a fortnight but I'm sure some must have been shorter, particularly in the early days. But they were always magical, and when we returned home I'd be surprised at how nothing seemed to have changed in all the time we'd been away.

At some point in those early years, the folks hired a bungalow in Sandbanks, just over the road from the Sandbanks Hotel. Another dream holiday for kids; yards from a beautiful sandy beach perfect for running, playing football and building sandcastles, great paddling and swimming, and a walk along the beach to Bournemouth pier with its amusement arcade. More kiddie heaven.

I was probably about nine when we first holidayed on the Isle of Wight, the ferry crossing a huge adventure in itself. We rented a small, semi-detached house in Bembridge, a few minutes walk from the beach; perfect for us to dash back and forth between house and beach for anything we needed. On the first day, we watched fishermen on the beach regularly pulling in fish and decided we wanted some of that action. We had a fishing rod but no large weights suitable for casting far out, so Dad took us to buy some. Back on the beach, no sooner had we started than the line broke and we lost the weight. This was repeated a few times and our stock of weights quickly ran out, so back Dad went to buy more. The line again broke a number of times and back Dad went until at some point the puzzled shop assistant asked what breaking strain we were using. Dad had no idea what he was talking about, but finally the penny dropped that our fishing line was nowhere near strong enough for the weights; so not only did he have to buy yet more weights but also some stronger line. In recent years he often chuckled about how daft he'd felt, and how we'd probably killed more fish through lead poisoning than we had caught, not hard as we only got one.

My other memory of family holidays on the Isle of Wight comes a few years later when we drove to Alum Bay for coloured sand to fill those glass ornaments the island is renowned for. There were loads of people on the lower slopes scraping away sand, but Big Brother fancied some red stuff, near the top of course. Up he went, only to freeze when he got there. After trying to coax him down for a while, Dad went to the café to ask for help. I remember the scene well; Big Brother pinned to the cliff face as people gathered, looking up at him, wondering whether it would all end in tears; Mum and Dad pacing nervously while Nan and Pop, who were with us that time, stared resolutely out to sea. A young lad came out of the café with an Alsatian dog and the pair of them scooted up the slope; in no time they were alongside Big Brother and the lad talked him up over the top to everyone's relief. Drama over.

A year or two later, we ventured further afield to Great Yarmouth with its wonderful long sandy beach and persistent strong wind. I bought a kite, a square of clear plastic with a red picture of a sputnik satellite on it, space flight being all the rage at the time, and it just shot skyward. I would lie on my back on our lilo and just stare mesmerised at the tiny spot that was my kite high in the sky. Once or twice, Dad bought me another ball of string that I would tie on and then, presto, the dot would be further away. I remember it coming down unexpectedly once, and I spent ages winding up miles of string while clambering, apologetically, over loads of people.

But about that lilo. We had an auntie on Mum's side who must have been relatively well off as she took holidays abroad in far off places like the South of France, and she would always bring back presents. One such gift was a double lilo, white with a flower design, on which I would lie for hours, reading comics and staring up at my kite. At some point, Big Brother took the lilo into the sea, and in no time the wind that was so good for kites proved bad for lilos, and he was heading rapidly offshore. Dad swum out to the rescue but soon had to turn back, only just having the strength to reach dry land himself. But we were lucky as a young man, a stronger swimmer than Dad, swam out and pulled the lilo back while, once again, Mum and Dad paced nervously on the beach. Bit of a theme developing here.

In 1967 we got really adventurous and headed to the uncharted lands of north Devon, Woolacombe to be precise. We rented a house, or part of a house, called White Breakers with a bay window looking straight down

140

onto the gloriously sandy beach; we loved the place. The water was very cold, blue skin the norm, but exhilarating as body surfing the Atlantic rollers really took your breath away; no namby-pamby wetsuits in those days. Together we made a large sand model in the shape of a crocodile, covered it with shells and, of course, gave it a name; Woolacombe Willy.

That was a wonderful holiday in a beautiful setting, and I have returned there a number of times since, but it would be many years before we again holidayed together as a complete family. The following year, Big Brother was deemed old enough to go on holiday with his mates and, as so often happened, I was allowed to do the same as him; after all a bunch of my friends were his age or older. It was truly the end of an era.

For my first non-family holiday I returned to the Isle of Wight with three friends for a cycling and Youth Hostelling week. Two of us stopped for a night or two at Hayling Island where Mum, Dad and Little Brother were staying with Nan and Pop at their regular bungalow, before making our way to Portsmouth and the ferry.

I learnt a number of things that week, but one stands out. One day we split into pairs as we wanted to do different things, the friend with me had a daily paper round making him the rich one of us. We were queuing at a fish and chip shop when he offered to buy me fish and chips if I bought him a Mars bar. This puzzled me, so he explained along the lines of "I have more money and am happy to share that with you as long as you're happy to share what money you have with me; that's what friends do". Can't argue with that.

A couple of years later that friend was to stun us all when he announced that he had joined up with the Royal

Marines. He was bored in his job as a trainee draughtsman and, while strolling around in his lunchtime, had been lured in by a recruiter. We felt he was mad, and all tried to talk him out of it, but to no avail. And we were all wrong. On returning from his basic training, an exercise that the majority fail, the weedy young boy we all knew had become a confident, fit, young man. A true lifer, he signed up for 23 years in all, rising through the ranks. I missed him not being around regularly but am happy that he found his world. And we still manage to keep in touch, if only occasionally.

The next year we bought a small van between us. To be precise, four friends who had jobs bought the van for £30 and I was given the task of 'doing it up'. It only had two seats and three of us would travel in the back, so I cleaned it up, bolted the spare wheel on the bonnet to make space inside, lined it with carpet underlay in an attempt to make it less noisy and found a mattress from somewhere so we had a place to sit. I wouldn't last ten minutes in the back of that van today, but we were young, and drove two hundred miles to Woolacombe with no complaints. The only technical problem we had was when the exhaust burst near Ascot half an hour into the journey; that was when I was introduced to the magic of Gun Gum and tin cans for fixing exhausts. We camped at a site in Mortehoe and spent a gloriously sunny two weeks basking on Woolacombe beach and exploring Devon.

That set the pattern for the next couple of years as my swimming friend with a car drove us around various parts of Devon and Cornwall. We would camp, spend most of our time on the beach exploring rock pools or swimming, and occasionally take a trip out to explore the area.

I have a fond memory of camping near St Ives when a powerful, truly Cornish, storm hit. We drove to Land's End and walked along the clifftop, all under a large tarpaulin, to experience the full force of the storm, as you do, but on returning to the campsite found the wind had shredded our tent and all our things were afloat in a big puddle. So, we packed up and drove into St Ives where we sat for hours in a launderette, drying all our clothes while dressed just in our swimming trunks. Afterwards, with the rain still pouring down, we repaired to the pub for beer and food before settling down to sleep in the car. But a few hours later, a red flare went up, a yacht was in trouble and the lifeboat was being prepared; we could hardly miss the action, so out we ventured into the rain once more to watch proceedings.

All ended happily, but we were soaked again and spent a fairly uncomfortable night in the car. The next day, in typically Cornish style, the sun burnt down and we spent our time on the beach, recovering and stitching together bits of tent.

During my teens I regularly found myself back in the Sandbanks area. On a hot bank holiday weekend, we would pile into the car and head down to the coast, spend all day on the beach at Studland Bay, then try to find somewhere to kip for the night; not easy when the beach was patrolled nightly. The next two days would be more of the same, invariably leading to bad sunburn, a small price to pay, before queuing for hours to cross the Studland Ferry and head home, red raw, hungry, knackered but happy.

Package tours had been around for years, but with limited appeal. Unless you were rich enough to fly, a trip to Mallorca would involve a long coach drive with ferry crossings taking some 48 hours, and accommodation could

143

be basic, so not everyone's cup of tea. But that all changed in the 60s and 70s when a number of Mediterranean countries, Spain in particular, saw a boom in hotel construction. At the same time, larger, faster planes arrived on the scene driving down the cost of travel, and suddenly Mallorca was just a couple of hours away. A final factor was the easing of restrictions on the amount of currency that could be taken abroad. For a large number of Brits, Torremolinos and Benidorm now seemed as accessible as Hayling Island.

In 1971 we got really adventurous, though not flying yet. My driving chum had invested in a newer car, a rather natty Cortina MkII, and was up for a camping trip to Spain. After a challenging drive over the Pyrenees, we arrived at our destination somewhere on the Costa Brava. I have only a few memories of that holiday. There was a bar that became our local where we had to sleep one night when, once again, we were totally flooded out; and we regularly attended a disco called The Custard Beast located in some caves on the beach. I discovered a liking for chocolate Lumumba cocktails and had my first experience of Happy Hour.

Then, a few days before we were due to leave, one of my friends developed serious stomach pains; we thought the drive might be too much so tried to get him on a plane only to be told that changing air pressure during the flight might kill him; quite unnerving really. So, with none of us speaking Spanish, we toured hospitals in and around Barcelona seeking help until, eventually, we got him admitted to one where they informed us that he needed an operation. We phoned his parents who flew out to be with him and then, after much discussion, the two of us who were due back at school flew home, leaving the driver in

144

attendance; his brother-in-law flew out later to accompany him on the drive home. All ended well, but definitely a holiday to remember, although for all the wrong reasons.

Meanwhile, long-haul flights were no longer restricted to the super-rich and, in January 1970, the Jumbo Jet took its first commercial flight. With its unique design and unprecedented size, the plane has been synonymous with long-haul flights until two years ago when they were dropped by most airlines, mainly in response to financial constraints brought about by the Covid pandemic.

The first scheduled supersonic passenger service for anther icon, Concorde, was introduced in 1976, with British Airways and Air France flying from London to Bahrain and Paris to Rio de Janeiro respectively. On hearing the unmistakable deep rumble of its engines, it was impossible not to look up in admiration at the distinctive delta shape and pointed nose as it passed overhead.

You had to be rich to fly Concorde, but the rest of us could still admire our British creation. It was small, carrying around one hundred passengers, and seating was cramped but that was irrelevant, it was fast. In 1996, a BA Concorde flew from New York to London in two hours, 52 minutes and 59 seconds reaching a top speed of 1,350mph. But the aircraft's noise and operating costs meant only 14 actually went into service and, sadly, in 2003 Concorde operations were finally ceased. I assume that supersonic flight will return sometime, if only for the mega-rich.

Holidays abroad were becoming more the norm. Over the next few years I visited a variety of destinations, generally in Greece or Spain. The selection criteria were simple: cheap flight, accommodation, food and drink; hot weather; good beach; clear warm water for swimming. We only used cheap charter flights that always left at the most inconvenient times, and I spent many tedious hours on airport floors waiting for a delayed departure that would get me home around sunup; I'm definitely too old for that now.

Shortly after meeting my wife-to-be I introduced her to the joys of camping. I don't think she was particularly enamoured with the accommodation, a small two-man tent, or the food arrangements, chocolate digestives and an apple for breakfast. But Soar Mill Cove near Salcombe is so picturesque, and the weather was glorious, so we had a great weekend. By then she must have been getting an idea as to the type of bloke she was with, yet still she persevered, so I must have done something right.

The next year I took her to the campsite at Mortehoe, just outside Woolacombe, where I had stayed previously with the lads. All went well until a little fog drifted in; the foghorn on the local lighthouse, just a few hundred yards away, started up….. and didn't stop all night. The following morning, we upped tent and moved to a small hotel over the road; that was our first holiday hotel and our last camping trip.

For the five years between our meeting and having kids we went away quite a bit. There were a number of continental holidays; Menorca, Portugal, Tenerife and the like; none overly expensive of course. We occasionally went with friends and kept to villas and self-catering apartments.

There were also regular trips in the UK; we avoided the school holidays and regularly headed to the South West for a week in February; never booking, we just turned up and asked around at local pubs or Tourist Information offices. One time in Dartmouth we ended up renting a boathouse that extended out over the river Dart, a beautiful setting but cold and damp. It had served as a rowing clubhouse, the bathroom had been the changing room and it was big, with a bath in the corner and dozens of coat hooks still lining the walls. Heating was by a single propane gas heater on wheels, so if one of us took a bath, the other would wheel the heater into the bathroom and sit reading while keeping warm. No expense spared.

Skiing wasn't a particularly common pastime then; we talked about having a go, but plans were put on hold when in 1988 we found we were pregnant. For our first holiday with child we returned to our hotel in Mortehoe. We weren't on our own though; a couple of friends came with us with their son who was the same age as our daughter, oneish. By then we were pregnant again and the other couple were expecting too; we both ended up with two kids, one of each, with birthdays close together and they all went to the same schools. We're godparents to the daughter. Nice.

Unlike many parents, we decided that foreign holidays would be put on hold for a while. Holidays are supposed to be relaxing, and the idea of airports with young kids seemed far too stressful compared to packing all you need in a car and driving a few hours. True, the British weather was never reliable, but that seemed a small price to pay, and we managed to enjoy ourselves whatever. We started in the southwest at the Heron House Hotel in Thurlestone, then a bungalow in Croyde Bay before moving on to the Isle of Wight and the Shanklin Manor hotel for a couple of years. Then we rediscovered Sandbanks, and more particularly the Sandbanks Hotel, and that was it for years to come.

The old place we had stayed at as kids was long gone; the land redeveloped with a beach café standing roughly where I remember us staying. At that time, the hotel was pretty much dedicated to kids having fun; the beach was all golden sand, gently sloping, and the sea crystal clear. Sandbanks seems to have its own climate and I often stood bathed in sunshine looking inland where black clouds hovered ominously.

There were entertainers on hand to keep the kids amused, and nobody cared if they came straight from the beach trailing sand and seawater through the hotel. A grass patch for sunbathing was regularly taken over for football; there were two tennis courts and a small putting green. Dads would build large sand constructions on the beach, with or without the kids. It was heaven for children and, best of all, they ate early and had a disco to entertain them in the evening, so for the first time in a while we got to eat in peace, and at a leisurely pace.

I would hire a dinghy for a little sailing, and one regular highlight that we all enjoyed was a rib ride, speeding across the water, jumping the bow waves from the ferries going into Poole. I'm easily pleased.

The Sandbanks Hotel has since played a major part in our family life and we returned year in year out, it became a home-from-home as we reunited each year with friends we'd made previously. Big Brother's family followed suit with even more visits than us, I had my fiftieth birthday there, and we took Dad to the sister hotel, the Haven, for his eightieth. One year, Wifey's family joined us, and her niece announced that she was going to get married there, and last summer, around ten years later, she did just that in a venue a few hundred yards away. So I guess you could say we like the place.

In 1995 I took a couple of months off; the weather was great, and we spent a lot of time with the kids, both in

148

the garden and taking an occasional local excursion. Outings were booked at a whim; a hotel on the Isle of Wight; a visit to friends in the Peak District incorporating a stop-off at Alton Towers; a stay in a luxurious hotel on the gloriously golden beach of St. Brelades Bay in Jersey. We just did what we wanted when we wanted, and it was sooo relaxing, leading me to reflect on what horribly stressful things holidays have become when, as is normally the case, you need to run to a timetable. Planning months in advance and spending loads of money means we have to enjoy holidays, whatever it takes; no wonder we need to get back to work for a break.

Around 2000, Son and I made a flying visit to see my globe-trotting uni mate in France, for a short, sharp introduction to skiing in les Alpes Maritimes. It was a great weekend and something we repeated a number of times later, including an extended stay in 2011 when the Iceland volcano eruption mangled our plans; the trip home was an adventure in itself and we were met in Calais by Wifey and Daughter who had to bring the car over, it being impossible for us simply to buy a passenger ticket. In 2012 they both joined us skiing, a great time was had by all, and we have since returned a few times during the summer months to enjoy Nice and Monaco.

As the kids got older, so our holidays became a tiny bit more adventurous though always in Europe. I like the more active stuff, so we had a few trips to resorts in Corsica and Sardinia taking in a bit of sailing and scuba diving.

Over the years, extended family holidays have also featured. For Mum's 70th we all hired a large house in Dorset, complete with snooker room in the basement. Big Brother's mother-in-law has an apartment in Estepona, and a group of us have rented apartments in the same

149

block a couple of times. Boozy times of course, but great fun, although we did nearly kill Dad by making him walk too far in the sun, the phrase "don't worry it's only about five times the walk to Ladbrokes" ringing in his ears.

I also enjoyed a few weekends with Dad and both brothers in Norfolk at the Blakeney Hotel, ostensibly bird-spotting but hilarious and slightly alcoholic father-son bonding sessions to boot. Before Dad died, we had one final trip where the whole family came along, which was rather nice. Our latest extended family venture saw us skiing in the French Alps; how things have changed.

Horrible parents that we were, we never took our kids to any of the Disney parks. Daughter remains a Disney fan to this day, and for her thirtieth birthday we took a family trip, together with Son and partner, to Disneyland Paris; and I have to admit that despite the total lack of interest I had in such places, I actually enjoyed myself. And Daughter hardly stopped beaming, which was reward enough.

For some years now, our overseas holidays have followed a similar pattern; all-inclusive in a reasonable quality hotel with comfortable well-furnished rooms; nice beach, not too crowded, preferably with scuba facilities, and within walking distance. That's about it really, not terribly exciting or adventurous but who cares?

Meanwhile, the global holiday industry has blossomed making most parts of the world accessible at not too high a price. Son likes to travel and has already visited places like Indonesia and Cuba.

So, there you have it. The world has become a much smaller place in my lifetime; flying is second nature while holidays to exotic places are relatively low-cost and commonplace. But this doesn't come without a price tag; in particular, the environmental damage caused through tourism can be terrible. It would be good if we could just follow the old conservationist's adage "take only photos, leave only footprints" but that rarely happens; humans tend to be messy and destructive wherever they go. Also changes made to encourage and support tourism can themselves cause the character of a place to suffer irreparably, which is a shame. But on the whole, I would say that as far as holidays and travel is concerned things are probably better now than in my youth.

15.

You'd Think Geography Wouldn't Change

Since I was brought into this world, not only has our history been transformed, but the whole layout of the place has changed dramatically as countries have come into, or gone out of, existence, or sometimes just changed their names for the fun of it. Here is a brief summary of some of those changes although I am sure to have overlooked many others.

In 1955, world maps still showed large areas of the globe in pink or red as part of the British Empire, but that was soon to change; some forty-seven of those countries have gained independence, meaning new governments, politics and alliances, new flags and, in quite a few cases, new names. A quick roll call is in order.

Between 1956 and 1959 Sudan, Malaysia and Ghana gained their independence. The 60s were the busy spell; Singapore gained their independence from Malaysia before twenty-four other countries went their separate ways, namely: Nigeria, Cyprus, Somaliland, Tanzania, Cameroon, Kuwait, Sierra Leone, Uganda, Trinidad and Tobago, Jamaica, Kenya, Zambia, Malta, Malawi, Maldives, The Gambia, Barbados, Lesotho, Botswana, Guyana, Yemen, Swaziland (renamed Eswatini in 2018), Mauritius and Nauru.

The pace of change slowed in the 70s although a further fourteen countries gained their independence from the British, namely: Fiji, Tonga, United Arab Emirates, Qatar, Bahrain, The Bahamas, Grenada, Seychelles, Dominica, Tuvalu, Solomon Islands, Saint Vincent and the Grenadines, Kiribati and Saint Lucia. The process came to an end in the 80s, the final six countries gaining their independence being Vanuatu, Zimbabwe, Antigua and Barbuda, Belize, Saint Kitts and Nevis, and last but not least Brunei.

It wasn't only the British who had developed a taste for running other people's countries though, and as the colonial age ground to a halt in Africa another thirty plus countries gained their independence from various European rulers. The French relinquished control of nineteen countries: the Kingdom of Morocco; the republics of Tunisia, Guinea, Cameroon, Senegal, Togo, Mali, Benin, Niger, Chad, Côte d'Ivoire (Ivory Coast), the Congo, Gabon and Djibouti; Democratic Republic of Madagascar, Popular Democratic Republic of Burkina Faso, Central African Republic, Democratic and Popular Republic of Algeria, and the Federal Islamic Republic of the Comoros. Spain gave back Morocco and the Republic of Equatorial Guinea while the Belgians handed over the Democratic Republic of the Congo plus the republics of Burundi and Rwanda. Finally, the Portuguese returned the republics of Guinea-Bissau, Mozambique, Cape Verde, The Democratic Republic of São Tomé and Principe and the People's Republic of Angola. And if that's not enough the Republic of Namibia and the State of Eritrea gained their independence from South Africa and Ethiopia respectively.

As the sun was setting on the age of European colonialism, another factor was significantly affecting the map of the world. After the Russian Revolution of 1917,

Communism, sharing with the many rather than being dictated to by the rich and powerful few, had appealed as a fairer and more appealing way of life than Capitalism, and a number of countries gave it a go although, sadly, in most cases reality failed to match the ideal once human nature kicked in and self-interest took the wheel. Created in 1921, the United Socialist Soviet Republic, or U.S.S.R., comprised 15 republics: Armenia, Azerbaijan, Belarus, Estonia, Georgia, Kazakhstan, Kyrgyzstan, Latvia, Lithuania, Moldova, Russia, Tajikistan, Turkmenistan, Ukraine and Uzbekistan. The Warsaw Pact came into being in 1955 in response to the creation of NATO, a military alliance between Western bloc countries. The Cold War was the result of this, bringing the ever-present threat of nuclear annihilation. It seems strange now, but we regularly received, through public service broadcasts or leaflets, instruction on how to react in the event of a nuclear attack. Strange times indeed. In my earlier years the USSR was a military superpower covering nearly a sixth of the globe, yet now it's gone.

East and West Germany were completely different countries; I was six when the East Germans started building the Berlin Wall. Ostensibly to keep 'fascists' out of East Germany, its real purpose was to keep East Germans from leaving. In 1989, political revolution in Poland and unrest across Eastern European states, culminated in the head of the East German Communist Party announcing that East German citizens could cross to the West whenever they wanted. I recall the night of the announcement, watching joyous TV scenes as people partied and took to the Wall with pickaxes and any tool that came to hand. The unification treaty followed in October1990, creating a single Germany while the Soviet

Union continued in decline and formally ceased to exist on December 31, 1991.

In the Caribbean, the Cuban Revolution had been going on for 5 years when, in 1958, the rebels took control of the country. Moscow-trained Fidel Castro ran the country along Soviet lines from then until handing over to his brother Raúl in 2011. Cuba is only 103 miles from Florida, and the close proximity of a state allied to their nemesis, Russia, still conjures up American ill feelings. Incidents including the disastrous Bay of Pigs invasion, and military brinkmanship, led to the Cuban missile crisis of 1962 when, for a time, the world genuinely appeared to be on the brink of nuclear war; but sanity prevailed. The country is generally still referred to as Cuba and their flag remains the same. Since those times Castro, and even more so his sidekick Che Guevara, have gained fame through the countless T-shirts and posters adorning student bedroom walls throughout the world.

For a time, many South and Central American peoples considered more left-wing ideologies; scared of another Cuba, the CIA carried out a number of nefarious covert operations to derail any insurrection and assist strong, conservative leaders of their choice to keep the lid on any such move. The result was often military dictatorships with a nasty habit of 'disappearing' anyone with the courage to speak out against them.

Back to Europe where there were other changes. The Socialist Federal Republic of Yugoslavia was run by its founder, Josip Tito, from formation in 1945 until his death in 1980. But with Tito's death and the fall of Soviet Russia, the republic disintegrated: Slovenia and Croatia both declared independence from Yugoslavia in 1991. War followed in Croatia as Serbs tried to create their own state.

Macedonia gained independence with little conflict although war again broke out, this time in the republic of Bosnia and Herzegovina as Bosnian Serbs wanted to stay with what was left of the Yugoslav Federation. It was at this time that the chilling term 'ethnic cleansing' came into wide usage. The upshot of all this upheaval is that in my lifetime, one country, Yugoslavia, has become seven: Croatia; Bosnia and Herzegovina; Kosovo; Macedonia; Montenegro; Serbia and Slovenia.

In 1993 Czechoslovakia separated peacefully into two new countries, the Czech Republic and Slovakia.

Only four communist countries remain today; China, the Republic of Cuba, Laos and the Socialist Republic of Vietnam. North Korea is unique, being governed on Juche socialist principles, described by the government as "Kim Il-sung's original, brilliant and revolutionary contribution to national and international thought".

Back to Africa. In 1961, following a referendum the previous year, South Africa broke its ties with Britain to become a republic. The country was shunned by much of the world for its apartheid system, which, after considerable political upheaval and violence, was finally abolished by the South African government in 1993. The following year, the country's first non-racial election was won by Nelson Mandela's African National Congress. Mandela had spent twenty-seven years in jail for his part in trying to overthrow apartheid; one man's freedom fighter is another man's terrorist. No change to the country's name, but a new flag was introduced symbolising the hopes and optimism of the new regime.

Current problems in the Middle East can, in part, be tracked back to 1916 and the rather hurried and haphazard way France and Britain agreed to carve up land previously under Ottoman rule, into new countries in two spheres of influence: Iraq, Transjordan, and Palestine were under British influence with Syria and Lebanon under French influence. This led in the second half of the twentieth century to growing Arab nationalism, the rise of strong dictatorial leaders like Saddam Hussein and Hafez Assad, and the emergence of countries dominated by small elite clans; all while most of the population lived in relative poverty. And, to add to the problems, Britain chose to create Israel in the heart of Arab lands. No wonder this area is in a permanent state of upheaval.

2011 saw the Arab Spring; a loosely related group of protests throughout the region, triggered by anger over government corruption, economic hardship, social exclusion and the like. The protests culminated in regime change in countries such as Tunisia, Egypt and Libya, but while there has been a degree of increased democracy and cultural freedom, increased instability and oppressions has followed, often exacerbated by interference from western governments worried about access to oil, but with little real understanding of the underlying issues.

Territorial disputes continue unabated around the world as countries look back in history to justify various claims, or to cement their position in the global hierarchy; the Chinese, Indian and Pakistan governments are regularly at odds, which is worrying really as all three have nuclear weapons. One thing is certain; human nature being as it is, more change is inevitably on its way.

Finally, for various reasons countless countries, areas and cities have simply been renamed; in my day for example we had Burma, Peking and Calcutta where now we have Myanmar, Beijing and Kolkata. Had I been able to buy a satnav back then, investing in lifetime map updates would indeed have been prudent.

16.

Spondoolicks

Money was never in abundance when we were kids; Mum and Dad provided the essentials, but if we wanted anything extra, then we understood that we would either have to wait for Christmas or birthday time, or else use our own cash, which tended not to hang around too long, so the only option was to work for it. I first tried this strange concept aged about seven or eight; Big Brother and his friends had heard that you got paid simply for wheeling golfers' trolleys around the local course, and they were heading off for some easy cash so I, of course, tagged along. Potential caddies turned up at the shack and added their names to a list; things were run strictly on a first-in-first-out basis, so it paid to arrive early. We turned up hours before any golfers and waited, bored stiff, but we all got a round, and I received my first pay. I can't remember how much it was, but I don't think it was enough to persuade me to do the job regularly, although I did go back a few times more before retiring.

Next came the paper rounds. Aged about ten, again following in Big Brother's footsteps, I took on a Sunday round for a local paper shop. This involved arriving early at the shop to choose one of the shop's rusty butcher-bikes with a large rack on the front, loading into a cardboard box the papers which had already been sorted and marked up with addresses, placing the box in the rack, and pedalling off to deliver papers to my eagerly awaiting clientele. The whole process took under two hours, and I remember, initially at least, being paid six shillings, about £6 today. In nice weather it was quite a pleasant way to start the day, although in the rain and cold it somehow lost its appeal, but I kept it up for quite a few years.

I took on a second, more lucrative, round a while later, again taking over from Big Brother (another pattern emerging here). This was a Saturday evening round delivering late editions of the Evening Standard that included the football results, essential reading if you wanted to check whether you were a millionaire before heading to the pub. Papers were delivered to the railway station where they were dished out by the distributor to his eager workforce. Customers paid cash for their paper, if they weren't in, then no Standard. Papers were 6d each but, depending on how happy they were feeling, customers often paid more. I received 1½d for every paper sold (probably under 10p today), so being paid 1 or even 2 shillings meant a huge bonus, in relative terms at least.

At the end of my round, I returned home with pockets full of change, checked the number of papers sold, counted the money, calculated how much I owed the distributor (unsold papers could be returned next week) and only then knew how much I had earned. Not only was this a relatively lucrative round, but it also taught some basics both about business and human nature. I soon came to realise that the people with least money were those most likely to give a tip.

At the age of fifteen, and with no help from Big Brother this time, I started my career in retail. The lead came from a friend of Mum's whose son worked in a local menswear shop where they needed a Saturday boy. After a short interview, the main point of which was to see if I could count, the job was mine. Eight hours a day, every Saturday, for the princely sum of £1 or around £20 today. But it wasn't just the huge salary that I gained from. Initially, the idea of working in a shop that generally catered for middle-aged men and their desire for 'fashionable' suits and ties might not have been all that appealing but, again, the job definitely taught me a lot. I had to be punctual, interact with customers including dealing with complaints, monitor stock levels, watch out for shoplifters, handle cash and measure customers who often had no idea what size they were. At such a young age, it came as some surprise when countless 'grownups' turned to me for advice on how well a suit fitted, whether they looked good in it or whether this colour tie went with that shirt.

Strangely, we had one claim to fame; allegedly, we were the only shop in Surrey selling Levi's jeans, and people came from far and wide to buy these radical vestments. There was only one style then, blue and presumably 501's, and boy were they tough compared to today's flimsy offerings; it took six months wear just to break them in. They were labeled 'shrink to fit' which was a great marketing ploy; the advice was to put your new jeans on and sit in a warm bath so they could shrink to fit perfectly to your body before taking them off to dry. Presumably, as denim goes out of shape pretty quickly, this approach had about the same effect as a quick wash in the machine, but it sounded far more radical and, doubtless to their parents' bewilderment, countless teenagers around the country would sit in the bath wearing their jeans.

There was also a summer job at a factory making suede skirts. My role entailed boxing up skirts and labeling them for dispatch. Not overly exciting but I was earning.

The next year I took a summer holiday job as a lifeguard at the local pool; hardly 'Baywatch', but a major step up on the earnings ladder. For the next five years or so I was able to earn extra money through most of the school holidays, working at a place that was already my second home, and usually being surrounded by my friends. What was there not to like? Not only that, but the money wasn't bad either and, it being the 70s with strong union influences, the conditions were good. Weekend work was paid double time and a bank holiday shift meant double time plus a day off in lieu i.e. triple time. Needless to say, I signed up for every bank holiday shift going.

It was not terribly exciting work, but prepared me for employment in later life, staring at the water waiting for something to happen. I claim no heroic feats, although did need to assist a few kids to the side over the years. I'd strut manfully around in my orange 'Lifeguard'-emblazoned t-shirt, or sit for hours in the tall lifeguard chair, watching. I also learned that a hangover can be treated by lying on the bottom of the pool with an air tank strapped on.

It was at the pool that I started to notice people's different attitudes to work. If the boss was looking for someone to sweep the car park, I was usually the first to volunteer; I just wanted a break from the monotony and the chance to get out of the chlorinated air, but this amused most of my colleagues who generally preferred to keep their heads down, do as little as possible and go home.

Not surprisingly, I did the occasional bar work, but my most challenging role came late in my school career, and on occasion during uni holidays, working as a window cleaner for one of Dad's friends. It was relatively well paid, but somehow opportunities mainly came up in the middle of winter. Starting work on a pitch-dark morning by plunging your hands into a bucket of icy water to prepare your scrim for the job ahead may wake you up, but it's not a particularly pleasant pastime. But I did come to appreciate the wonders of the human body as, after ten minutes of agony, extra blood pumping through the veins led to warm mitts in the harshest of conditions.

But that wasn't the challenge; the problem was that I didn't like heights. I'd set my ladder against the building and slowly head skyward hanging on to my scrim, much to the amusement of the team who teased that I would meet myself on the way down; not sure about their use of words but the meaning was clear. At the top, my imagination would run wild, conjuring up pictures of my body lying crumpled on the paving below or impaled on some ominous fence spikes. Illogical as it seems though, as long as I had hold of something, anything, I was perfectly happy; my fears would evaporate even though that plastic gutter in my hand had no chance of holding my weight in the event of an accident. Draw what conclusions you will about my intelligence.

There never really seemed to be a problem earning a little extra cash in those days. Little Brother played in the Colts for the local cricket club who were based in the Woods, and I think his first earner came at the age of about ten when he was paid for keeping the score at home games. I believe the team each contributed 3d, a total of 2s 9d (about £2.40p today); it might even have been double that as I'm not sure if the visiting team were also asked to contribute. One day the club captain escorted Little Brother home to explain how he'd used one of his

163

sixpences to play the one-armed bandit in the clubhouse and won the jackpot, probably the equivalent of about £80 today; the nice chap had come to confirm where the money had come from. Not bad for a day's work.

Later, he would regularly man the petrol pumps at the garage over the road from our house; sitting in the kiosk until a customer pulled up, then putting petrol in the car, offering to top up the oil and water or clean the windscreen, taking the customer's money and returning with the change and, occasionally, receiving a tip. All this while the customer stayed seated in the car; how things have changed. He got me a job there but, once again, it was mainly in the middle of winter which wasn't so much fun. Sitting in a small freezing hut while sheltering from swirling snow, then going out to fill cars when the icy cold petrol pump nozzle would stick to your hand left a bit to be desired; still it was money.

Little Brother also came up with a more novel earner. I believe it was after winning a miming competition at the local disco that he and his mate were asked to perform similar routines for cash, the closest any of us came to a glitzy showbiz life.

Thinking back, my brothers and I didn't seem to have any problem earning a bit of extra cash, just as long as we were willing to put in the effort. Things definitely seem a bit different today. Steering well clear of the usual old codger call that kids today don't understand the meaning of work, the main differences seem to be around regulation and supply and demand. I have no idea what, if any, regulations were in place, but restrictions on how old you had to be to work, the amount you got paid, the hours you could work or health and safety never came into it. Doubtless at times we were exploited by modern standards, but we were just happy to get our hands on some extra spondoolicks.

So, was it better then than in current times? I suppose this has to be another draw. Today, increased employment regulations mean people are less likely to offer work on a casual basis, and there will probably be more competition, including from older folk who also need the cash. On the other hand, if you can find a job it may well be better paid and with better conditions than in our time.

17.

The Wonders of Radio

The British Broadcasting Company was created in 1922, since when anyone who owned a radio set had access to public information, news and entertainment. It blossomed during wartime, providing not only an invaluable source of information but also entertainment programmes to boost morale; most of course used to spread government propaganda. 'Desert Island Discs' was first broadcast in 1942 and there were programmes like 'Music While You Work' and 'Workers Playtime'. Dad regularly talked about 'Dick Barton – Special Agent', a radio drama based on the exploits of an ex-commando and his chums; from 1946 it went out every weekday evening in fifteen-minute episodes and I can picture him as a young man huddled near to the radio, totally engrossed and straining to catch all the action.

In the daytime hours at least, unlike the TV, there was always something to listen to on the radio. Also, unlike the TV, you could listen while continuing with whatever you were doing; Dad would take a portable radio to work so he could listen while decorating, and Mum regularly had the radio on in the kitchen as I sat playing on the kitchen floor. She would listen to music or boring talk shows like 'Woman's Hour', but the one that always got me was the shipping weather forecast. I had no idea what it meant, but sat mesmerised as the reader went through lists with names such as Cromerty, Dogger, German Bight, and Rockall, describing conditions along the line of "South or southwest 4 to 6, occasionally 7 at first and 3 later; moderate or rough becoming mainly moderate; rain; good, occasionally moderate." They were talking gobbledygook about far off places, but somehow it still seemed interesting.

Led astray by Big Brother, I was lured into the illicit world of undercover listening. Lying in bed with my small transistor radio, complete with single earphone, I tuned into radio stations like Radio Caroline and Radio Luxemburg well into the night, probably about 9 or 10 o'clock. And, from 1964, one particular comedy programme became unmissable; 'I'm Sorry I'll Read That Again' or ISIRTA to its fans. Starring Tim Brooke-Taylor, John Cleese, Graeme Garden, David Hatch, Jo Kendall and Bill Oddie and opening with 'The Angus Prune' tune, the humour was totally mad, but I loved it. After 1967 it was broadcast on Radio 4, the BBCs new channel for spoken word programmes, so I was already tuning in to the old fogey station. With bad puns, continual references to rhubarb tarts and ferrets, ridiculous songs and input from the live audience it was all gloriously insane and, of course, far too politically incorrect for today. What a shame.

All music on the BBC was broadcast on the Light Programme until 1967 when, in response to competition from now legal commercial outfits, the BBC had a revamp and the Light Programme was split into three; Radio 1 for continuous pop music, Radio 2 for easy listening and Radio 3 for classical music. Mum would always be first up, and as she started pottering around the kitchen, she would turn the radio on. By the time I started senior school she was a regular listener to breakfast shows; Jimmy Young until he retired and Terry Wogan took over. We would have preferred Radio 1, but somehow these guys seemed to start the day in an acceptably relaxed manner.

Sunday lunch is the other time I remember the radio always being on. Initially, Mum would have it as background while she prepared the food, but then it was moved to the table and kept on as an accompaniment to the sounds of our eating. I wasn't keen on the likes of 'The Billy Cotton Band Show', parent music introduced with the call of "Wakey-Wake-aaaay!"; but there were entertaining comedies like 'The Navy Lark' and 'Round the Horn'.

For a number of my teenage years Radio 1 was my listening of choice, the likes of Noel Edmonds and Kenny Everett being essential weekend listening before I deigned to arise from my bed. But slowly, as our own collection of recordings grew and portable cassette players arrived on the scene, the radio became less important, and now I rarely tune in except when I'm driving, and then I'm most likely to be listening to Radio 4 rather than music. Times change.

This is not really a subject where the kids are better or worse off today. My first draft for this chapter concluded that; "with digital radio and the Internet, there is far more choice today, but kids probably prefer things delivered via visual media; I would say to them to, at least once, try the experience of listening to a drama or sports commentary on the radio. Close your eyes and let your imagination provide the pictures, you might just enjoy the experience". But Son's partner has since pointed out that, fogey that I am, I have completely ignored podcasts that have gained in popularity, particularly during Covid times, so perhaps, as with the rising appeal of vinyl recordings, old-fashioned aural entertainment is making a comeback.

18.

My First Gap Year

So, I'd finished with the childhood joys of life and was heading out on the next stage of my journey; what to do? I had my university place booked and was pretty sure I'd be going, but needed time to confirm definitely that I was 'doing the right thing'. Perhaps an overseas adventure, or maybe amass a little cash to support me through the impecunious student years to come. The phrase was yet to be coined, but I was having a Gap Year.

I needed to earn some money, but lifeguard work was only available in the holidays, so I decided to try the record and hi-fi shop in the High Street. Strolling boldly in, I presented myself to the manager who, to my surprise, offered me a job. So now I was a hi-fi and record salesman. That was when I got Dad to buy the second-hand Akai reel-to-reel recorder; a good move as he then spent countless hours recording all his old records. The job had its perks, for instance we could take home albums from work to record, so during this period our music collection increased substantially. I did pay for a number of records too, one of which was the album 'Goodbye Yellow Brick Road', theme music for this period of my life.

Then, my working life took a twist. Christmas was approaching when a friend of Mum's told her of a job at a nearby prep school; apparently the PE teacher had died just at the start of the school year and they had been

169

unable to get another in time, so had filled the role with a sporty lad who was now going off to do something else; perhaps I might be interested? The only time the headmaster was available to interview me was early morning on New Year's Day, but he told me that he understood the inconvenience and that I should still enjoy myself; and I did.

The interview was at 9 a.m and, true to his word, the Head was sympathetic. After small talk, the heart of the interview went something like this. "What are your main sports?" "Swimming, football and basketball." "Hmm. The boys have swimming lessons at the local pool, football was last term, and we don't play basketball. How are you with hockey?" "To be honest, I've never played it." "Hmm. Well, I suppose it's a bit like football with sticks. When can you start?" I was paid £20 a week, which wasn't bad at the time, but the true wonder was being paid for not working at half term and the Easter holiday.

It was definitely an experience. One of my fondest memories is of a hotly contested cricket match with another local school. I was umpire and, of course, had a white coat to wear over my tracksuit, the one Mum had bought me for swimming about five years previously. The visiting umpire had a white coat too, under which he wore his MCC blazer and tie, cavalry twill trousers and brogues. New to this umpiring lark, I had read somewhere that it is very easy to lose count of the number of balls bowled and, to avoid this, the umpire should keep six stones in their pocket as a counting aid. The match progressed and the opposition's star batsman was slaughtering our bowlers when, last ball of the over, he was clean bowled. But he only got halfway to the pavilion before the visiting team's scorer came scuttling out all afluster; it transpired that the

170

crucial ball had been the seventh of the over. Impossible, I thought, counting my stones; but sadly, there now were seven, as it seems I had picked up five stones and a piece of mortar that had broken in two. Oops. Us umpires met mid-wicket, and I decided the best form of defence is attack. "It seems to me," I led, "that while this is my mistake, the result should stand, just as it would if your batsman had scored a six." I was somewhat surprised, and not a little relieved, when the other, far more experienced, umpire agreed. The game continued, and with their star gone we won. Over tea and sandwiches, we discussed the event and my fellow umpire suggested we took the right decision although we both agreed to research it further.

Some weeks later, after the rematch where we had been firmly put in our place, and again over tea and sandwiches, the other umpire brought up the event. "After further investigation it would appear we made the right decision regarding that seventh ball." "Yes definitely." "Did you look it up too?" "Oh yes. Definitely the right decision." "Where did you look?" "Hmm?" "Where did you look? Wisden I suppose?" "Of course. Where else?" I was definitely developing the bluffing skills that I would need to progress when I moved on to Big Boys' work.

I never did get to travel during my gap spell, but then it had always been highly unlikely anyway; in those days it wasn't easy to arrange a quick trip around the globe; besides, I was hardly what you would call adventurous, and I knew nobody who would have joined me on an expedition. So, I stayed and built up my cash reserves instead. Lifeguard work, cleaning windows, occasional bar work and manning the petrol pumps all added to the funds until the big day came. My one big expense was the aforementioned £30 invested in my first car.

I was also doing bar work at a local pub at the time, and a couple of weeks before I was due to head off, the landlord came over for a chat; my plan was to travel up on the Friday, the day before he was having a big wedding anniversary bash which sadly I would miss, but if I wanted to put the word around my chums, we could have a sendoff on the Thursday; late lock-in of course. The day came and the pub was packed with friends and family, many of whom I hadn't seen for ages; it didn't need the Internet to get a party advertised. With so many people I assumed the lock-in was a non-starter and consumed rather a lot of lager, only to find closing time came and went. Totally bloated, I moved on to my short of choice, whisky and dry ginger. Not a good move. People kept buying drinks, which was okay in itself, but every time they ordered me one, the landlord went through the same process, "one being paid for, one because he's off to university and one because he's missing our anniversary, oh and some dry ginger." So every glass was a treble with a small dash. I had a great time but needless to say ended the worst for wear, and can remember making my way home around 2 o'clock, supported by Mum and Dad, and totally at one with the world.

19.

You Can't Beat a Good Book

I love books; always have. The earliest books I can remember are the Janet and John and Ladybird series, although fiction soon grabbed my attention and I eagerly consumed anything that came my way. I loved The Famous Five books by Enid Blyton although never really got into the Secret Seven, enjoyed Just William and Billy Bunter stories and couldn't get enough of the adventures of Biggles with his pals Algie and Ginger; although I never realised how prolific a writer W E Johns had been, apparently there were 98 Biggles books. But I wasn't really fussy, give me any book and I would finish it in no time.

Aged about ten, I started reading the James Bond books, and only in later life would I come to understand why my friend's mum had casually asked whether my parents were alright with me reading such stuff; not really appropriate material for one so young. On finding an author I liked, I would devour everything by them before moving on; not necessarily a good thing as, for a number of authors, a pattern tends to emerge, and they become predictable. All the James Bond, Agatha Christie and Sherlock Holmes books were eagerly consumed before my tastes broadened and I turned to more gruesome fare with works by the likes of Alfred Hitchcock and Dennis Wheatley. I lapped up ghost and horror stories, one of my favourites being the short story 'Casting the Runes'. Alistair

MacClean and Hammond Innes came next, more boys' adventure stuff.

Senior school saw my introduction to more cultured fare like 'War of the Worlds', '1984', 'Animal Farm' and 'To Kill a Mockingbird', and I particularly enjoyed Graham Greene's 'The Power and the Glory' going on to read all of his other books. The same happened with John Steinbeck after I read 'The Grapes of Wrath' and 'Tortilla Flats'. We're talking fiction here, but it was through Orwell, Greene, Steinbeck and Lee, that I started to become aware of political differences and inequality around the world.

Having been introduced to the genre of science fiction, a whole new world of books then beckoned. There were classics like Jules Verne's 'Journey to the Centre of the Earth' written over 100 years earlier, but it was more contemporary works like 'I Robot', 'Fahrenheit 451', 'Brave New World' and 'Dune' that led to another reading binge as I ploughed through numerous books by Isaac Asimov, Ray Bradbury, Aldous Huxley, Frank Herbert and many more.

Science fiction was one thing, but I was not so sure about fantasy books that seemed, not to put too fine a point on it, childish drivel. Then, at the ripe old age of eighteen, I picked up 'Lord of The Rings' and was instantly hooked on Frodo Baggins and Middle-earth. I'd read tons of books involving action and adventure in the real world, and original ideas were becoming scarce, yet with fantasy books, once you can suspend reality and accept that by wearing a ring you become invisible, then storylines become almost limitless.

I took a break from fiction, reading little until the 80s when I had the pleasure of joining the army of commuters making the daily trip to London. A forty-five minute train ride each-way gave plenty of time to get stuck into a book, and for most of my forty years commuting that's exactly what I did. My tastes became fussier, and authors whose books seemed formulaic were dropped; at some point the quality of writing became almost as important as the story itself.

I rarely leave a book unfinished, but once read they are categorised as either 'good', meaning that on completion they would be put on the shelf for lending out or re-reading later, or 'train rubbish' to be either consigned to the bin or donated to the charity shop. I read tons of classics by Dickens et al and discovered authors like William Boyd, John Irving, Kazuo Ishiguro, Iain Banks, John Updike, Gabriel García Márquez and many more whose books are still on the shelf.

I had a few commuting friends with similar, sometimes quirky, literary tastes, and we would swap books. I'd not read any travel books before an old school and footballing friend lent me 'Attention All Shipping: A Journey Round the Shipping Forecast' by Charlie Connelley. It's a tour around all the strange places I had heard on the radio while sitting on the kitchen floor as a child; Cromerty, Dogger, German Bight, Rockall and the like; believe it or not it was a real treat. Another commuting friend who spent his days at the Treasury lent me 'The Ascent of Rum Doodle', a cult spoof mocking the 1956 world of stiff upper lip British mountaineers. Our tastes were definitely eclectic, bordering on the pretentious at times; once, as a fellow commuter brandished a copy of 'The Da Vinci Code' my footballing chum remarked "Ah, Dan Brown, literature for the masses". Oh dear.

In 2007 Amazon launched the Kindle. Momentarily the idea of a small electronic device holding numerous books had its appeal; but I didn't succumb, coming to the conclusion that at least part of the appeal in reading was holding the book and turning each page; Oldie that I am, I remain forever bound to the paper version.

Recently, some more educational stuff has found its way onto my reading list. I particularly enjoy history books, but also read the occasional science book, providing it has been written in layman's turns. While enjoyable, this has highlighted a sad fact; in my youth I had an excellent memory and could recall a vast array of facts in minute detail, but today my short-term memory is such that, no sooner do I read something really fascinating than I have problems recalling it. Sad really, although it does mean I can reread a book and get almost as much pleasure from it as the first time.

Anyway, this was only meant as a brief aside, so time to wrap up. Without doubt books have made my life richer, particularly in my youth when I would take myself off and while away hours, my mind wandering around an ever-growing world of wonder. Many people don't feel the same way and consider reading to be a waste of time, a view even more common today with kids who prefer to get their stories delivered at speed in visual format. But they are missing so much. Take the 'Lord of the Rings' films for example. Yes, they can be impressive, but there are technical limitations in producing such a film and you are always watching the director's interpretation of the story while sharing the experience with millions of others. By reading, you remove the technical limits and can create in your head your very own personal version; surely that's always got to be better?

To me, bookshops of old were marvellous places to wend away an hour or two exploring who knows what, but sadly declining sales have seen their demise and they are now few and far between. This is a sad thing, and one area where I feel today's kids are at a disadvantage, even if they don't know it.

20.

Bovvered?

Perhaps I'm fooling myself, but I think I'm quite a nice bloke. 'Nice' is not a particularly flattering sort of word really, suggesting a sort of wishy washy, bland, alright sort of thing; but in our current world I'll settle for it, and wish there was more niceness around.

Earlier, I referred to my friend's public speaking victory at school, talking on the subject of smiling. We don't smile enough anymore, he surmised, smile at a stranger and they'll wonder what you're up to at best, at worst you might get thumped. Hold the door open for someone following you by all means, but don't expect them to acknowledge the fact. Help an old lady across the road and she'll be frightened you're after her handbag. It was true then but even more so now.

Wifey was brought up in the East End of London and often reminisces about the good old days when communities looked after each other, smiled and said "hello", even to strangers; and it was considered safe to leave your door unlocked. True, the notorious Kray brothers might have run the patch, but apparently that didn't stop people being caring, friendly and quick to smile.

In the 80s, comedian Harry Enfield introduced us to teenager Kevin who found just about everything 'unfair'. It was funny at the time, but the world now seems full of people, not just teenagers but adults who should really know better, bleating about how unfair everything is. Lose at sport, fail a job interview, get allotted the wrong seat in a restaurant, lose an election and it's always unfair and never down to personal failure, a legitimate series of events or perhaps an accident; any outcome other than that desired is unfair and usually someone else's fault.

Historically the British have been proud of their views on fair play and democracy. Lose an election? "We lost, there's always next time". Lose a football match? "That's the game. Congratulations to the victor". Corruption was something that happened in strange lands overseas, the British being above that sort of thing. True, we may have been just a tiny bit naïve on that one, but no more.

Attitude starts at the top and filters down. As long as our leaders are good role models, we have nothing to fear. Oh dear. "Fake News" is often now the first response of politicians when they are accused of wrongdoing, but for years they have found the best form of defence is attack, "it's all lies!" I can recall the speech that MP Jonathan Aitken gave in April 1995 in response to a joint Guardian/ Granada TV investigation concerning shady dealings with affluent Saudis. "If it falls to me to start a fight to cut out the cancer of bent and twisted journalism in our country with the simple sword of truth and the trusty shield of British fair play, so be it. I am ready for the fight. The fight against falsehood and those who peddle it. My fight begins today." Stirring stuff indeed. He sued, gave his version of events and the trial collapsed; he was subsequently found guilty of perjury and perverting the course of justice and jailed for 18 months of which he served 7.

MP Neil Hamilton also threatened to sue after being implicated in the cash-for-questions affair, where

Mohammed Fayed claimed to have paid MPs to raise specific questions in Parliament on his behalf. Hamilton dropped the case and faced no criminal charges, although he seemed to be generally associated with sleaze thereafter. Yet, somehow, he and his wife managed to get invited on a number of television shows such as 'Have I Got News For You' where he was regularly the butt of jokes concerning 'brown envelopes'. I know my views regarding Hamilton, but I'm not sure what it says about the BBC.

Then in 2009, following a Telegraph investigation the MPs expenses scandal broke and we got an insight into the mindset of quite a number of our leaders. The Conservative MP for Totnes was found to have spent £87,729 in four years towards the upkeep of his mansion, taxpayers' money having paid for, among other things, a wrought-iron fireplace and tree surgery. And the MP's response? Apparently, he is reported to have said that he didn't know what the fuss was about, people were just "jealous" of his "very, very large house". And he supposedly rounded off with "what right does the public have to interfere with my private life? None."

So, for some time now, I have had a fairly cynical view of politicians who, too often, claim to be working for the greater good while really being driven just by human nature and self-interest. Of course, that's not a fair assessment for them all, but it's true for quite a few. That said, the aftermath of the 2016 EU Referendum surprised even me. A simple majority was what was required, and a simple majority was achieved, unless you somehow believe that 52% is not a majority. Six painful years later, after the largest "it's not fair!" episode in British history, during which a large number of Remain voting MPs doggedly tried every trick in the book to stop, or at least delay Brexit, outstanding issues remain, exacerbated by the arrival of Covid and the Russian invasion of Ukraine. A period of volatility and challenge was inevitable, but had these people accepted the result and worked together to implement it, I'm sure the pain would have been significantly less.

In conclusion then, it will come as no surprise that I consider the old days as definitely better with respect to general attitudes. Too many people seem unable to accept any outcome other than that which they desire, and the idea of 'society', 'the greater good' or 'democracy' holds little sway; and I can only see things getting worse. It would be nice simply to blame the kids, but unfortunately this has been handed down from the grownups who really ought to know better.

21.

The Gilded Halls of Academia

There are many words I could use to describe the thoroughly enjoyable three years I spent at university, but none of them would apply to my first day in the land of academia. Following my sendoff, I awoke later than planned with a horrendous hangover, my head throbbed, and my stomach was churning. It would be six years before I would be able even to smell whisky without feeling sick. And it was raining, hard. I had breakfast, finished packing and loaded the car. That last part didn't take long as most of my possessions were in an old, battered canvas holdall; there was also an ex-army kitbag for shoes and the like, my acoustic guitar and a Philips cassette recorder that would sit on the front seat and provide music for the trip. Everyone had gone to work or school by then so, with no tearful farewells, I shut the door behind me and set off on my adventure. In the rain.

It was a lovely drive, a bit over 200 miles through the Cotswolds, Gloucester, Hereford and the like, although I didn't really get to appreciate this at the time. My old Morris Minor had a low maximum speed that was rarely achieved on account of the winding country roads, pouring rain and a hangover that refused to die. At some point I decided to stop and buy lunch, so pulled into what was probably a Little Chef and splashed out on fish and chips and a coffee. Feeling marginally better, I was soon back on the road. And still it rained.

After a long and tedious haul lasting some eight or nine hours, my expedition came to an end. I had no idea what to expect of the place, but was definitely underwhelmed. It was still raining, and the town had all the run-down characteristics of an out-of-season seaside resort; drab, with shabby buildings leaving a lot to be desired. I found my hall of residence, a converted Victorian guesthouse, parked and went in. It was still raining but at least my hangover had finally abated.

First impressions weren't good, and it got worse when I saw my room. Of course, freshers had the worst rooms and mine was right at the top, in the attic basically. I knew I would be sharing, but had no idea with whom; but emanating from the room, the door of which was open, was a thick cloud of Brut aftershave. What next?

My new friend was from the Rhondda Valley, a place of which I had never heard but soon would learn all about as he, rather magnanimously, invited me to join him and his friends at the night's main entertainment, 'up the hill' at the main university hall. It transpired that I had more in common with his three mates than the lad himself, and they became good friends throughout my tenure.

After a not-too-bad meal (my accommodation included all meals so no need to learn to cook) we headed off, taking in a few pubs before heading up. Hangover now banished, the beer went down well, the company was entertaining and, with Thin Lizzy playing live, it proved a most enjoyable evening. Back to hall where I made my way up into the attic and slept like a log, waking to a view, albeit through a very small window, of sun sparkling off the sea. Perhaps my initial response had been a little hasty? Words from a childhood song come to mind "Muddah, Faddah kindly disregard this letter"

There followed Freshers' Week, the aim of which was to introduce new students to university life. I quickly got to work out the layout of the town and the location of various key parts of the university; admin office, lecture halls and seminar rooms, student bars, sports facilities and the like. It was a week of socialising and making friends. My fellow students fitted two main categories, those who had lived a bit and were used to the occasional drink, and the more protected types who had never been away from home and were new to alcohol; many of the latter group definitely suffered most as they came to grips with their new life. There was a fayre where numerous sports clubs and societies vied for new members; I joined the Surf Club and Photography Club.

I was soon to realise my ignorance of life outside my home patch. "Where are you from?" I casually asked two girls. "Glasgow" came the reply. "So what's life like in Glasgow?" to which they both burst into laughter. One was from Swansea, the other from Hereford, but my knowledge of accents was non-existent. Oh dear. It also became clear how much dislike there was for the English, and southerners in particular. I was told that we are all run by people in London with no knowledge of, and even less concern for, the rest of the population; even if Britain was devolved into 50 autonomous authorities, they said, I would still be run by Westminster, so I'd be alright. Definitely food for thought, and a first step on the new path of enlightenment on which I was bound. But my new friends didn't seem to hold this against me personally, and we just had another beer.

At some point I visited the university shop to buy basics such as pens and a notepad, together with the obligatory uni sweatshirt and college scarf; then shopping in town where I splashed out on a new denim jacket. I was ready to work.

One key event, the hall initiation ceremony, took place in the car park after the evening meal on the first Thursday. Freshers were invited to attend, wearing nothing but swimming trunks and, with very few refusals, we lined up like sheep in a basement shower room where each of us had a large number written in black shoe polish on his chest. When your number was called, you went out into the car park, in the rain, and the hall chairman invited you to sit in an old bath full of something unpleasant, reminiscent of farmyards. He made a brief speech welcoming you to the hall, 'anointed' you with a pint glass full of the gloop and invited you to join him for a beer afterwards in the local pub. On rising from the bath, you were cheered by the other lads before making your way back to the shower room to clean up.

Now I know all this sounds, well, pretty stupid, and such events have become controversial these days as they are said to adversely impact those bullied into participation, but to me the process was harmless and served its purpose; we had started the evening as a bunch of individuals, on our own, nervously learning our way around, but at the drop of a hat we had a home. Forty students lived in the hall, and suddenly most could be relied on for help. Anyway, those who refused the ceremony were made welcome too, it just seemed to take a little longer. In the local pub a few days later, one of the town lads was picking on a rather scrawny fresher; the would-be assailant was lippy and brave before noticing a dozen students converging from different parts of the pub, at which point he decided it was probably time to leave. Presumably, the potential victim considered a few minutes in the gloop to be time well spent.

The hall soon became 'home', although the lifestyle took some getting used to. We shared bathrooms; there were only about six in all, so it was not always easy to get one. In particular, on a cold wet Wednesday afternoon, when many returned from sporting activities, it was a bit of a race, and rinsed out wetsuits would leave a ton of grit in the bath. In one of the bathrooms on our floor there was a mysterious electric clothes dryer; it was coin-operated, but the mystery was that someone by-passed the meter with a short cable making it free to use; and within days of it being rewired, the 'fix' would be back. This happened through the two years of my residence, and I never found the identity of our mysterious benefactor, although my roommate always liked fixing things.

Another example of low-key criminal innovation that appealed to me concerned the use of pay phones. Two students would agree a time for a call, both using payphones; the caller would dial the operator and ask to place a reverse charge to the other phone; the operator then called the other number to ask if they were willing to accept the charge, unaware that it was another payphone, before completing the connection, after which the conversation would be free. Ingenious.

I was pleasantly surprised to find my timetable wasn't exactly crammed; eleven lectures plus four tutorials a week, all one hour long, the rest of my time to be spent in the library or my room reading up on the subject. In contrast, those studying science degrees were in lectures or labs eight hours a day, from 9am to 6pm; except for

Wednesday afternoons, which were kept free for sports activities or anything else you fancied. Having so much free time seemed a good thing, but now, when kids are paying for the service, I can't help thinking many with my timetable will question the fairness of paying the same for 15 hours of personal attention as someone receiving 36 hours.

It soon became clear that the challenges of life in the gilded halls of academia were not to be quite as I had anticipated. Not only was there not as much work as I had expected, but quite a few of my fellow students seemed, not to put too fine a point on it, a little bit dumb at times. They were all very bright from an academic viewpoint, but common sense was not always that common. Not only that, but because of my gap year, and my familiarity with public houses, a lot of my fellow freshers were younger and less worldly than me, and could come over as rather childish, proudly keeping track of the number of drinks they had imbibed before throwing up or doing something none too clever. Still, I knuckled down, soon found friends of a similar ilk and proceeded to enjoy those aspects of uni life that I had honestly not really considered.

A major change in my life came on the very first day at uni. I had hitherto been a lager drinker, but at that time lager was noticeably more expensive than ale, so for the sake of economy I immediately switched to bitter, forced my first few pints down until eventually acquiring the taste and, as they say, the rest is history. It was said there were over fifty pubs in the town, supposedly one more than the number of churches. Looking back, I can't remember counting them, but I did my best to visit as many as possible, although this became harder as, being on a limited budget, we tended to gravitate towards establishments that we felt at home in and then found it hard to drag ourselves away. There was also a number of student bars we could frequent; not the same atmosphere as a real pub and the 'glasses' were plastic, which didn't appeal to us aficionados, but they were cheaper, so on occasion we would force ourselves. As a student I had to stick to a budget of course; I remember this being £1, about £8.50p today, or 4 pints for a weeknight out and £2 for a weekend night.

I have never been fitter than during those three years. I played digs league football and basketball for the hall; five-a-side football for the Rhondda Ratcatchers, having been declared an honorary Welshman by the chums I met on my first day; surfed whenever the opportunity arose; played water polo for the university and squash at least once a week. To fill the spare hours, I also bought an old kayak from a fellow student for a bit of sea canoeing, although it's just dawned on me that I have no idea how I eventually got it home. Finally, there was the fifteen-minute brisk walk two or even three times a day uphill to the university for lectures and social events.

Each hall of residence had a hall chairman, a role filled by a second-year student, those in their final year being far too busy. Hustings were held, and potential candidates gave a speech as to what qualities they could bring to the role, then the residents elected their man. For some reason, our hustings were traditionally held with the speaker sitting at a desk in the sea with water up to his chest.

The chairman was not only responsible for somber rituals such as initiation, but also for hall discipline in the event of there being any 'incidents'. On quiet Sunday afternoons, with little else happening, there might be a hall trial, presided over by the chairman. The heinous crimes would be read out, the prosecutor would make his case and the defendant or his representative would reply before the residents attending passed judgment. A typical sentence for a guilty verdict would be for the miscreant's bed to be placed in the middle of the prom with the offender tied to it with a placard around his neck reading something like 'Guilty of evil thoughts'. If nothing else, events such as these gave the passersby something to wonder at on what was otherwise. a very boring day.

The topic of class never really crossed my mind until our first Sociology tutorial, when we were asked what class we considered ourselves to be and why, followed by whether we considered university to be a middle class institution. We all tried to impress the tutor with our deep thoughts; I eventually came to the conclusion that I was working/middle class and yes, university was a middle-class institution. At the time, a number of pubs sold boxes of matches with 'intellectual' quotes on the back and a few weeks later I saw one bearing the lines "Sociology, the study of those who don't need it by those who do".

But we did have a pretty broad cross-section of society and not everyone got along. International Politics at the uni was highly rated and, as a result, a number of army chaps attended; they didn't get along at all with the more left-wing types. Some, strangely, bought loads of Socialist Worker newspapers just to dump them in the bin, after which the salesperson would simply pocket the cash and retrieve the papers for resale. Welsh students happy to be British, were regularly in dispute with the Welsh Nationalists. A basketball-playing friend on my course was from Harrow where he had attended a state school and developed a distinct dislike for the other one; this became apparent in the company of another course attendee, an ex-Harrow boy whose father had furnished him with a brand new, red E-type Jag for passing his exams. These and many similar differences were always bubbling under and provided entertainment for people watchers, but it was all very low key, handbags-at-dawn stuff at the worst. Even the town vs gown disputes rarely got serious.

Every February, a major event in the university calendar was Rag Week, basically seven days of excess justified by the aim of raising cash for charities. Our Rag was actually very successful at raising cash and didn't do badly on the madness either. There were three-legged pub crawls, raft races on the river, a procession of floats running the gauntlet as students and townies pelted them with flour bombs and all sorts; sporting events, concerts, fancy dress, eating and drinking competitions and much more; all accompanied by large amounts of alcohol. The largest form of income was through the sale of Rag mags, containing jokes and articles of generally bad taste, most of which would not be allowed today.

Parents of one of my friends owned a guest house in Blackpool, and it became an annual ritual that four of us would drive up for a weekend, be very well looked after as the guest house was empty in February, and take in a variety of northern hospitality and beers while selling Rag mags. A small percentage of sales could be claimed to cover travel expenses and we always managed to finance the outing, so everyone was happy.

During our first drive up, we stopped in Liverpool to try our luck. We hadn't been touting our wares long before an inquisitive bobby came to ask what we were up to. We explained, and he warned us that this wasn't the most salubrious area to be in, and that we should take care; he

190

then stood with us for a while as a host of dubious looking characters strolled past, even telling a few who he obviously knew by name, that they might like to contribute, which they dutifully did, albeit reluctantly. So nice to have the support of the local constabulary.

Something similar happened in Blackpool the next day when a more senior officer gave us permission to sell there, but we made the mistake of selling him a mag and about an hour later one of his constables came to tell us we weren't allowed to sell after all. Apparently, the boss had thought he was being nice to local students but, on realising that we were from out of town, he didn't want to encourage us. Still, we had sold quite a few by then and repaired to a local hostelry where sales continued to boom.

Our first Blackpool trip was courtesy of my old Morris Minor; it had become a bit of a luxury, but my plan had always been to sell it when the tax, MOT and insurance all came due for renewal. I was rather chuffed to make a 50% profit when it went for £45 but a little sad to see my old friend driving around town without me.

I discovered the error of my ways at the end of term when, for the first time, I had to make my way home by train. In the 60s, recommendations from the Beeching report had been implemented and an axe taken to the rail network with many unprofitable lines closed down; consequently my route home was: 1. Train to Shrewsbury; 2. Wait for a train to Wolverhampton; 3. After a further wait, board a train to Birmingham and wait again; 4. Catch a train for London Euston; 5. London Underground to Waterloo and wait; 6. Train home from Waterloo. In contrast my first drive had been a short sprint. Not only was the journey pretty horrible, but also the trains were short, and at the end of term were very crowded, so leaving early was advisable; not so easy following a last night of celebrations. Needless to say, it wasn't long before I decided a new car was essential.

I say 'new', but at a cost of £65 that's not the best word for it. It was a Renault 4, painted a rather horrible dustbin grey, with a dashboard gear change similar to the Citroen 2CV and a dented and very rusty bonnet. After acquiring and fitting a replacement, lime green, bonnet from a scrapyard, I was given some spare paint by one of Dad's friends who also let me use his warehouse and spraying gear; in no time I had a gleaming, bright orange, apparently a colour all the rage for bulldozers, motor, that would see me out for the rest of my uni tenure.

I decided to stay in the hall of residence for a second year. The best rooms were large doubles on the seafront with big bay windows overlooking the sea, and as this luxury seemed to outweigh the benefits of privacy, I opted to share again. After a stirring speech, delivered from a wet desk, my mate had been voted chairman and as such had first choice of room. Many an hour was spent sitting in the window looking out at the people passing, our gloriously sunny beach or, more often, grey waves crashing on a grey shore. There was a pier, not spectacular but still a feature; starlings would flock there in their thousands and their impressive flying displays or murmurations have recently featured in a number of wildlife programmes on TV.

There were scientists in our midst who would occasionally be called upon for their expertise in matters of importance. My roommate produced homebrew, and it took much scientific debate to create a recipe for the strongest stuff possible while retaining some semblance of beer; one time, they smuggled the beer into one of the labs in order to speed up the brewing process by spinning it through a centrifuge. All Greek to me. Self-catering scientists would pool their knowledge before foraging for free food, seaweed, mushrooms and the like.

As with my school years, I'm afraid to admit that for three years I didn't take a lot of interest in affairs outside our little bubble, but in 1975 two events did catch our attention. Firstly, there was a referendum as to whether we wished to stay in the EU; it was only a trade deal and a vast majority voted 'yes'. Then, in April 1975, we watched as the story unfolded of America's ignominious final retreat from Vietnam, the fall of Saigon and their hasty helicopter retreat from the US embassy, leaving their allies to face the oncoming North Vietnamese. To a large number of students, the Vietnam War had always been wrong and this event was seen as a fitting end.

In my final year I became aware of an uncomfortable truth, I would soon need to think about working for a living. It transpired that most students on my course envisaged accountancy as a career, but not me. Careers advice was limited as our lecturers generally had little experience of life outside of academia, and in the end I plumped for Marketing; mainly because that didn't seem to need any specific knowledge. The Milk Round was on us, with company representatives visiting universities to extol the virtues of their employers and sign up potential candidates for further interview. I requested interviews with a number of companies taking part, bought my first suit and tie and rolled up for my first ever big boy job interviews. These events were educational, but I suspect my lack of enthusiasm may have shone through; there were a number of follow-up interviews but, for one reason or another, they never led to a job.

Suddenly my Finals were upon me. A relatively intense period of study followed, usually incorporating a short pub break near closing time before reading into the night. This was not particularly successful, and my first two exams were a disaster. We didn't know what constituted a pass, but the fact that I had only answered 50% of each paper, and I had little faith in those answers that I had managed, didn't bode well. The marking process was opaque in those days, but rumour had it that failing one exam resulted in your final mark being automatically downgraded one step; failing two meant a double downgrade; fail three and you were out; no degree. Now, while I admit I had not been over-industrious on the studying front, the sudden realisation that after three years I might leave without a degree was worrying, and for the first time I felt a little stressed.

One thing that didn't help was my hayfever. From the age of about ten, I'd suffered every year between May and August enjoying all the symptoms, itchy eyes, sneezing, streaming eyes and nose; lovely. Some years were better than others, but unfortunately the uni years were not good. Needless to say I was overcome with sympathy from my friends who would sit sobbing while saying "I'm so happy!" Who needs enemies? But one good thing did come out of this. I'd been a smoker for a number of years, and the environment had led to increased tobacco consumption, but during the hayfever season, I would regularly wake up with a particularly horrible throat, which ultimately provided the incentive needed to kick the habit.

I particularly remember events around the last of my Finals exams, Statistics, on the morning of Wednesday 8th June. I really needed a good one, so a last big effort was called for. But I faced challenges. The Monday had been a bank holiday to honour the Queen's Silver Jubilee, the weather was glorious all weekend and the pollen was horrendous. So, I was locked away, sneezing, crying and nose running, studying while the town buzzed with tourists and sunny bank holiday enjoyment. Yippee.

I was the first in my social group to complete my finals so, while I wanted to celebrate, everyone else was beavering away and I had no company. In the end I went to a near-empty cinema and sat on my own, clasping my handkerchief and sniffling away, while watching 'Cross of Iron'. Rather a sad anticlimax really, but a good film.

Of course, I did get to celebrate, and the last couple of weeks of my uni life were pretty good. One unfortunate incident happened late one night in our main local at the time. To set the scene; late night, loads of happy people, music and me. After more than a few pints of Banks' mixed, and while eating a celebratory pack of pork scratchings, I ran my tongue around the inside of my mouth and was slightly puzzled to feel a slight lack of teeth. It appeared that the scratchings had caused me to snap off two large and perfectly healthy molars! Luckily, I could feel nothing then, and they caused me no discomfort later on sobering up. Back home I had them both crowned and the dentist told me to expect the crowns to last at least ten years; I still have them today. They don't make things like they used to.

But that was it. I was awarded a BSc Hons degree, lower second class; commonly referred to as a drinking man's degree. Could I have done better? Possibly, had I put more effort in, I might just have managed an upper second but no more than that. Firsts were as rare as hen's teeth in those days, and only obtained by students who lived and breathed their subject, not a description I could really apply to myself; I was happy.

A few weeks later I returned with Mum and Dad for the graduation ceremony. On the eve of the event, we went to the pub where I introduced them to the landlord, one of a few who had taken care of their little boy, and drank too much of course, something I would regret. The next day was gloriously sunny, and there was I, wrapped up in my suit plus a gown and mortarboard hired for the occasion; the ceremony was long and tedious, I was too hot, had a horrible hangover and felt sick throughout. I was green and in much the same state I had been that October morning three years earlier; the circle that was my university life had closed.

The theme music for this phase of my life has to be Pink Floyd's 'Dark Side of the Moon'. Shortly after my arrival at uni, a live performance was broadcast on BBC radio and I lay on my bed in my attic room, listening spellbound. I was familiar with their earlier music from the days of Syd Barrett, but this was something else and I have been a fan ever since.

Both my kids attended university. Unlike me, they did the sensible thing and went for interviews and a look round. We went along for both, and I have to say that many aspects of the trips filled me with nostalgia and perhaps a little envy. Lecture theatres, halls of residence, student bars and countless posters advertising various activities all seemed so familiar, although the presence of en-suite bathrooms in a hall of residence did come as a shock.

Yes, much was familiar, but there have also been many changes since my time. Most obvious is the introduction of tuition fees in 1998. In my day, students were only responsible for living expenses, and grants to help with these costs weren't uncommon.

Of far greater significance than tuition fees, I would argue, is that the entire ethos of universities has changed. Back in 1974, further education was provided by two types of institution: universities focussed on the more academic subjects; they were attended by a small minority who were encouraged to study anything that interested them; working for a living was a secondary concern and would come later. Polytechnics, on the other hand, tended to serve their local communities offering more in the way of vocational-oriented qualifications accredited by professional bodies. To many, the universities were elitist, superior and up themselves, but in the labour market academic qualifications increasingly became the main prerequisite for a good job, with employers fighting over uni students and ignoring the rest. In 1992, to address this growing imbalance, the polytechnics were reclassified as 'new universities' offering degree courses; they also catered for sub-degree qualifications although these BTEC subjects have since mostly been transferred to colleges of further education.

The impact of this change has been huge. Far more kids now have the opportunity to earn a degree and go on to a 'graduate job', which is good. On the other hand, with so many graduate job hunters on the market, academic qualifications become a must-have for pretty mundane and menial jobs, further working against those without the right bits of paper. And universities have become businesses in their own right, competing for students, or more precisely the money they bring; the overriding priority of any modern education now is getting that job, a bit like cramming before an exam.

So are things better now? With regards the number of people offered the opportunity of a university education, things most definitely are. But considerable expectation management is necessary. While the number of graduates has increased, the number of 'graduate level jobs' hasn't, so don't expect too much; many young graduates have to take a lowly starter job before working their way up. There seems always to be a shortage of scientists and engineers, so kids worried about employment opportunities should take a technical degree; but these tend to be hard work and, understandably, not so appealing to the majority. And I find it strange that kids who don't enjoy school lessons rush to sign up for a university course that is little more than grown-up school with partying thrown in.

We had it better when it comes to costs, but I suppose funding such large numbers in further education means tuition fees are inevitable. My guess is that many kids will come to the point where they feel university costs outweigh the benefits and choose not to go. In this digital world, weird and wonderful ways of making a living are materialising all the time; I mean, I have no idea what purpose influencers serve; and I expect more ways of earning a living will continue to pop up, making that all-important university education slightly less essential.

22.

The Exciting World of Politics

Possibly Groucho Marx said, "Politics is the art of looking for trouble, finding it everywhere, diagnosing it incorrectly and applying the wrong remedies." Politics isn't everyone's idea of fun; we accept it as a necessary evil while criticising the way it works, spouting off occasionally about things we think are being done wrong while feeling there's not a lot we can do about it. I've drifted through life aware of individual political events, but seen these more as a sideshow than something for me to waste my time on. But, like it or not, politics has a huge impact on our lives and, in many ways I often didn't notice, has changed considerably during my lifetime. So, for that reason I decided it warranted inclusion here. As always, feel free to skip this chapter and move on if your eyelids are already beginning to droop.

While humans have evolved to reap the benefits of living and working in large groups, this brings challenges as to how such groups function. A common characteristic of mankind is that self-interest often trumps the greater good and, left to follow their own ends, any group is likely to sink into anarchy before the strongest takes control, a state of affairs not considered beneficial by most. So some form of leadership is required. Our version of democracy has evolved over the years since 1215 when King John signed the Magna Carta; the good bit is that we get to choose the body of people who run us, the less good bit is that they are all politicians.

We all have a picture of the type of person who should be in charge, but they generally have better things to do with their time; perhaps innovating, creating, helping us live longer, running large successful companies, passing on their knowledge, excelling at some sport or another; in fact anything rather than getting involved in politics. It's a particular type of person who feels they know what is best for the rest of us. Regardless of political leanings, many of our politicians share a similar background of private school and an Oxbridge degree, reading Philosophy, Politics, and Economics a common feature.

Our first-past-the-post election system ensures that the two main parties take it in turns to run the country while smaller parties, like the LibDems and Greens, have a disproportionately small share of seats in Parliament compared to the number of votes they achieve; arguably unfair, but providing greater stability than proportional representations where governments are often based on coalitions which regularly collapse, leading to a never-ending cycle of elections.

One feature of our system is that the opposition will find fault in almost everything proposed and implemented by the government of the time, reversing much of the previous bunch's policies as soon as they get their chance to govern, so making the implementation of long-term projects challenging. Short-termism is the easy path for politicians who are generally looking for quick wins to curry favour.

Then of course there's the civil service, the bureaucrats who many think actually run the country. In 'Yes Minister', Sir Humphrey suggests that civil servants should tell ministers as little as possible so that they can't tell anyone else what is going on. A line from a sitcom perhaps, but not necessarily that far from the truth. The main aim of the civil service is to maintain the status quo, regardless of the leanings of the party in power, while keeping out of the limelight, remaining anonymous and avoiding responsibility at all times. Achieving these aims has been a challenge recently since, like him or not, Boris Johnson proved to be a disruptor trying to change things by controlling the power of unelected civil servants. But to keep it simple, let's just assume that it's the government that runs the country and move on.

Personally, I always thought the idea of communism was OK. Give what you are able and take what you need; we're all in this together. Sounds good to me, but I soon realised the flaw in this; the theory is great but goes horribly wrong as soon as humans get involved. Self-interest rapidly comes to the fore and, to quote George Orwell's Animal Farm, "all animals are equal, but some animals are more equal than others". Shame.

So my own political views are slightly left leaning, if a little confused: as a society we have a moral duty to look after the vulnerable while at the same time avoiding being ripped off by scroungers. As a rich nation we should help those from poorer countries; bona fide refugees are, of course, a special case, but there is a limit to the number of other people we can take in, and we should aim to help poorer countries to prosper rather than just opening our doors to all-comers. Taxation is a necessary evil, and nobody should be exempt; those with more should pay more. The idea that people with money can buy a superior quality of education or healthcare seems wrong, yet I have paid for private medical treatment and would have sent my children to private school had I thought they needed it. As I said, my views are a bit confused.

I was born ten years after the end of World War II. Post-war Britain was a land of austerity but also of optimism. We had seen off the Fascist threat, food rationing had just ended, the Empire still ruled a considerable part of the world, our nascent welfare state with the jewel in the crown, the NHS, was growing in maturity and we were a shining beacon of democracy for the rest of the world to envy. What could possibly go wrong?

In the 1955 general election, the Tories maintained their grip on power and would do so for 43 of the next 67 years. It wasn't long, however, before things took a knock when the British, French and Israelis were forced by the Americans to back down in their argument with Egypt during the Suez Crisis of 1956, highlighting the fact that Britain was no longer the superpower it imagined itself to be.

The Tories started the 60s in charge, first with Harold Macmillan followed by Alec Douglas-Hume, but change was on the horizon, not only in who was running the country but also in how they were perceived by the electorate. In 1963, Secretary for War John Profumo resigned after admitting that he had lied to the House of Commons regarding his affair with a woman who, it transpired, was also seeing a Russian military attaché known to be a spy.

This is possibly when attitudes of both the press and the general public towards our leaders started to change. Hitherto, politicians had generally been treated with a fair amount of respect and deference, but now their actions, decisions and motives were increasingly under the microscope and open to question. This was the decade of social change, free love, flower power, peace and the pill; in 1964 liberalising Labour, under Harold Wilson, took the floor.

With Wilson at the helm, social services and welfare blossomed with the abolition of prescription charges on medicines, an overhaul of the benefits system and an increase in state pensions. Spending on the NHS increased from 4.2% of GNP in 1964 to about 5% in 1969, generating a boom in building of hospitals and local GP medical centres. Local authorities were authorised to provide free family planning advice and contraceptive devices. Other social reforms addressed a variety of issues including abortion, the death penalty, homosexual acts, censorship and the voting age. Labour built a considerable number of council houses while introducing schemes to encourage and support the lower paid in buying their own homes. New restrictions were placed on the rights of immigrants to the UK, and the Open University was created. In 1970, after a bit of a dip, the economy was again on the up and Harold Wilson called an election, with opinion polls predicting an easy win with a 12.4% majority. Not for the last time, the polls were wrong. Enter Ted Heath.

Throughout the seventies, Britain was considered the sick man of Europe with poor economic growth and terrible industrial relations; 29 million workdays were lost to strikes in 1979 alone. It was a time of rampant inflation, 26.9% in August 1979, with the cost of basic items increasing drastically each year and workers demanding wage increases to match. Heath's Tories were in charge for the first four years of the decade, during which the coalminers' strike of 1972 caused a reduction in output from power stations; electricity supplies to homes and businesses were reduced through rota disconnections, leaving many without power for up to nine hours a day. Further industrial action from the miners followed, and the government introduced a three-day week in order to conserve fuel in response to the 1973/74 oil crisis.

British voters had had enough and, in 1974, decided to give Labour another go, first with Harold Wilson, and then James Callaghan. But industrial unrest continued, culminating in the Winter of Discontent in 1978/9. Tanker drivers went on strike leading to fuel shortages and garage closures. Striking ambulance drivers, gravediggers and refuse collectors added to the misery, and even members of the Royal College of Nursing downed tools, with many more following suit. The misery was compounded by the coldest winter in 16 years.

I was completing my education at the time, then starting my first big boy's job, lived with my parents and had no financial commitments to speak of, so was able to continue my drift through life relatively unscathed. Power cuts were inconvenient, but living by candlelight and torch could even be a bit of a novelty; on passing various groups of strikers, we hooted our support, their wage demands seemed fair to most of us if we didn't stop to think about where the money was actually to come from; and life went on. We were young and yet to learn the realities of life.

In 1973, after much lobbying and numerous rejections, the UK was finally allowed to join the European Economic Community (EEC). This was seen by some as an opportunity to address our economic woes, but Harold Wilson wasn't so sure and in 1975 held a referendum to ensure the move had the support of the population. It did, with over 67% of voters, including myself and Margaret

Thatcher, saying 'Yes'. It seemed a no-brainer, after all it was only a trade agreement so what was wrong in that?

1979 saw the start of a whole new era as Margaret Thatcher came to power. Loved and loathed in equal measure, she brought a rare quality to politics, the will to see through what she had started. She took over a failing system that had evolved over decades as both Conservative and Labour governments had progressively increased the level of state interference and control in the lives of the people, and she created a roaring economy, no longer sick but, to many, an example of how things should be done.

A proponent of the economic doctrine of monetarism, and that individuals should take more responsibility for themselves, she reduced government interference in the economy, selling off state-owned enterprises like gas, electricity and water. Believing that the unions undermined parliamentary democracy and economic performance, she curtailed their power through the introduction of legal restrictions. She introduced monetarist free market reforms, deregulated the financial markets, reduced the dependence of individuals on the state, cut expenditure on social services such as health care, education, and housing and gave council house tenants the right to buy their homes.

It wasn't easy at the start. Rising unemployment and the ongoing recession made her very unpopular in the early years, but she was thrown a lifeline when, as part of a long-running dispute over sovereignty, the Argentines invaded the Falkland Islands in April 1982. Her rapid and unflinching military response led to victory in ten weeks and her approval ratings rocketed which, together with growing economic recovery gave her a landslide victory in the 1983 election. I was in the Falklands in 1980, weeks after Foreign Secretary Nick Ridley had visited to float the idea of a 'leaseback' proposal that had been secretly discussed with the Argentines. Apparently, his reception was hostile, and on his departure he was booed by crowds singing 'Rule Britannia'. One of the most common complaints I heard was that, though Falkland Islanders were generally of British stock, they had fewer rights to UK residency than people from Commonwealth countries. Personally, I think our claims to the islands a little tenuous anyway, and it seems the British government were looking for a way to unload responsibility when the Argentines jumped the gun.

The conflict that followed saw the death of some 255 British military personnel with many more wounded, and cost around £2.7 billion (£9.6 billion today). If some acceptable form of future 'leaseback' had been found, every one of the 1,800 Falkland Islanders could have been paid £1 million compensation and offered UK residency and there would have been no war; nearly everyone would have been happy, except possibly Margaret Thatcher who might have lost the next election. But of course that's not the way things work.

A further sign of the times; on 12 October 1984, during the Tory party conference in Brighton, the Provisional IRA detonated a bomb at the Grand Brighton Hotel in Brighton, killing 5 and injuring a further 31.

In 1989, proceedings at the House of Commons were broadcast for the first time, something we now take for granted.

To this day Thatcher is a divisive figure. For the winners she could do no wrong. A growing number of people took the step onto the property ladder, money was flowing, and a large percentage of the population had become shareholders, profiting from their cut-price shares in gas, electricity and the like. Disruption and misery caused by regular, often unannounced, industrial action was a thing of the past, and the pound was on the rise, with holidays abroad and imported goods suddenly costing less. The future was rosy.

But for the losers things weren't so good. The trade unions had been neutered, in particular through two bruising episodes. The Miners' Strike of 1984/5 brought protests across the country as other unions took to the streets to show their support, often leading to violent skirmishes between strikers and police, but the Miners eventually had to admit defeat. Unprofitable mines were closed or sold off, leading to tens of thousands of job losses and decimating mining communities where, to this day, Margaret Thatcher is a figure of hate.

Similarly, in the year-long Wapping dispute of 1986, print unions failed to stop Rupert Murdoch from moving production of the Sunday Times to a new site in Wapping, where new technology allowed journalists to input copy direct rather than employing printers. Depending on your perspective, this was either progress or an unwarranted attack on the workers leading to unemployment for thousands. Through the introduction of laws restricting actions available to unions, and by demonstrating that she was willing to use the police if pickets attempted to close a plant down, Margaret Thatcher's policies left the unions hog-tied for decades to come.

Even Margaret Thatcher's greatest fans can't claim that everything she did was good. As financial regulation was relaxed and overseas banks and financial institutions set up home in the City of London, vast sums of money flooded in and soon some people were earning more money than they ever thought possible. But this didn't come without cost. It ushered in an age of excess, of brash obnoxious yuppies flashing their cash as mockingly personified by Harry Enfield's character Loadsamoney, while those at the other end of the wealth spectrum found it harder than ever to make ends meet.

Despite being the longest-serving premier of the 20th Century Margaret Thatcher's popularity fell markedly and, in 1990, she 'chose' to resign. The reason generally cited for her downfall is the introduction of the poll tax replacing the domestic rates system to raise cash to fund local government. This tax ignored the value of a property and was calculated on the number of adults living there. As low-income households generally tend to house more adults, the outcome was that the rich paid less and the poor paid more. Many chose not to register, or refused to pay, taking to the streets in often violent protests, the worst being the Trafalgar Square riot on 31st March 1990 attended by around 200,000 people and degenerating into a running battle with hundreds of protestors and police officers injured. The tax was introduced one week later but repealed in 1993, replaced by the Council Tax.

Thatcherism had led to a widening of the gap between rich and poor and she was seen as out of touch with the less well off; some of her statements were considered racist; all facts that turned support away. Also, many Conservatives were not happy with her increasing Euroscepticism that led to a split in the party that has lasted to this day. It was time for her to go.

Margaret Thatcher left Downing Street to be replaced by John Major who won the leadership contest not so much on merit, rather because he wasn't Michael Heseltine. Among other things, Major committed British troops to the first Gulf War and privatised British Rail. He also signed the EU Maastricht Treaty, a treaty that greatly expanded the remit of the EU, introducing the concept of European citizenship and freedom of movement; it came into effect in November 1993. Since the late 70s all EU states had signed up to the European Exchange Rate Mechanism (ERM) linking the exchange rates of member countries and preparing the ground for a common European currency.

But on September 16th, 1992, labeled Black Wednesday, despite frantic government intervention, the value of the pound fell below the lower limit specified by the ERM and the UK was forced to leave. This was the death knell for the Conservatives who had won re-election on a pro-Euro platform and were seen to have wasted billions of taxpayers' money in a pointless effort to support the pound. Ironically, this could well have led to the British economic boom of the 90s, bringing gains that significantly outweighed the costs of Black Wednesday while European countries floundered under restrictions imposed by the EU. It's a funny old world. But that was John Major done for.

The 1997 election saw another landslide result, but this time for Tony Blair and the enigma that was New Labour. By this time the black and white of British politics was becoming distinctly grey. Labour had always stood for the rights of the working man, while the Tories represented the upper and middle classes. But some of Margaret Thatcher's policies, such as encouraging council house tenants to buy their homes, had won her a degree of working-class support. Labour had always struggled to get into power and now the odds were even more against them. Tony Blair's answer was to pinch a number of policy ideas from the Tories and Liberal Democrats, carry out a marketing rebrand exercise and bingo, New Labour was born.

All very well, but while the Tories were pulling themselves apart in perpetual argument as to whether they were pro- or anti-Europe, the other side were now locked in battle between old and new style Labour; Chancellor Gordon Brown representing a more traditionalist approach. Critics describe Tony Blair's style as presidential and talk of 'sofa government' where decisions that should have been made in Cabinet were instead taken by a group of favourites, many unelected advisors, gathered in the Prime Minister's office.

Among other things, Tony Blair implemented policies on Human Rights, National Minimum Wage and the Freedom of Information. Referenda were held resulting in the devolution of powers to Scottish and Welsh parliaments, and spending on public services was significantly increased. He also gave the Bank of England independence in order that interest rates could be based on economic rather than political criteria. But to many he is remembered as the man who opened the door to uncontrolled immigration and who played the role of George Bush's poodle in supporting the Iraq War on the basis of duff data regarding Weapons of Mass Destruction. Time to go, and so he resigned in 2007.

Chancellor of the Exchequer, Gordon Brown, took the reins. His approach was far more traditional and for a few months he enjoyed high popularity ratings, particularly for his handling of two attempted al-Qaeda inspired terrorist attacks. But that didn't last long. As PM, he oversaw the government response to the 2008 financial crisis, when a vast amount of money was spent bailing out failing banks; a costly exercise, seen by some as saving the very people who caused the problem at the expense of those who suffered most. The economy went into recession. Then, in 2009, the expenses scandal hit with revelations of widespread abuse by MPs. The case most remembered is that of Tory grandee Sir Peter Viggers, not short of a bob or two, who claimed expenses for building a floating duck house in his grounds. But abuse was cross-party and public affection for politicians plumbed new depths. The nail in the coffin was a woeful Labour performance in British elections for the European Parliament. Gordon Brown fought off a leadership challenge only to lose the 2010 election.

Enter David Cameron. While the Tories won most votes, it was a hung Parliament as they didn't have an overall majority, so they entered into an agreement with the Liberal Democrats and, for the first time since the end of the War, the country had a coalition government. Personally, I think this may have been a good thing as it kept the brakes on more extreme Tory policies, but many would disagree, and the LibDems paid particularly dearly for it in the 2015 election, deserted by supporters for reneging on their earlier promise to abolish university tuition fees. David Cameron promised a one-nation, compassionate Conservative party for all and, true to his word, whether following his own beliefs or through LibDem pressure, he was responsible for a number of liberal policies including the introduction of same-sex marriages. The economy he inherited was struggling following the 2008 Crash and so, with old Etonian and Oxford chum Chancellor George Osborne, he implemented a policy of austerity that, depending on your viewpoint, either saved the economy or caused untold harm. With a surprise overall majority, he was able to drop the LibDems and the future was rosy. What could possibly go wrong?

Cameron was confident that the population were generally in favour of remaining in the EU so, with this in mind, he sought to finally bury the long running arguments within his party by letting the people decide whether we should stay. Well, that wasn't too bright was it?

The campaigning that followed was eye-opening, at least to me. Both sides were disingenuous in their use of the English language, but two particular things are burnt into my brain. My jaw nearly hit the floor when, with Project Fear in full flow, George Osborne warned that leaving would result in the horror of falling property prices. Not only was this wrong, as property prices soon hit an all-time high but, more importantly, it totally ignored the fact that this news was good for half the population who can't afford to buy, and an immediate cause for a Leave vote!

And then there was that '£350m a week for the NHS'. At best, this figure was open to interpretation, but instead of pointing out that it was nonsense, and that the government also needed the cash to fund other non-NHS commitments, Remainer MPs responded with the fact that, taking into consideration rebates and the like, it was only £250 million. And they repeated this over and over again, totally oblivious to the fact that, to your average Joe, 'only' £250 million was still a pretty large wad to be 'giving away'. Somehow the government wasn't quite as in touch with the population as they thought and the people didn't vote as expected.

Doubtless had the outcome been a vote to remain, the message would have been "you've had your vote, this is a democracy so put up and shut up", but instead what followed held British democracy up for ridicule the world over as countless people lined up to declaim the outcome; the result was 'unfair'; the electorate were stupid and had been conned; we should have another vote etc. etc. etc. My rather naive hope is that our democracy lives on, that people will realise that they can have a say and bring about change, that their vote is important and should always be used, but the cynic in me suspects that voter apathy will return, and it even seems possible that we find ourselves going down the same road as other countries where it is normal to take to the street and try to overthrow the government whenever you don't get what you want.

One thing that I have yet to understand concerning the whole Brexit exercise is the stance of the unions. For years, cheap labour has helped us thrive while achieving the economists' Holy Grail of growth without inflation, but in the words of 60s comedian Charlie Drake, "what about the workers?" Companies can produce cheaper goods thus boosting the economy; if you have money, you can buy more for less. But a continual flow of cheap labour also has a negative impact on the wages of local lower paid workers who are likely to have higher living expenses than the visitors, but are faced with either accepting lower wages or pricing themselves out of work, the result being a cap on wages. Furthermore, the introduction of working practices like zero-hour contracts has only been possible due to the surplus of labour arising through this situation. Bearing in mind the effect that this was likely to be having on their members, I have yet to understand why the unions were so much in favour of remaining in the EU. I suppose I must be missing something.

It could be argued that, as leader of the country, David Cameron should have kicked off the debate by stating the pros and cons of each side and explaining his preference before taking a more neutral leadership role. By leading the country rather than promoting one group, he may have been able to keep a lid on the level of ill feeling that has been generated on both sides, and might even have kept his job. But, as we know, he didn't.

Irrevocably tied to Remain, he had to resign to be replaced by Teresa May who had the job of implementing the People's will. Basically a Remainer too, her heart wasn't really in it and, by trying to keep everyone happy while remaining as close as possible to the EU, she managed to upset everybody and was soon forced to leave. Enter Boris Johnson. Like his hero, Winston Churchill, he seemed to be the man of the moment, the only person with the drive and charisma to clear the drains and flush through the process that had become totally bogged down.

With a very small majority, only possible through working with the DUP, and with many Remain-voting MPs obstructing his every move, Johnson faced considerable challenges in getting Brexit changes through Parliament so, in October 2019, he called a snap election. The Tories won with a majority of 80 seats, their largest since 1987, winning 43.6% of the popular vote, the highest percentage by any party since 1979. They decimated the Labour representation, most noticeably winning many northern seats where Labour had been the party of choice for decades, named by commentators as the 'Red Wall'. The Labour party is still struggling to agree what went wrong, but much of the change is generally put down to support for Brexit, and it remains to be seen whether allegiances will shift back once the exercise is complete.

But, just like his hero Churchill, Johnson soon ceased to be the man of the moment and, in the wake of Partygate, was unceremoniously dumped by his party. To

214

the open-mouthed amazement of politics watchers around the world, a farce followed which saw two new PMs in a month, an unnecessary upset on the financial markets and a revolving door of ministers entering government only to leave weeks later; and all this while the government should have been focusing on serious issues like the cost-of-living crisis and Putin's invasion of Ukraine. The reputation of the Tories has been shredded and commentators are predicting catastrophic results at the next election. Who knows, we may be witnessing the death throes of our longest lasting political party. Then again, as they say, a week is a long time in politics.

I can't finish this section without a few words on the House of Lords. This institution dates back to Saxon times when a group of 'wise men' were brought together to advise the king. According to the Parliament website the House has three main roles namely: reviewing all bills (draft laws) before they can become law; investigating public policy, often through select committees appointed to consider specific policy areas and regularly involving questioning of expert witnesses working in the field which is the subject of the inquiry; holding government to account by scrutinising the work of the government during question time and debates in the chamber, where government ministers must respond.

To many, the House of Lords is an anachronism, a bunch of doddery old codgers, unelected yet able to interfere in the work of a democratically elected government; supporters argue that they fill a key role as when they caused cuts to tax credits to be delayed until protections for low paid workers were in place. Throughout my life there have regularly been calls to reduce their influence or abolish the House altogether; after reforms in

1999 for instance, 666 hereditary peers i.e. those who inherited their title, lost the automatic right to sit and vote in Parliament.

In conclusion, if you consider anarchy not to be a particularly attractive way to run our country, then you have to accept that some form of government is essential. Personally, I've drifted along disinterested in politics for much of my life; fairly indifferent to the impact it had on my world. In my defence I, like many, live in an area that has voted the same way seemingly forever, and only a traumatic catalyst could bring about change.

I read recently how, particularly in western democracies, millenials are more disillusioned in politics than ever before; can't say I blame them, but I do hope they manage to stay engaged. Though it might not always seem obvious, we do still live in a democracy where we can get rid of duff politicians at the ballot box; the Internet has provided powerful tools in getting messages heard and, love or loathe the result, the Brexit referendum demonstrated that the status quo can be disturbed. So, while politics is probably no better or worse today than it was when I was born, there might just be a greater possibility of change than in previous years, although of course that could just be an illusion. The nature and quality of any change is dependent upon the type, character and motives of the people who can be bothered to get involved, and therein lies the challenge.

23.

Great British Weather

Doubtless you may consider me a sandwich short of a picnic when I say that I love the British weather. Don't get me wrong, I've had my fair share of misery waiting for trains that won't turn up due to the wrong sort of weather; of packing windbreaks and thick sweaters for British summer holidays; of scraping ice from the car windscreen before realising, wheels spinning, that I can't get out of the drive anyway; of gazing forlornly out on the pouring rain from our tent in a quagmire of a camp site; of tenderly applying after-sun to red raw skin and of repairing damaged fences wrecked by strong winds. But that aside, I love the British weather. It is a continual source of wonder to me that the location and geology of our little island can produce such a variety of totally unpredictable weather.

Just a couple of weeks ago I saw a weather forecast where the south was sunny and dry while Scotland was experiencing heavy rain and temperatures 10 degrees lower. A few days later this was reversed, and the highlands were expected to have the warmest weather. Then yesterday, as I sat indoors, looking out on falling rain with the temperature probably around 18 degrees, a smiling young BBC weatherman reminded me that, this time last year, temperatures recorded in Cambridge Botanic Garden had reached 38.7°C, the highest ever recorded in the UK. Unbelievable. Going off at a tangent for a minute, can anyone explain why weather presenters are always happy, even when predicting horrible weather; why they always talk about what will happen rather than what just might happen but probably won't; and why, after they got the forecast spectacularly wrong, they fail to apologise for their mistake the next day?

Despite our temperate climate the UK has experienced a variety of extreme weather in my lifetime. True, more often than not these have affected places further north than Surrey, but we have had a few too. Winters definitely seem milder than I remember from my childhood. With no central heating and little insulation, we would regularly wake to find ice on the inside of our bedroom window, and getting dressed in the winter was not the most enjoyable of pastimes. I was seven when the Big Freeze of 1963 occurred. It started with four inches of snow on Boxing Day with a further ten inches three days later; by New Year we were snowbound. Heaven to young kids maybe, but the opposite for the rest of the population. Temperatures remained close to or below zero until March, there were regular power cuts, mains water pipes froze so people had to collect water from road tankers, and dustmen were unable to do their rounds. This was the last time that the Thames froze over, an amazing event in the eyes of one so young. We lived a five minute walk from the river, a place of adventure and mystery; to a seven-year-old it seemed very wide, and the idea that we could just walk across it to the other side was incredible. A car rally was held on the Thames, cars were used to tow skiers on the ice and the Navy had to use an icebreaker to keep Chatham dockyard accessible.

Forty-six years passed before I experienced similar levels of snow in the UK. One Friday in January 2009 I discussed with our builder his plans to start work on our extension the following Monday. I asked whether the forecast snow might delay the project, but he just smiled, knowingly, and assured me this would not be the case; only heavy rain would give them problems. On Monday I awoke to see a covering of snow outside, shaved and dressed, ate breakfast, put on my coat and stepped out to clear the car for the drive to the station. Out into snow over twelve inches deep, with drifts nearer eighteen inches. In retrospect it was rather stupid to even attempt brushing the snow from the car, but that's what I did for a few minutes before realising I was going nowhere. The car stayed in the drive for the next week, and it was three days before I could get to the office, and then only by walking to the station as roads remained impassable. It was actually quite enjoyable for a few days, peaceful and very pretty, but we were glad when the thaw came and things were back to normal a couple of weeks later. We didn't see the builder for about ten days.

I was thirteen when floods hit the southeast in September 1968. We were lucky in that the water never reached us. Although living not far from the Thames, this was no threat to us as we were uphill from the river and there was a flood plain able to absorb a lot of water as the river burst its banks. School was closed of course, so we did what any self-respecting kids would do, got on our bikes and headed off to see the excitement.

It was September and not cold, so we were pretty oblivious to the fact that we were soaked through. I remember cycling with my not-yet-Marine buddy, through water a foot deep, down a main road to a point where we could look down on a bungalow with brown water from the River Wey gushing from its windows and doors. I like to think we offered any help we could, but can't remember doing much; at that age we were probably more impressed by the spectacle than the misery people were experiencing. More than 1,000 locals were made homeless, and apparently in some parts of Molesey the water was 8 feet deep.

Had you suggested to anyone living in Britain in 1955 that, not too long in the future, they would experience droughts and hosepipe bans they would have looked at you as if you were barking mad. If nothing else we always had more than enough rain, particularly in the summer months when big events at Wimbledon, Ascot, Henley, and Epsom, any cricket match, school sports day or summer fete were likely to be interrupted by rain, and spectators were well advised always to pack a brolly. Yet I now receive emails regularly from my local water company, asking that we refrain from using too much water if we want to avoid a hosepipe ban as resources are stretched.

May 1975 saw the start of one of the most severe droughts on record for the UK. It lasted 16 months, the driest 16-month period in over 200 years. For a number of years, I had been working as a lifeguard at the local pool in my summer holidays. In 1975, obviously with money to spare, another sign of how times have changed, the council decided to station lifeguards on a pond where people often swam. A colleague and I were asked to fill the role. All very exciting really; we had a little hut where we kept our inflatable dinghy and could shelter from the rain, had there been any, and a radio for contacting the Town Hall should we need emergency services. Every morning we'd call in to check the radio was working; "Kiwi 48 to base. Kiwi 48 to base."

Those were the days. The only problem was that it all turned out to be rather embarrassing, particularly because not many people actually swam there, a dozen in one day would have been considered a rush, and often nobody came. But I did get to read a lot, and we had numerous pleasant chats with friendly dog walkers, usually concerning the question of why on earth we were there. Then of course there was the drought, which meant the water was only about three feet deep anyway. Still, as a hard-working university student it was pleasant to be paid to paddle a dinghy around in the sunshine and recharge my batteries a bit. Believe it or not, we were asked to return the following year with much the same outcome.

These days we have a depressing pattern whereby places like York and the Lake District regularly experience the misery of flooding while in the south we have near-drought conditions. While this is partly due to natural phenomena, the situation has been exacerbated by man. Floodplains are invaluable in providing a safe space for rivers to overflow when they become overfull, yet in recent years numerous cases have come to light where planning permission has been given for houses to be built on such lands. Successive governments have encouraged the growth of the economy in the south, leading to a rapidly growing population and more and more open spaces being concreted over in order to provide accommodation and office space, yet infrastructure has never kept pace with the growth.

Whether through greed or stupidity much of the beautiful green spaces in the south are now gone for good. Yet providing this ever-growing population with water, or the ability to dispose of unwanted water, has always been of secondary importance, presumably because it brings cost rather than profit to developers. Much of our water system still depends on a system built in Victorian times. Surely it's not beyond the wit of man to devise an economically viable solution whereby excess water causing serious grief up north can be channeled to the arid south, perhaps alongside the long-awaited HS2 rail link?

During a BBC weather forecast on the 15th October 1987, weatherman Michael Fish made a statement that he would live to regret. His exact words were "Earlier on today, apparently a woman rang the BBC and said she heard there was a hurricane on the way. Well, if you're watching, don't worry, there isn't!" A few hours later hurricane force winds made landfall on the south coast and proceeded to wreak havoc, resulting in the death of eighteen people while causing huge devastation, including the loss of some 15 million trees. Technically, Michael was correct as, apparently, it was not actually a hurricane because it didn't originate in the tropics, but I don't think he got away with that.

We woke in the night to the sound of our dustbin lid being blown off, so realising it was a little blowy I closed the window and went back to sleep. The next day I retrieved the dustbin lid and walked round the corner to the station heading for work, but I didn't get far. It transpired that numerous fallen trees were blocking the line and there were no trains, so I went home for a coffee and to plan my next move. There was no next move. Watching the news the enormity of the event became clear; vast areas of the south resembled a bombsite and we were going nowhere. According to the local radio, not only were the railway lines blocked but all roads out of our area were closed by fallen trees, and anyone with a chainsaw or 4x4 capable of dragging heavy weights was asked to meet at various locations in order to start cutting our way out. I had neither, so put my feet up for a couple of days.

Without doubt the weather has changed during my lifetime with far more extreme stuff. Average temperatures have increased, more storms, more floods, and meteorological records broken at a rate Usain Bolt would be proud of. Perhaps the feature I find most irritating is the unseasonal winds that seem to blow harder throughout the year in the style of a good autumn storm. You can't help wondering what on earth is going on. But, for now, let's steer clear of the whys and wherefores, and just make the observation that, during my lifetime, the regular occurrence of unpredictable extreme events means the weather seems generally worse than it was in my childhood.

24.

My Introduction to Big Boys' Work

Fun though it had definitely been, university life was now truly behind me; time to grow up, look for a real job and get a Career. But not quite yet. I decided on one final Uni summer holiday, three months of shifts at the swimming pool while wandering off to various places whenever the urge took me. But that had to end, and I started looking for the route to grownupness.

There being no Internet, jobs were advertised in the national papers, mainly The Telegraph, Times and Financial Times. Applicants wrote letters, yes by hand, sent them by mail and waited for a response to drop on the mat a few weeks later. This may sound a little tortuous today, but at least applicants usually received a response even if only to say "...unfortunately we are unable to offer you....but wish you good luck..." I landed a few interviews through this route, but none came to anything.

I remember one day sitting with Dad, discussing my situation over a pint, talking through my options and my search for job satisfaction, but he just looked puzzled before commenting, "if work was supposed to be fun, they wouldn't have to pay you to do it." So profound.

Summer came to an end and my lifeguard skills were no longer needed, unemployment was high, and I had little option but to sign on the dole. This was an experience in itself and every Wednesday I visited the employment exchange to discuss any change in my circumstances and any possibilities that might have come up.

On rare occasions, Dad's window cleaning mate provided a day's window cleaning work that I was supposed to declare so that the amount earned could be deducted from my dole money, a process that obviously discouraged claimants from taking on work as it would leave them no better off despite their efforts. A number of overhauls of the system have since been attempted but I don't think they have it quite right yet.

One event that I do remember from this period is attending an interview in Ilford. I didn't get the job, but did drop in to see Mum's sister who lived close by. We chatted and she made an interesting observation that I shouldn't be looking to work for large companies, in her view I was much better suited to smaller organisations. In retrospect I realise how right she was, but that didn't stop me focusing on larger companies, after all that was where the money and jobs seemed to be.

Although the labour exchange promoted local jobs, I didn't expect there to be much for me, so I was surprised when something did come up; an engineering firm about ten miles away was looking for a management trainee. So, I dug out the suit and tie, had a smart haircut and, freshly shaved, headed off for interview. Things went well, and the job was mine, starting salary a princely £3,000 a year; Big Boys Work was well and truly up and running.

I spent about six months as a trainee before taking on a management role. Previously, the company had always promoted engineers into management, but they were trying a new approach, training non-technical managers, and I was their guinea pig. It soon became clear though that there was no real training programme in place;

I was simply to spend time in various departments to gain an understanding as to how the company operated.

Department heads would often be mystified as to what was expected of them, or even worried that I might be a Head Office spy checking up on them, so it was time to take control. First day in a new location, I would initiate a conversation with the department head along the lines of "I am here to learn how your department works and fits into the company structure; I'm not reporting back on any aspect of your department; I'm happy to take on any job that helps you out, or observe any process that might help my understanding, but please don't feel you have to invent tasks just to keep me busy. If there is nothing for me to do or see, I will happily sit in the corner and read my book." I was amazed to get away with it, but most department heads embraced this approach; I learned a lot while not having to fill time with pointless tasks, and also got to read quite a few books.

In 1978 'Sultans of Swing' was released, introducing us to the distinctive style of Mark Knopfler and Dire Straits. It was a tune you couldn't get away from, played regularly on radio and TV, and if you entered a pub you could guarantee to hear it on the jukebox. I loved it, and this is my theme tune for the period.

So, during this first foray into the world of Big Boy's Work what lessons did I learn? Two come to mind. Firstly, and useful to know, people in senior roles may not always have the level of self-confidence or intelligence that you might expect.

Secondly, while I had considered employment as a mutually beneficial arrangement where the employer gets something done and the employee is happy to provide their labour in exchange for the money they need to survive, it's not that simple. At Uni I had been impressed by the story of the Volvo manufacturing process whereby a team took responsibility for all aspects of building a single car, with management and workers pulling together and taking pride in the final product. Sounded a great idea; surely everyone gains from creating quality stuff? Unfortunately, this was not the way in union-dominated Britain, where management and unions were continually at war and the output inevitably suffered. After much haggling, the union allowed me to attend a soldering course for shopfloor workers. Six minutes before the end of day a bell would ring indicating it was time to clear up; a second bell three minutes later signalled time to wash hands, gather coats and belongings and prepare to leave; the final bell was like a starting pistol as everyone rushed for the door. If I was near to completing an exercise, I would work a few minutes longer so I could start something new the following day, an approach looked on with suspicion by my colleagues who felt I shouldn't work a minute longer than I was being paid for, and who couldn't understand why I wasn't joining the race for the door.

During this period an event occurred of even greater historical significance than my first real job. One of our customers at the time, by way of the MOD, was the Shah of Iran. The Iranian Revolution culminated in his exile in 1979 and Iran became an Islamic state. At the time, I think that this was just a commercial setback from a company viewpoint, and I doubt many people would have foreseen where it would lead in the years to come.

I'd been in the job about fifteen months when we were taken over by another, larger and more efficient company. The job had been interesting at times and the

227

people were friendly, but I felt things changing and decided it was time to move on.

Moving into big Boys' Work is a significant time for us all. Were things different then than for kids today? On leaving university I received little advice on the real world outside. I had an Economics degree yet absolutely no idea how to use it. In retrospect, it's extraordinary to think how little I knew of things like the City of London, banking, investment, insurance and the like; basically no understanding at all. And I had no real idea of other areas where an economist might seek employment. Of course, I must take some responsibility for this state of affairs; advice was probably available, I just wasn't really thinking about work. Then again, as most of our lecturers were generally academics, their experience of the outside real world was generally limited too, so any advice given might have been of limited value.

In contrast, universities today have much greater ties with outside businesses and organisations employing graduates, with work placements often included as part of the course. This benefits not only the student, who gets experience of the outside world and the chance to impress a potential employer, but also the employer who can assess potential employees and grab the good ones. All in all, a better state of affairs than in my time I would say.

25.

An Ode to the Silver Screen

Going to the pictures was a regular part of my life as a kid. There were two cinemas, the ABC Regal and the Odeon, both of which had seen better years. Each only had one screen, with upstairs and downstairs seating; we could never afford upstairs. They stood only a few hundred yards apart but, strangely, people tended to have a particular affiliation with one or the other; we were mostly Regal folk. The Regal in particular would have been impressive in its day, but that day was long gone, and describing both establishments as 'tired' would have been an understatement. The seats were saggy and creaked when they tipped up, carpets were threadbare, and in the winter the heating left a bit to be desired. The golden age of cinema was over and many earned their label as 'fleapits', but somehow they were still magical.

My first visit to the pictures was with Dad and Big Brother to see 'Tom Thumb'. It was released in 1958, but I guess we probably went a year or two later. I can't remember much about the experience but then, some 30 years on, with kids of my own, there it was on TV. The kids loved it; we recorded it, and then watched it over and over again as is the way with kids and videos. It's a musical including performances by a young Terry Thomas and Peter Sellers as the baddies, and I have to admit that despite the corny story, iffy dialogue, fifty-year-old special effects and the fact that it's a musical, I rather enjoyed it.

One Saturday morning, aged about six, I ventured out to investigate the ABC Minors. It was great; huge screen, cheering kids, loads of cartoons and some adventure or another. That was it. Sold. For years to come there was hardly a Saturday morning when I couldn't be found at the flicks. There were always plenty of cartoons, Bugs Bunny definitely my favourite, but also loads of action; mainly cowboy and indian or war films. A regular favourite was an old black and white version of Batman, probably the 1949 serialised 'Batman and Robin'. Each weekly episode ended with a cliffhanger leaving us wondering how our caped hero could possibly escape; perhaps he was tied up in the boot of a car plunging down a ravine, but miraculously next week's episode would start with him untying himself and jumping out just in time. Even at such an early age we sometimes felt a little cheated by such creative license, but we forgave them.

My next visit with Dad was to see the first James Bond film, 'Dr No'. I suspect he wanted to go and thought Big Brother was old enough and as so often happened, I tagged on. I'm not sure the film would be considered suitable for an eight-year-old today, but there you go. Disruption of US rocket launches by some mystery weapon with the aim of kicking off a war with Russia; an exotic Jamaican setting; a criminal scientist with artificial hands, an army of baddies and an underground base; a chase through mangrove swamps; attack by a flamethrower tank; an attempt to kill Bond with a tarantula; all coming to an explosive climax with a last-minute escape before the baddies' lair goes up in smoke. Not only that, but bikini-clad Ursula Andress emerging from the sea. I mean, I can see why Dad wanted to go, but I loved it too. James Bond has now been an integral part of the British film industry for fifty-eight years and is still going strong. Amazing.

My cinema viewing peaked in the late 60s and 70s. Between ages twelve and seventeen, hardly a week passed without a trip to the flicks. Monday evenings we'd be there. Most of my friends were older than me, although a number were smaller, and we would approach the ticket lady in negotiation mode; one week persuading her that we were all old enough to see an X-rated film, the next arguing that at least some of us were under 16 and warranted half price tickets. Looking back the variety of films we saw is quite staggering. Programmes generally comprised two films; this was the era of the 'B' movie, usually uninspiring but often unintentionally hilarious.

In my uni town there were two rather dilapidated cinemas that I would occasionally attend when at a loose end. My marine biologist chum recently reminded me that, allegedly, biology students would visit these in order to find subjects to study; 'flea pits' indeed, but now presumably long gone. Possibly due to the large number of students in the town, they would often feature some pretty obscure films; burnt into my brain is a weird Andy Warhol horror double-bill of which one story concerned Dracula's move to Italy where he felt the blood of 'wirgins' would be more freely available than in Transylvania; presumably he considered morals in his homeland to be more lax.

During the 80s my visits to the cinema became far less frequent and since we had kids, I can't remember seeing any film not considered suitable for younger viewers.

Like so much else in my life, technology has wrought much change in the world of film and the cinema. Animation played a key part in my early favourites, Walt

Disney leading the way since 1937 when he produced his first full-length traditionally animated feature film 'Snow White and the Seven Dwarfs'; every frame hand-drawn and coloured by a team of animators. Animation was later paired with live-action as in MGM's 'Tom Thumb'; but Disney hit the jackpot with 'Mary Poppins', although a similar approach with 'Bedknobs and Broomsticks' was not so successful. Later, 'Who Framed Roger Rabbit' was a particularly enjoyable adult-oriented blend of live-action and animation with guest performances from characters like Bugs Bunny and Daffy Duck.

Stop motion animation has been around ages, just think of the original 'King Kong', but it has been refined more recently with the help of computers, and there are now many high quality, feature-length stop motion films like Tim Burton's 'The Nightmare Before Christmas', or Aardman Animation creations 'Chicken Run', and 'Wallace & Gromit: The Curse of the Were-Rabbit'.

Pixar was founded in 1986, the year Luxo Jr. went down a storm when premiered at a computer animation graphics conference. Luxo, the lamp that jumps across the screen at the start of each Pixar film before bouncing on the 'I' in PIXAR until it deflates, is now one of the most recognisable company mascots worldwide. Pixar's work was originally confined to TV until, in 1995, they released their first full-length film, 'Toy Story'. It was an instant success and their 3D style, more associated with computer animation than cartoons, has become hugely popular. At the time of writing this, they had released twenty-three full-length films. Pixar was taken over by Disney in 2006 but the brand lives on.

Characters in Pixar films tend to be larger than life, are often non-human and only vaguely resemble the original article, if one exists in the first place. On the other hand, live action/CGI films combine human actors with animals that have been created entirely by computer, based on footage of the real thing. The resulting characters can appear unnervingly realistic except that they follow the script perfectly and might act slightly strangely for animals, perhaps speaking and philosophising. Disney has recently produced remakes of a number of earlier classics, like 'Jungle Book', using these techniques.

In my youth, special effects were confined to fairly basic tricks like projecting a moving background behind the actors, using miniature models and explosives to create large battle scenes or suspending actors on wires to simulate flying. We didn't really believe that what we were watching was real, the illusion was just part of the entertainment. Sci-fi and Fantasy films were often the drivers for special effects, and I particularly remember those created by Ray Harryhausen for films like 'It Came from Beneath the Sea', 'Mysterious Island' and 'Jason and the Argonauts'. Then, in 1977, along came 'Star Wars' and we were blown away. Combining extremely detailed miniatures, animation and a revolutionary system of computer-controlled motion photography, George Lucas and artist John Dykstra created realistic effects that set the gold standard for the next twenty years or so.

As the digital age really took off, so too did the world of special effects, and we have since been flooded with a whole variety of offerings. These mainly fall into three categories; computer-generated imagery or CGI, compositing which transposes a visual element from one background to another, as where an actor in a studio is filmed walking in front of a green screen before the image is transposed to, say, an underground cave scene, and finally, motion capture where dots that a camera can trace are painted onto an actor's face, or cover a suit they wear, in order that data captured by the cameras can then be mapped onto a 3D skeleton model using motion capture software.

Technology has also significantly changed the way in which we receive our regular film fix. When I was young, films were few and far between on our two TV stations, and those that were available were usually pretty old. If you wanted to see a recent film you went to the cinema. New releases were a major event and, if you missed it first time round, you never knew when you might get a second chance. Things started to change in the late 70s with the launch of videotape players in two formats, Betamax and then VHS; the marketing battle ultimately being won by VHS with Beta fading into obscurity. Laser disc players followed shortly after, but these never matched the popularity of VHS. The technology was now in place for films to be viewed at home, and a huge market grew as consumers rented or bought personal copies of films to be viewed at their leisure. The media expanded into DVDs and Blu-ray, but the principle remained the same until the next game changer in 2007 when video distributor Netflix started providing content over the Internet through streaming.

Driven by technical innovation and commercial entrepreneurship, the way in which films are distributed and made accessible to audiences worldwide has changed almost beyond recognition in my lifetime, to the point that audiences willing to pay, now have access to nearly all but the very latest films on demand, anytime, anywhere. And, with large flatscreen TVs and surround-sound systems commonplace, we can now almost produce the cinema experience at any time of day or night, without the inconvenience and expense of actually going to the cinema. But cinemas have not sat idly by watching their customers drift away, they too have had to innovate. Since my day, when a cinema would offer the same single film for a week, we now have multiplex cinemas offering not only a number of films at the same time, but also more flexible schedules. Cinemas are far more attractive venues with comfortable seating; sometimes incorporating restaurant facilities or the option of ordering a bottle of wine while you view. They have also invested considerably in technology to enhance the customer experience; iMax, for example, claims 'the world's most innovative movie going experience' with 'awe-inspiring images' and 'heart-pounding audio.... pumped into a theatre that has been customized for an optimal experience.'

It doesn't stop there. Not only is there bound to be further technical developments, but also the cinemas themselves are under threat. The more people opt to do their viewing at home, the less business there is for the cinemas. This issue was already bubbling under before the pandemic when cinemas remained closed and audiences were forced to stay at home; revenues for both the cinemas and the studios plunged. In response, the studios started to release films to streaming companies as soon as they hit the big screen; Warner Bros, for example, released all of its 2021 films straight to streaming service HBO Max. The cinemas are now open, but we must wait to see the long-term effect of this 'temporary' move.

But, in the face of so much change, the film industry has continued doing what it does best, churning out films. They have variously been rubbish; brilliant; offensive; thought-provoking; frightening; exciting; sometimes happy and sometimes sad. In other words, no change. Despite modern twists, the same genres exist, and totally original storylines are rare. In this nostalgia fest it would be remiss of me not to credit at least some of the films that entertained me over the years. The number of potential candidates is huge, and if I were to repeat the exercise tomorrow the list would doubtless be noticeably different. There being so many, the remainder of this chapter is little more than a list of films and stars, but if that's not enough to ignite some memories, you might like to move on now to the next chapter.

A host of good cowboy films was already in circulation by the time I was born, but that didn't stop them making more. I was fond of Spaghetti Westerns, in particular 'The Good, The Bad and The Ugly' and 'Once Upon a Time in The West'. More thoughtful films like 'Soldier Blue' and 'Dances With Wolves' showed the native Indians not as menacing savages but as human, victims of occupation while 'Butch Cassidy and the Sundance Kid' was highly entertaining and 'Blazing Saddles' was a marvellous, if now widely misunderstood, spoof simultaneously taking a pot at both all the old cowboy movie clichés and racism.

As kids we were brought up on a diet high in war films, with many a miserable wet winter Sunday afternoon given over to family viewing of some black and white epic or another; classics like 'Bridge on the River Kwai', 'The Cruel Sea', and 'The Dam Busters'. Most concentrated on the heroic exploits of outnumbered British and American soldiers; all Germans or Japanese were 'bad' and, except where showing a stiff upper lip in the face of adversity, humour was a rare ingredient. As time passed, war films became more varied and nuanced. 'The Great Escape' was great, anti-war films like 'Mash' and 'Catch 22' went down well and storylines broadened as in the likes of 'Kelly's Heroes' and 'The Dirty Dozen'.

The Americans regularly return to the Vietnam War for inspiration with results sometimes controversial and often gutsy; disturbing introspection with a bit of guilt thrown in. They are stories not only of the horrors of war itself, but of the treatment and experiences of veterans on their return home. Not exactly light viewing, but riveting just the same. My shortlist comprises 'The Deer Hunter', 'Good Morning Vietnam', 'Full Metal Jacket', 'Platoon', 'Apocalypse Now' and 'Born on the Fourth of July'.

I was a child of the Cold War that provided inspiration for many spy films. Since the release of 'Dr. No' in 1962, there have been 25 other James Bond films and I admit to enjoying most of them, although was never a fan of George Lazenby or Timothy Dalton. There were many subtler, but no less enjoyable, spy offerings such as those based on Len Deighton's books like 'The Ipcress File' and 'Funeral In Berlin', or numerous works of John le Carré; 'Tinker Tailor Soldier Spy' and 'The Spy Who Came in from the Cold' spring to mind.

Action films, while not the pinnacle of sophisticated culture, have always appealed to me. But flash-bang action alone is not enough; a macho, charismatic hero is essential together with a fair sprinkling of humour. We cheered in 1969 as Michael Caine and his boys coolly liberated gold bullion from an Italian armoured car and in three Minis, red, white and blue of course, raced through gridlocked Turin along paths, down steps and through a sewer pipe before finally driving up a ramp into a moving converted coach. British guts and ingenuity had prevailed. The Americans tend to do this type of thing well. Think

Indiana Jones in 'Raiders of the Lost Ark', John McClane in 'Die Hard', Axel Foley in 'Beverley Hills Cop' and Martin Riggs in 'Lethal Weapon'. All pure nonsense of course, but hugely entertaining just the same, to the point that between them, these characters now feature in seventeen feature films, all box office hits and regularly repeated on multiple TV stations around the world.

Serious drama tempered with humour is how I would describe what is possibly my favourite film, 'One Flew Over the Cuckoo's Nest'. In the same category I would place films like 'Rain Man' and 'The Last Detail'.

Then there are the Sci-fi and fantasy offerings. My interest in this genre started in the 60s when I began to appreciate the boundless escapism on offer to anyone willing to put reality on hold for a while. There were huge murderous plants in 'The Day of the Triffids', sinister Martian influences in 'Quatermass and the Pit', and a trip through a scientist's bloodstream in a miniaturised submarine in order to cure a tumour in his brain in 'Fantastic Voyage'. Humans were a subordinate a species in 'Planet of the Apes', and I never really understood what '2001: A Space Odyssey' was really about but it was visually stunning. This genre is truly limitless and has been boosted hugely by developments in the world of special effects. To mention just a few more of the biggies, in no particular order; 'Blade Runner', 'Star Wars', 'Alien', 'E.T.: The Extra-Terrestrial', 'The Lord of the Rings' 'Ghostbusters', 'Back to the Future' and 'The Terminator'.

There seems to be an age, generally early teens, when we discover a strange need to be scared, and develop a liking for horror and ghost films. It happened to us, and I have witnessed the same in our kids. Generally, it's not long before the novelty wears off although the occasional fright doesn't go amiss. After 'The Curse of Frankenstein' in 1957, Hammer Film Production dominated the horror film genre for the next fifteen years or so, coincidentally covering my adolescent stage. Compared to modern horror films these were pretty tame, but to me the biggest novelty was that the goodies were no longer immortal. Up till then, I knew that the hero and most of the good guys would survive unless they heroically sacrificed themselves for the cause, but now you couldn't tell who would be left standing come the end of the story. There were films like 'Dracula' and 'The Plague of the Zombies' but the one I think I found most frightening was an adaptation of the Dennis Wheatley book 'The Devil Rides Out'.

Hammer's dominance, and my interest in the genre, waned in the 70s with the arrival of more modern, and often more gruesome, stories like 'The Exorcist' and 'The Texas Chain Saw Massacre'. But if you were into gore, the 80s saw the arrival of some real classics. The decade started with teenagers being stalked and murdered in 'Friday the 13th', so popular that eleven sequels followed. 'The Evil Dead' revolved around demonic possession, and in 1984 Freddy Krueger introduced himself, complete with disfigured face, brown fedora, striped sweater and that leather glove with six-inch razors as fingers. That was just the start of the Nightmare on Elm Street franchise. Horror-comedies also did well with the likes of the spoof 'Scary Movie', 'Gremlins' and 'The Lost Boys', which gave vampires a bit of a makeover.

The British sense of humour has often confused the non-British and, looking back at the range of British comedy films that I've enjoyed, frankly I'm not surprised. In the 40s and early 50s, Ealing comedies ruled with films such as 'Passport to Pimlico', 'Whisky Galore', 'The Lavender Hill Mob' and 'The Titfield Thunderbolt'. These were truly 'British' with relatively sophisticated scripts poking fun at various aspects of society, and starred the likes of Alec Guinness, Joan Greenwood and Margaret Rutherford. In the late 50s and 60s they gave way to comedies based on innuendo, slapstick, class differences and schoolboy humour redolent of seaside cartoon postcards. Leading the way were the 31 Carry On films made between 1958 and 1978. This was a time when political incorrectness ruled, and in the 70s the Carry On baton was passed to a variety of not-so-funny soft porn comedies like 'Confessions of a Window Cleaner'; a typically conservative British response while, for a short time, hard core porn went mainstream in parts of America.

But the range of British comedy cinema has developed significantly over my lifetime. We had films like 'Dr. Strangelove', satirising Cold War fears of nuclear annihilation, and the surrealism provided by the Monty Python team in 'Holy Grail', 'Life of Brian', 'The Meaning of Life' and 'Jabberwocky'; I rather liked Terry Gilliam's 'Time Bandits'. There have been horror comedies like 'An American Werewolf in London' and 'Shaun of the Dead' and more thoughtful comic drama, along the lines of 'Educating Rita', 'Local Hero', 'A Private Function' and 'Shirley Valentine'. Black humour abounds in films like 'Trainspotting', 'Lock, Stock and Two Smoking Barrels' and 'Death at a Funeral', and I have to admit to having enjoyed the occasional romcom like 'Four Weddings and a Funeral', 'Bridget Jones's Diary' and 'Notting Hill'. Then there's 'A Fish Called Wanda', not to mention animations such as 'Wallace & Gromit: The Curse of the Were-

Rabbit', pirate radio nostalgia-invoking 'The Boat That Rocked' and more obscure offerings like 'Withnail and I'.

If that isn't enough, we have imported and lapped up a plethora of comic offerings from the USA. Bill Murray has starred in a fair number of good films; 'Ghostbusters' and 'Groundhog Day' immediately spring to mind but I particularly liked 'Mad Dog and Glory' with Murray, Robert de Niro and Uma Thurman. While he could never be accused of under-acting, Jim Carrey films are usually an experience; three in particular come to mind, namely 'The Mask', 'Liar Liar' and 'Lemony Snicket's A Series of Unfortunate Events'. My niece and nephew say I remind them of Steve Martin, which would be alright if it wasn't for the fact that most of his characters tend to be, well, kind-hearted wishy-washy losers. Surely that's not me? 'Parenthood' really struck a chord, as did spaghetti western spoof 'Three Amigos', along with 'Bowfinger' and 'Dirty Rotten Scoundrels'. Then there's Mel Brooks' creations 'The Producers', 'Blazing Saddles' and 'Young Frankenstein', all hilarious but totally bad taste and off-the-wall humour. To be honest, the list of good American comedy films is huge so just to name a final random enjoyable few: 'Airplane', 'Meet The Parents', 'There's Something About Mary', 'Mrs. Doubtfire', 'Raising Arizona', 'The Blues Brothers' and 'Sleeper'.

The 50s and 60s were the heyday of high budget film musicals. I had little interest in them at the time, no self-respecting lad would, but Daughter has developed a love for them all, and I find I now begrudgingly enjoy an occasional viewing of films like 'West Side Story', 'High Society' and 'Singin' In The Rain'. The 60s and 70s saw family musicals like 'Mary Poppins' and 'Chitty Chitty Bang Bang' while slightly more grown-up fare came in the form of 'Grease', 'Dirty Dancing', 'Footloose' and 'Fame'. These were OK, but my favourites from the genre are 'The Rocky Horror Picture Show' and 'Little Shop of Horrors'. I think the 90s were lacking in musicals but, come the millennium, we had a remake of 'The Producers', plus the likes of 'Hairspray', 'Mamma Mia!' and 'La La Land', and now we seem to be in an age of biopics with 'Bohemian Rhapsody', 'Rocketman' and 'What's Love Got To Do With It' so far, presumably with more to come.

Finally, having mentioned some of the films that have given me great pleasure over the years I must pay homage to the stars that have made these productions so enjoyable. The list is huge but, with apologies to the many I have overlooked, and in no particular order, here goes: Michael Caine, Sean Connery, Maggie Smith, Danny de Vito, Peter Cushing, Christopher Lee, Sigourney Weaver, Bill Murray, Bruce Willis, Julie Christie, Mel Gibson, Tom Hanks, Julia Roberts, Susan Sarandon, Robert de Niro, Al Pacino, Albert Finney, Faye Dunaway, Robert Redford, Charles Bronson, Tim Curry, Judie Dench, Julie Waters, James Coburn, John Mills, Alec Guinness, Bette Midler, Ben Kingsley, Benedict Cumberpatch, John Cleese, Jack Nicholson, Hugh Grant, Anthony Hopkins, Dustin Hoffman, Jeff Bridges, Michael Douglas, Harrison Ford, Meryl Streep, Eddie Murphy, Helen Mirren, Jodie Foster, Shirley MacLaine, Johnny Depp, Samuel L Jackson, John Hurt, Paul Newman, Will Smith, Brad Pitt, Morgan Freeman, Colin Firth, Idris Elba, Ewan McGregor, Glenda Jackson, Alan Rickman, Daniel Day-Lewis, Catherine Zeta-Jones, Liam Neeson and so many more.

So, the world of movies has changed incredibly in my lifetime, yet we still enjoy watching films and the basic storylines haven't really changed so much. Watching a film today is not the novelty it was, but without doubt technical advances make the viewing experience better and more immersive than in my youth. Whether the stories or acting were better then than now is a matter of personal taste, but on the whole, I think things may have changed for the better.

26.

Gap Year 2 - Islas Malvinas

By the time I got to university, exciting, long-haul travel adventures were gaining in popularity. People would drive Route 66, backpack across Australia or hike through exotic Asian lands in order to 'find themselves' before becoming slaves to more mundane things like work, paying the rent or nervously watching mortgage rates. If I'm honest, such excitement wasn't really for me; I was a home boy. Then, almost by accident, my one travel adventure came along. I intended covering the event with a few paragraphs in the travel chapter, but then realised how it fits into the evolving theme of the book concerning, as it does, a place that few people had heard of before 1982, and reflecting significant changes to come in my world. So now it is a separate, and long, chapter and I fully understand should you choose to skip it and move on to the next, which is much shorter and focuses on changing fashions.

Spring 1980, and I was going through a restless phase. I'd tried working for a couple of years but didn't really like it. Meanwhile, my marine biologist chum from university had been working as a guide in the Galapagos Islands, sailing on schooners and having a great life as far as I was concerned. Sadly, the Ecuador government put an end to that and he was back home; but a new adventure beckoned as his former boss started a company to showcase the wildlife of the Falkland Islands. We met for a beer one evening and he talked through his plans which sounded far more fun than office work. "We could probably do with more crew," he said "why don't I see if you can come along?" Seemed like a good idea at the time.

We met again a few days later and he said I was welcome to come along; that came as a bit of a surprise I admit, but heck, why not? At some point in the evening he asked if I actually knew where the Falklands were; I had thought they were probably Scottish, the name sounded a good match for the Shetlands or Hebrides, so it was a bit of a revelation to find that they weren't so far from the South Pole. Oh well, in for a penny in for a pound. So began my one and only big travel adventure.

To Hamble for an interview; basically a few beers with the skipper and mate, and the job was mine; unpaid delivery crew, but at least I'd get fed. In return I was to take regular watches and help fit out the boat on the journey; it was a retired trawler with all its fishing gear stripped out, but cabins needed 'refining' for our guests.

I was regularly reprimanded for referring to 'the boat'; the skipper insisted boats have oars and 'Copious', for that was her name, was a ship or motor yacht. Rather grand for a tired old 70ft, orange-painted North Sea trawler, but she was solid enough and used to rough seas; she regularly wintered in the Arctic carrying polar bear-studying scientists.

The crew comprised the owner/skipper, a rotund chap with a liking for gin; the mate who was around my age and had learnt his trade on Shell tankers; the cook, a very slight young lady with short curly hair; my chum with a few years' experience of sailing the Galapagos Islands, and me. There were two paying guests, a largish lady of indeterminate age and a young lad who had just left school and was going to Argentina to visit family friends for a bit of polo before commencing a military career in the family regiment. Sounds like the characters in an Agatha Christie novel.

The trip comprised three main legs, the first being south to Senegal. We departed early September having waited a few days for a lull in the weather, but the skipper misjudged that, and we were struck mid-Channel by gale-force winds. It was pitch dark when the wind really hit us and, being round-bottomed, the boat rolled relentlessly, while bucking up and down through the waves as huge breakers smashed over the wheelhouse. Not at all pleasant, but being easily led I wasn't particularly bothered, I took my lead from the crew who appeared unfazed, all part of a seadog's life. But I soon realised I was going to be sick, so gingerly stepped outside. The boat kept rolling and, despite the dark, I could see the white foam of the waves first rising to greet me before falling away as the boat rolled back. Hanging on for dear life, I emptied the contents of my stomach into the sea and immediately felt much better; from that moment on I could deal with just about anything, calmly munching a fried egg butty down below in the smelly engine room in the roughest of seas. Baptism of fire over.

But one of the passengers wasn't so lucky. The lady was regularly launched from her bunk, and after a few hours of this treatment she was black and blue. The skipper decided to make a detour to lay up in Alderney where I believe they mutually agreed that she wasn't really up to the rigours of the trip and so she disembarked. Now we were six.

246

We made a brief stop in Tenerife enjoying a boisterous evening in a couple of dockside bars with some friendly Russian fishermen. They spoke no English and we spoke no Russian, but that wasn't a problem. That night I discovered that cockroaches could fly. While everyone else seemed oblivious, I was mesmerised by the number and size of these beasties whirring just above head height back and forth across the bar. The things you learn.

Next stop Senegal. Sailing off the African coast at night was a bit nerve-wracking; it's surprising how many suspect boats you see on the radar when you're alone on watch in the middle of the night having read of pirate activity in the area. We had a rifle on board, but I've no idea what we would have done with it had we been attacked. We weren't. Dakar proved a real eye-opener for an untravelled lad like myself; hot, dusty and bustling with humanity, some looking quite piratical to be honest. We found a bar with a weird and wonderful mix of clientele from the docks, a bit like the Mos Eisley Cantina from the first Star Wars movie; but they were welcoming and sold beer, so that was good enough for us.

The cook had proven less than brilliant, and so the skipper bought her a ticket home and packed her off in a taxi to the airport. Now we were five, but with a rather important situation vacant. My chum had cooked a bit, but I didn't have a clue, so we offered to take the job on between us, him cooking and me washing up. We were no longer unpaid, but instead shared the cook's wages between us; affluent times indeed. The new cook headed off to the local market in search of provisions, returning a couple of hours later to inform us that he'd bought a tuna, conjuring up images of tins from the supermarket. So, it came as a bit of a surprise when two local guys, together with a crowd of onlookers, turned up noisily carrying between them a huge fish; they look so different out of the tin. Suddenly we were fishmongers and set about chopping the thing into various manageable chunks for storing in the freezer.

For my first experience of the tropics, one novelty was how early and how quickly night fell; one moment the sun was shining brightly, next it was pitch dark. The area around the port was poorly lit and often the first you realised someone was near was when they smiled, all slightly disconcerting at first. We'd been warned that pirates had spies around the docks, and so treated all questions asked with suspicion, although they probably were just genuinely interested in where we came from and where we were going. Anyway, our old tub and crew didn't exactly look like rich pickings, and after a few days ashore we took to the sea again, unmolested.

The second leg was a cruise of some 2,200 miles, southwest to Brazil; no real challenges, just long slow rollers. Distractions were rare. Once we saw on the radar a tropical cloud approaching; it was a hot sunny day, yet in about thirty minutes from the time we spotted it, this cloud came straight at us, whipped up the sea so waves crashed over the bows, dumped a load of rain, and then in minutes was gone; most strange. Schools of dolphins would join us and ride our bow wave just for the fun of it; on hearing the 'whoosh' of a blowhole being cleared, we'd rush out to watch the performance. Priceless. At the time my friend, somewhat unwisely, was reading 'Survive the Savage Sea', a book about the ordeals of a family who survived 38 days in a liferaft after a pod of killer whales sunk their yacht. One night I came on watch to find the bridge empty, and I could hear him talking to himself outside. Going to investigate I realised he was saying something like "Go Away!", although using slightly more colourful terms. We had been joined by a pod of killer whales, around ten times the size of dolphins, and they too were riding our bow wave. The sight was awesome, although I could understand my friend's concern, and wasn't completely sorry when they went their way.

We were mid-Atlantic when we heard that actor Ronald Reagan had been elected as president of the USA, and on nearing the equator my friend announced that anyone crossing for the first time had to perform the crossing ritual in order to keep Neptune happy; both things seemed equally sensible. But with time on our hands, we all complied; the inflatable dinghy was filled with seawater and we took turns to sit in it while my friend, dressed in red long johns, flippers snorkel and mask, while carrying a black umbrella (don't ask, you're probably thinking the same as I did at the time) pronounced the appropriate words. Presumably Neptune was happy as the rest of the trip passed without incident.

We took along tons of music of course, all on cassette, and my theme music for the voyage comprises two favourite albums; Meatloaf's 'Bat Out of Hell' was the ideal remedy for hours of mid-ocean boredom and solitude spent alone on watch through long dark nights, while Jimmy Buffett's 'Changes in Latitudes, Changes in Latitudes' seemed to capture the essence of the trip.

The crossing to Recife took about ten days. First impressions of Brazil were positive; compared to Dakar everyone seemed so much happier. Few people looked as if they had any money, and I'm sure that if we'd wandered into the wrong area we would soon have been liberated from ours, but there always seemed to be a party atmosphere, with music and someone blowing a whistle or beating a samba rhythm on a homemade drum.

That night we visited a couple of dockside bars, which was when I first realised how important football is to the Brazilians. Two guys were arguing heatedly over the names of the full England squad for the 1966 World Cup; having agreed on all but one. Realising that we were English, they just assumed we must know and asked us to adjudicate. To keep the peace, we just guessed, and everyone was happy; it would have been so much easier with the Internet.

The following day we went ashore taking our passenger along. The town has a river running through with a number of bridges making it easy to work out your location in relation to the docks; or so I thought. We had work to do on the boat, but our passenger chose to stay and explore. Hours later, and now pitch dark, he hadn't returned, and we began to get concerned until, finally, he turned up. Apparently, having completely lost his bearings and speaking no Portuguese, he had wandered aimlessly around before coming across a newspaper office where someone who spoke English called a taxi to take him to the docks. Having told his story this young, soon to be, although I suspect not overly keen, trainee officer, smiled and made the observation "not so sure I'm going to make that good a leader of men". The next day we started on the final leg, southbound to The Falklands.

After a brief stop in Vitoria to drop off our passenger, we chugged into Rio de Janeiro. What a moment. The sun shone down, the sea sparkled indigo, the huge statue of Christ the Redeemer looked down from Corcovado, and Sugarloaf Mountain completed the picture; it was truly breathtaking. We dropped anchor and the mate, my friend and I took the inflatable dinghy ashore to sort out the landing paperwork, tying up at the yacht club. With nobody in sight, my friend said something like "this is the life, no British weather and no bloody George and Dragon", the pub where he occasionally did bar work. From behind a bush came a voice, "not the George and Dragon on Kingston Hill? My daughter works there." Small world indeed. Out stepped a British ex-pat who had been living in Rio for years. This proved most fortuitous, as he and his family took us under their wing making sure our stay was a good one; they were incredibly generous and hospitable even to the point of putting me up when I passed through on my way home.

There followed a frenzied few days; during the daylight hours we had chores to carry out but still had plenty of time to go ashore, visit the beach or wander around the city; come nightfall my friend and I, together with the mate, were back for the social life, returning slightly the worse for wear, around sunrise. A short nap, and then up to start again. This took its toll, and by the time we left Rio we were drained.

During our stay we did have one bit of excitement. Returning from an excursion to a nearby island for a picnic and swim, we spotted a boat with people waving frantically, obviously in distress, so we steamed to the rescue. They were probably a little bemused when our fore hatch was thrown open, a couple of speakers appeared, and 'Rule Britannia' blared out across the water. My mate always believed in having the right music for the occasion, as witnessed by Son thirty years on when we were visiting him in France for a bit of skiing and the Icelandic volcano eruption extended our stay; no sooner had we heard the news, than the house was filled with Jimmy Buffett singing

251

'Volcano'. But back to the rescue. The boat was slightly larger than ours, and its engine had failed, so our skipper offered them a tow. An operation that proved challenging, with the rhythm of the waves causing the other boat regularly to fall back straining the rope to the point that it broke, catapulting back and taking my friend off his feet, leaving him with a hefty bruise. But he survived, we all got back safe, and some very grateful people were returned to dry land.

Rio was an exciting city, although definitely a place of contrasts. The landscape was spectacular, the people smiley and happy, and there was a buzz as if everyone was ready to party. On my way home from the Falklands I saw the New Year in on Copacabana Beach where the atmosphere was electric, the finale being a waterfall of fire cascading down the outside of a hotel on the beach. I heard later that this was totally illegal, but the hotel owners always ignored the law, and a policeman would turn up on New Year's day to collect the fine.

This seemed to sum up the place nicely. Great wealth was on show, but also great poverty as in the favelas perched on surrounding hills overlooking the city. Crime levels were high. One night we were at a street bar when a man came up and tried to steal the mate's manbag (yes I know); there was a quick tussle during which the mate responded with a truly Anglo Saxon mouthful similar to that used mid-ocean to persuade the killer whales to leave, then the handle came away from the bag and the would-be thief fell backwards before getting to his feet and sprinting off, only to join his friends at another street bar fifty yards away, where he carried on drinking as if nothing had happened.

Another night and, running late, we urged the taxi driver to hurry; he jumped a number of red lights earning himself a good tip. Only later did we find that this was routine, as residents were told not to stop at red lights at night unless it was essential, as there was always a risk from car-jackers. I was warned that if I hired a car and got into a confrontation with another driver,   not to stop. Apparently, not only did macho Brazilian men idolise racing driver Emerson Fittipaldi, but they also thought they could drive like him, causing numerous accidents; they generally had a fiery temperament, and many carried a loaded pistol in the glove compartment for resolving differences of opinion. At least that's what I was told.

After leaving Rio we delivered our passenger to Vitoria; now we were four. The first few days of our final stretch southward were uneventful before things became more challenging. The first problem was wet sheets. We'd been cruising a few days when I noticed seawater running down the sides of my cabin, soaking my bed. On investigation the reason became clear. Built of solid oak beams sealed with black pitch to keep things watertight, MY Copious was capable of dealing with cold rough seas; but the design didn't take into consideration the blazing sun of the tropics. In equatorial waters, we had noticed soft tar oozing between the boards, but at the time did not realise the implications. As the water got cooler the wood shrunk, leaving gaps for water to trickle through. Nice. Once we realised the cause, this was not deemed a major concern and perhaps the wood swelled up again with the water, as I can't remember it being a permanent issue. Anyway, on we went.

Our first real challenge came approaching the River Plate. At its mouth, the river is nearly 140 miles wide and a continuous stream of shipping steams in and out at all hours of day and night. It was dark and there was thick fog as we approached; imagine crossing a busy road at night in such conditions. But we had our radar, on which we could see loads of little dots on the screen, probably each representing a very large ship, so all was relaxed. Until, that is, the shelf holding the radar box fell off and, with a thud, the radar was no more. I spent hours in the bow, ears pricked for any sound that might warn us of approaching boats, and I've rarely felt so relieved as when the sun came up and the fog lifted. On we went.

I can personally vouch for the fact that the South Atlantic can get a little choppy. It was blowing a bit, and the boat was being thrown around when I came back on watch after an eight-hour break to find our position hadn't changed; steaming full ahead we hadn't moved. "Not to worry," my chum told me, "as long as the bilge pumps keep going everything will be OK". He left me on watch and went below, returning shortly looking a little on the ashen side. "The bilge pumps have packed up."

It took a while to take this in and to consider our options, of which there were none. We were 500 miles from land and away from main shipping lanes with no chance of rescue. So, we opened a couple of beers and discussed just about anything else. I think this is the point when my view on life became more fatalistic, when your number's up your number's up. Anyway, you'll have realised by now that things worked out; with a repair akin to using a pair of tights as a car fan belt, the problem was fixed, and we carried on; or at least stood still a while longer before eventually continuing south.

The final challenge came a few days away from the Falklands. At some point, having been on the same shelf as the radar box, our satnav gave up the ghost too. We knew we were generally going in the right direction, but the islands were a tiny target; if we missed it would be next stop Antarctica, and we had little fuel left to boot. The mate was fairly confident that he could plot our course 'the old-fashioned way' using a sextant; but it wasn't that easy. Continual low cloud cover meant sightings of celestial bodies were rare, at least that's what he claimed, so we gave up on that idea.

Then someone suggested RDF, or Radio Direction Finding, using radio transmissions to calculate our position. We managed to tune in to Falkland Islands Radio who were playing 'Teddy Bears Picnic' at the time, problem solved. Well nearly. We eventually did find the Falklands but were quite a few miles away from target and, embarrassingly, the reception party waiting to greet us had to wait a bit longer. Worse still, as we finally cruised majestically up to the jetty, our captain had a quick oops moment, accelerating rather than hitting the brake and causing the welcoming committee to scatter quickly back from the jetty. We had arrived!

We quickly retired to a bar where I got talking to the crew of the British Antarctic Survey vessel John Briscoe. They were returning to the Antarctic the following day and looking to recruit a postman, the current one having just quit and left for home; did I fancy it? When not handling mail in and out I would help scientists to weigh penguins, measure ice thickness and so on. This sounded fun, but although I had thoroughly enjoyed my time at sea, I was really looking forward to a few days on dry land and reluctantly turned the offer down; a decision I have lived to regret, moreso as we come to understand the effects of global warming and the shrinking expanse of Antarctica. But there you go, chance missed.

Arriving in the Falkland Islands in 1980 was like going back in time. Some 1800 people lived there, the majority near Port Stanley, but others spread around the islands. Most buildings were made from wood with corrugated metal roofs, the cost of importing bricks and the like being astronomical. With no television, the locals relied on the BBC World Service and Falkland Island Radio for news; we were interviewed for the latter after our arrival, apparently a major event. There were a few miles of tarmac road, usually empty, and drivers would cling to their steering wheel in the rare event that they passed another vehicle.

The phone system was very basic with all calls coming through a switchboard operator. Our phone number was 'Falkland Islands 2 and 2 rings'. If the phone rang once, that could be for next door, if it rang twice, it could be for us but we would wait as a third ring meant it was for the house on the other side. The telephone operator knew everybody and would take messages or reroute calls if necessary. Later I was amused to see a story in the papers concerning the Falklands War. Supposedly, a bunch of intrepid British soldiers approaching a farm were discussing how to find whether it was occupied by Argentine troops. Showing great ingenuity, one asked for ten pence to phone the farm, which he did, to be told by the farmer that the Argies had left. Well, great story as maybe, but just slightly questionable. Where were these phone boxes and who would use them? Shock horror, it would appear you can't always believe what you read in the paper.

The Falklands climate is temperate with average temperatures around 2°C in winter and 9°C in summer; it is windy more often than not, with frequent gales severely restricting the survival chances of trees. The landscape is rugged but there are some lovely sandy beaches; the water is cold, naturally. But the wildlife is truly impressive, seals, dolphins, whales, birdlife of all shapes and sizes. On arrival, the skipper paid us off and we moved into Woodbine House, the abode my friend's old boss was renting. Now the boat had arrived, the boss planned an introductory tour of the islands, and he invited us along as guests; no need to do anything, just enjoy the view and an occasional tipple.

Things went well until we landed, I know not where, to pick up four passengers. One, the owner of Birdland, a wildlife park in Bourton-on-the-Water, owned the two Jason Islands and he, together with three companions, wanted dropping off there. We were invited ashore to eat, and consumed much wine before all returning to the boat, only to be woken a few hours later by a loud thumping. I slowly forced myself awake, but my mate, with many more sea hours experience than I, just leapt from his bunk yelling, "We're aground", before dashing off. It transpired that we had anchored in a kelp bed, and overnight the anchor had dragged; sure enough, we were up against the shore and the tide was going out. Quickly launching the inflatable dinghy, we took the anchor out a way before dropping it, the plan being to winch ourselves off, but to no avail.

The tide continued to recede, and we were high and dry. Our passengers seemed to have slept through all the excitement and were a little surprised to come for breakfast in a cabin leaning at 45°. An embarrassing few hours were then spent waiting for the tide to return while the passengers presumably wondered what they had let themselves in for.

Having successfully dropped the passengers off we then went on a tour of the islands. The few people we did meet were warm and welcoming, possibly just glad of a little company, but the main attraction was the wildlife. Approaching one island I was amazed to see a bank of short, wind-stunted trees full of black-crowned night herons; hundreds of them. To me, herons were solitary birds to be found standing motionless in water, so to see so many in the trees was really weird; and they totally ignored us.

Another time I sat for ages on a clifftop while a few yards away magnificent black-browed albatross, with wings spanning seven or eight feet, hung motionless in the air seemingly just for the fun of it; one slight twitch of a wing and they would dive or swoop away at speed with no apparent effort; truly majestic. There were penguins of various breeds and sizes going about their daily business, completely oblivious to our presence, seals and sealions likewise.

Sheep farming was the main industry on the islands; mutton figured prominently in the islanders' diet and was nicknamed '365' for the number of days a year they ate it; but we did visit one island where they bred beef. Not quite like popping into Sainsbury's for a joint though; we'd radioed ahead to place our order and on arrival it was ready, one cow in four pieces. A quick look on the Internet suggests the average size for beef cattle is in the region of 1,200lbs to 1,400lbs so it seems likely each greasy quarter weighed around 300lbs, and we had to manhandle them, first from the jetty into our little dinghy and then, in rolling seas, from the dinghy up onto the deck of the boat. Suddenly the offer of a free trip as 'guests' seemed a bit of a ploy. Still, we managed, and steamed home where my mate and I took on the role of butchers, hacking the meat into various chunks before consigning it to the freezer.

A few miles outside Port Stanley is Moody Brook, site, at the time, of the town barracks housing a contingent of some forty Royal Marines. We were invited for social drinks a couple of times and very pleasant it was too; the Marines are a close-knit bunch, and a number of these guys knew my swimming club mate, which definitely helped. A little over a year later, Argentine warships would steam into Port Stanley, and I wonder whether any of the guys I met were still there and, if so, how they must have felt.

To get the real naturalist experience, my mate and I spent a few days on Kidney Island, a short trip offshore of Port Stanley. There was nothing there but an old hut for shelter and loads of wildlife. We were dropped off before trudging cross-country to find the hut and were slightly disconcerted to discover a huge turkey vulture perched on the roof glaring down at us as if contemplating a future meal. The island is small, about 80 acres in all, much of it covered in tussac grass growing up to 10ft tall and creating a network of strange passageways. You never know what you might encounter around the next bend.

Strolling among sleeping elephant seals was an incredible experience if you could stand their fishy breath. The bulls are enormous, around 15ft long and they can weigh in at 3 tons; when disturbed they 'dash' to the sea so the only thing to avoid is getting caught between them and the water as they stop for nobody. One morning we couldn't get out of the hut, the door being jammed shut by a large elephant seal asleep against it. We rattled the door and yelled until he finally woke and shuffled off.

Colonies of magellanic, macaroni and rockhopper penguins all went about their business taking absolutely no notice of us while dolphins and seals swum nearby. One memorable aspect of our stay was nightfall, when tens of thousands of seabirds returned home; sooty shearwaters live in burrows, and we would sit in the dark listening to them hit the ground with a thump before scurrying off underground.

When the time came for me to leave, I took a plane to Argentina landing at Comodoro Rivadavia. As far as the Argentines are concerned, Islas Malvinas are part of Argentina so no need for an entry visa or any time-wasting immigration procedures, just straight on to a connecting plane, next stop Buenos Aires. Realising I was British, the taxi driver taking me to my hotel talked animatedly about John Lennon; I couldn't understand a word so tutted, raised my eyebrows and wondered what the ex-Beatle had done now, only hearing news of his assassination later; heaven knows what the taxi driver made of my unsympathetic response. I spent a none-too-comfortable night in a hotel; my first experience of air conditioning and I couldn't work out how to turn the temperature up, so woke decidedly chilled; also, it was summer in the southern hemisphere, nice and warm, loads of beautiful flowers and pollen enough to set my hayfever off for the second time in one year. Deep joy.

Next, an 800-mile bus ride to Iguazu; a journey taking some twenty-four hours during which time I met nobody who spoke English. My fellow passengers smiled, and some tried to communicate a little but without much luck. It's surprising how depressing it is to be surrounded by happy chattering people when you don't understand a word being said. We passed through lots of beautiful countryside with tons to look at, but it was still a relief to arrive at my destination.

Iguazu Falls is by far the most beautiful place I have ever had the pleasure to visit. Marking the border between Argentina and Brazil, the falls are set in lush green jungle teeming with colourful and noisy birds, butterflies, lizards and much more. They comprise a few large falls, plus between 150 and 300 smaller ones depending on the water level. By luck I visited at a time when the river was in full flow, and the sight was breathtaking. On the Brazil side you can only look across the river at the falls, but on the Argentine side a series of walkways go over the river; from one viewpoint I was able to look down on the tallest waterfall, Devil's Throat, some 90 metres wide with an awe-inspiring drop of 80 metres, and it genuinely took my breath away. All this against a setting of bright green trees, a brilliant blue sky and burning sun producing myriad rainbow prisms sparkling through the spray. Unforgettable.

But it was time to go and I had a problem; the border crossing to Brazil was by boat and the soldier manning the post obviously wasn't a fan of the British. He looked puzzled at first, leafing through my passport for an entry visa. Realising the problem, I explained that I had no visa having come from Islas Malvinas; he threw my passport down, said something incomprehensible, and started dealing with the next person. Someone in the queue explained that he'd said something like "if the British gave you your entry visa they can give you your exit visa". I sat for a while pondering my next move; a row with the Argentine military seemed unwise, so eventually I snuck onto the boat. So far so good, but on the other side I wondered if I might have been just a little hasty; there was a short road through the jungle up to the Brazilian border post and I had no idea what their reaction would be when I arrived without an exit visa; I imagined being refused entry to Brazil and living in that strip of land forever. But no worries; the Brazilian border guard spoke English, listened sympathetically to my tale, roundly cursed the Argentines, stamped my passport and welcomed me to Brazil. Phew.

There followed bus rides to Santos where I played football on the very beaches where Pele had honed his skills, then up to Rio for a Christmas and New Year on Copacabana Beach; a bizarre event considering the weather back home. Then came a big decision; I had enough money left for a flight back home, or alternatively could fly to Miami and bus up to Minnesota, visit a friend and borrow the money for a flight home later. No competition really, northward I went.

On arriving at Miami airport, I queued behind a little old lady and witnessed an unpleasant customs official gleefully pull everything from her bag before leaving it for her to repack. He called me over with a nasty smile and I could read his mind, "rucksack; long hair; beard; scruffy clothes; drugs; time for some fun." I readied myself for a long stay when he called over a colleague, obviously an expert at dealing with this sort of layabout. He was young and friendly, chatted briefly before waving me through, to the obvious annoyance of his chum. Welcome to America.

I left the airport to hunt for the Greyhound bus station, wandering around some rundown areas before finally finding the place. It was very early and the streets were deserted, which is probably just as well, as I found later that this was a dodgy neighbourhood soon to be the scene of some fairly violent riots. I bought a ticket to

Minnesota and settled down on the bus in preparation for a 2,000-mile road trip.

There was a rapid turnover of passengers and as we got further north, people began to look at me a little strangely. The weather was getting colder and people boarding wore more, and heavier, clothing while my attire was more suitable for the beach. Changing bus around halfway, I took the opportunity to dig out some warmer clothes, though these were still inadequate. By the time we reached Chicago roadside thermometers were showing a temperature of -20°C, and it got even colder in Minnesota; so just about the first thing I did was to buy a pair of boots and some thick socks, although I figured the rest of my clothes would do if I wore them in layers.

Minnesota was another strange experience, with temperatures freezing yet not initially seeming cold, something to do with the air being drier than we have at home. You could still freeze to death in a few minutes though. It was good to catch up with my friend, his wife and brother who, by coincidence was also visiting; but the weather restricted the amount of sightseeing I could take in. I stayed a week and then headed home, touching down at Gatwick early one Friday morning. Little Brother was working from home that day and picked me up from the airport. Driving through Esher at about noon, we stopped at The Bear for my first British pint, or two, then home. Adventure over.

I later phoned my mate's mum who told me that, just after I'd left the Falklands, David Attenborough had passed through on his way south to film in South Georgia. My lot had invited him and his team for a meal at my former home, Woodbine House and, apparently, an enjoyable evening was had by all. Before leaving,

Attenborough asked if he could do anything for the party on his return to the UK, and my friend asked him to contact his mum and let her know how things were going. A few months later she received a call that went something like: "Good morning, this is David Attenborough and I have a message for you from your son." "Oh (expletive deleted), do you think I'm stupid? You're back then." "No, it really is David Attenborough." "Yeah right, and I'm a monkey's uncle. How was the trip?" "Honestly, I really am David Attenborough and I really did meet him in Port Stanley. Honest." After a while she realised that the voice sounded less like me and an awful lot like the great man himself, she apologised profusely, and they had a long chat. Nice that he took the time to follow up as promised.

In the years since then a lot has happened. The Falklands War in 1982 means far more people are aware of the islands. The population has doubled, although I'm not sure if that includes the permanent presence of some 1,000 British military personnel. Since the evolution of satellite TV, televisions are commonplace, and communication is far easier. A few years ago, there was a story of a farmer in the Falklands who had an accident in an isolated spot and was able to alert the locals through contacting a British emergency service - after the telephone box saga this story might be questionable, but I'm inclined to believe it. I assume the old telephone exchange has been brought up to date and who knows, there may even be a phone box.

Forty years after the Copious capers, the Falklands are firmly on the tourist trail; Tripadvisor even has reviews for Kidney Island, with one describing it as "great for kids to explore and have fun". Somehow this depresses me. I shouldn't begrudge others the great experiences I enjoyed, but I have my reservations; my friend and his boss had been eased out of the Galapagos Islands by the Ecuador government who saw the financial opportunities of large-scale tourism, and apparently the place has since changed for the worse. I would hate to see the same happen to the Falklands.

Further south, the Antarctic ice is melting at an alarming rate, the full effects of which on both humans and the local wildlife, have yet to be seen.

Recently I saw the Argentines were again pushing for the British to relinquish control of the Falklands. After the lives lost and financial cost of the war, I suspect that British public opinion will not back such a move, at least for the timebeing.

In 1984, the Brazilian and Argentine national parks containing the Iguazu Falls were designated UNESCO World Heritage Sites, which I suppose should be good, although from articles I have read the sites have been developed considerably since my visit which can be good or bad depending on your tastes and need for modern luxuries. I remember a news article from a few years back, concerning the effects man has on the environment; it showed some very depressing pictures of the falls with just a slight trickle of water spilling over. The story stated that extensive jungle clearing and building in Paraguay had diverted much of the water, resulting in this rather sad outcome. That may well be the case, but I have also seen recent pictures of the falls in full flow. It seems that the size of the falls is dictated by the rainfall and there is generally plenty in the area, although in 2006, following a very rare and severe drought, the falls virtually dried up. Perhaps that was when the photos were taken. Whatever the truth, if you ever get the opportunity to visit Iguazu, it is worth checking the likely conditions before you book.

So, to the question was it better then than now? Personally, I have to say yes. The areas I visited were less full, and the environment less affected by humans than is the case today. There was a lack of all the modern conveniences that people now take for granted, and I like that. But maybe the islanders think that being dragged into the twenty-first century, with all that brings, is an improvement, and I suppose tourists enjoy the trip; so perhaps honours even once more.

27.

Fashion Through the Years

It will come as no surprise to anyone who knows me, when I say that I am not exactly what you'd call fashion-conscious. In the early 70s I discovered a liking for Levis and Fred Perry polo shirts and now, fifty years on, I'm sitting at my computer wearing Levis and a Timberland polo; say no more. The kids mock my hairstyle; the colour has changed from toddler blonde through brown to sophisticated grey, and the length has varied, but basically the same style throughout my life, a fringe with a parting on the right. They are horrified when the flip-flops come out, and I have relied on brown boat shoes for as long as I can remember; if it ain't broke don't fix it I say. But if not exactly a dedicated follower myself, I have witnessed a fair few changes in fashions and thought it would be fun, and might add to the nostalgia, to note a few of the things I can recall.

Arguably, modern men's fashion started in the late 50s with the Teddy Boys and their bootlace ties and drape jackets; brothel creepers or winkle pickers were de rigeur. They tended to follow American tastes, listened to Rock & Roll, and had greased quiffs. Dad loved to tell of the time when in a café, aged about four at the time, I announced loudly to all and sundry "when I grow up I want to be a Teddy Bear Boy". This seemed to amuse him. By the 60s the Teds had expanded to incorporate leather jacketed, motorbike-riding Rockers.

Youth culture really took off in the Swinging 60s, triggering a hugely diverse wave of fashions. Carnaby Street became the centre of the world for new trends and the media was forever showing pictures of the 'in crowd', recounting stories of their sinful, drug-fuelled hedonistic lifestyle. Us ordinary lads might have been impressed with a few things, the mini skirt for instance, but pictures of guys in bright coloured embroidered kaftans and silk neck scarves left us cold. To be honest it just sounded like a different planet.

For many young dudes in the early 60s, The Beatles led the way fashion-wise; suits without lapels, accompanied by thin ties, was their original trademark, plus the Beatle haircut of course. With passing years the hair grew and their clothes became more varied ranging from psychedelic and sheepskin waistcoats to John Lennon's white suits; Lennon also made round metal glasses suddenly fashionable.

On the heels of the Beatles came the Mods. Not a music group, but a collective term for a bunch of folk with similar lifestyle tastes. They wanted something smarter than the Rockers and turned to Europe for inspiration. On their scooters, Lambretta or Vespa, they favoured olive drab parkas, sometimes with a fur-trimmed hood and often with a large Union Jack on the back. They tended to dress smart; Italian tonic suits, Ben Sherman shirts often with a tie, or a Harrington jacket for a more relaxed look. Big Brother was in this camp for a while; I just liked the shirts, although a few years ago I did buy my first Harrington; after all it was described as timeless.

Towards the end of the decade, Hippie and Bohemian styles took over for many youngsters. Girls wore long flowing cotton dresses in bright colours with tie-dyed and flower patterns. Other than that, most of the hippie attire was unisex. I was fond of my skin-tight loon pants, totally impractical with no pockets and large bell-bottoms. Full immersion in the hippy look required various items like corduroy jeans, sheepskin vests, mariner's caps, headbands, sandals; all often adorned with patches and badges with peace symbols, flowers or slogans. Anything army surplus was considered hip; in particular greatcoats and canvas backpacks.

I did like leather jackets though, not the black Rocker style but the brown sheepskin-lined bomber pilot sort. Sadly, these were very expensive; lower quality black ones were much cheaper so naturally that's what I went for. I remember travelling to Stockwell on the back of my mate's Lambretta to buy it; at a time when at least some kids were becoming quite polarised, there was I using a Mod form of travel to buy Rocker clothes, I was already confused. I remember the trip simply because it poured with rain most of the way, as I sat cold and miserable staring at my mate's parka-clad back; but I got my jacket. Sadly, as I don't actually feel the cold much, even when winter set in it was rarely cold enough for me to wear what I considered to be my trendy purchase; bit of a waste of money really.

Jeans have always been my preferred legwear. When we were kids, Mum furnished us with green-stitched, black jeans, complete with zip pockets that I thought were cool, even if we didn't use the word then. I graduated to blue denim and was fifteen when I discovered Levi's, since when I have always been a bit choosy when it comes to jeans; not the frightfully expensive ones of course, but Levi's, Lee and Wranglers have taken their turn. These days it's always Levi's. As I got older, I'm not sure Dad really approved; his view was that jeans were workwear and strictly for the kids. One slight deviation I remember is Oxford Bags, popular in the 70s; these were jeans although you could get more formal trousers if you so desired. They hugged the bum and crotch but billowed out around the legs, and we wore them for a short spell before realising how stupid they looked.

Facial hair is one easy way that a chap can assert his individuality, and it's free. I first joined the hirsute brigade during the summer holidays of my sixteenth year, sporting a drooping Mexican-style number that grew quite well other than at the corners of my mouth which stayed bare; truth be known that probably looked a bit daft, but I didn't care, I was a man! Of course, when the holidays were over it had to come off, returning as a permanent fixture as soon as I left school.

Both brothers were mustachioed too, which seemed to cause problems for some folk who were unable to tell us apart. Strange how people perceive you; over the years I have been told that I am the spitting image of a whole host of people, Nigel Mansell, Tom Selleck and Bob Carolgees to name just three. They all look totally different except for one thing; each had a moustache and it seems that people are unable to see beyond the facial hair.

Moustaches were popular through the 70s and 80s, particularly with male pornstars but there you go; we thought we were pretty cool, the three musketeers. For a couple of brief spells I toyed with a beard, not having to shave was great but the look wasn't really me. A couple of times, including on our honeymoon, I went clean shaven for a while, otherwise my moustache was a permanent fixture for about twenty-five years until it finally had to go when the grey bits started ruining the effect; I suggested it looked like a badger, Wifey said more like a skunk. For a short while the kids had a problem adapting to the new look as they'd only ever known me with a moustache.

Looking back at old photos I have a couple that I think look pretty cool, but in the vast majority my moustache does me no favours; that's the funny thing about fashion, what seems great at the time often appears less so in retrospect.

During the 70s, sportswear became acceptable daywear with tracksuits, training shoes, t-shirts and polo shirts all in vogue. I recall my first ever pair of Adidas Rom training shoes; white leather with three light blue stripes. Compared to previous shoes they were incredibly comfortable and became my footwear of choice for many years to come. I also remember buying a black vest with a large silver star on the front; I wore it for my one and only rock band performance under a grey cardigan, hand-knitted by my Nan; this may not sound too impressive now, but I somehow thought I cut a bit of a dash.

That was the era of platform boots, jumpsuits and boob tubes, while hotpants definitely caused a bit of a stir. There were wide kipper ties, tartan was everywhere, and Saturday Night Fever ushered in the age of disco fashion, all sparkly sequins and white suits. Fashion has a habit of occasionally coming up with something that really shouldn't exist, and in the 70s that happened with matching shirt and tie sets; the shirts had huge collars, were often flowery and always horrible. Sometimes you could even get a matching handkerchief.

271

As the 70s came to a close, the kids managed, once again, to really get up their elders' noses when punk burst on the scene bringing the advent of punk fashion; all ripped jeans, safety pins and black rubbish bags.

The 80s was the age of the yuppie, bringing us power dressing with flash suits, silk ties and braces for the men, huge shoulder pads, big hair and lots of expensive looking jewelry for the women; Wifey had an impressive set of curls when we met. Hawaiian shirts, which I liked, became popular, as were mullets with many of the guys; not me I hasten to add.

The age also brought us grunge, a sort of fashion counterculture whose proponents would wear anything they felt comfortable in; for the boys it was the likes of plaid shirts, unkempt hair and ripped jeans while the girls took to oversized cardigans, denim overalls and thick tights while starting to wear Doc Martens with everything. I was too old for it by then, although some of the new fashions bore a spooky resemblance to my own wardrobe. Grunge particularly appealed to my sense of humour when I read an article suggesting that the whole ethos was to create a look that youngsters could carry off effortlessly, but that would just make the older, still-want-to-be-trendy types look ridiculous. It was a stand against a particular type of person, usually moneyed and past their prime, who dictated what was 'in'. But of course, as time passed, the fashion industry got a grip on the genre and introduced the 'proper' way to wear grunge, complete with inflated price tag.

One fashion that appears to have caught the imagination big-time is that of tattoos. These had always been seen as the sign of either a misspent youth, a life at sea or experience in the military; they were generally the province of men, proving they were 'ard, although the occasional woman I'd met displaying them often seemed scarier. But now all that's changed; led by the likes of David Beckham, the rich and famous seem not to feel they've made it until they have a tat or two on show; and not only discreet little numbers but sleeves or other displays covering large areas of skin. Gone are the days of LOVE/HATE or an iffy skull and crossbones, current offerings are veritable works of art with their creators gaining global recognition.

I had never appreciated the enormous range of tattoo styles. There's the Traditional that marked achievements at sea, like having a King Neptune to show you had crossed the Equator, if only I'd known. There's New School, Neo Traditional, Tribal, Blackwork, Dotwork, Geometric, Illustrative, Sketch, Watercolour, Japanese and many more. While I quite like small discrete tattoos and some of the less overpowering tribal styles, I can't understand why you'd want to cover vast amounts of your body with ink. A tattoo on young, tanned skin covering firm muscle doesn't look quite the same when the skin gets old and stretchy, and the muscle goes flabby. Still, it's a free world.

But like it or not, tattoos can have an impact on your life. I recently saw an article in which a trainee doctor, planning to become a surgeon, said that his sleeve tattoo shouldn't affect his employment opportunities; people, he said, didn't think twice about a mechanic with tattoos but may not have the same views regarding an inked surgeon. He's absolutely right of course. I had a similar view when I left uni; why did it matter what I wore to an interview, after all it was the person they were employing and not their clothes. But, of course, I turned up in a suit because that's what the people who were making the decisions expected. I hope the trainee surgeon isn't disappointed. In a few years' time, people won't think twice about his tattoos, but we're not completely there yet.

What little interest I may have had in fashion in my early years died out by the 90s, so I'll stop there. Fashion has been little more than a source of humour to me as when, for example, I looked on in wonder while people paid to have their skin died an odd orange colour, somehow believing it looked like a 'healthy' tan. But I have come to appreciate that this multi-billion industry has its not-so-funny side too. We hear more and more of the psychological issues arising through fashion; body-shaming and young girls with eating disorders as they struggle to achieve the shape that they are told they should be.

Then there's cosmetic surgery to achieve the perfect look by stretching out those unsightly wrinkles, chopping off the saggy bits, pumping up lips to enhance that becoming pout through the injection of rat poison and of course, using surgical implants to reshape natural assets. It used to be that most of the participants were leathery ladies or wrinkled Lotharios simply unable to cope gracefully with the advancing years, but more recently, customers have become younger; it all seems horribly unnatural to me, and a bit sad that so many people lack confidence in their own bodies, but for the fashion world to flourish it is essential that people are dissatisfied with their natural look.

Also, stories of exploitation abound in the world of fashion; hardly surprising bearing in mind the young attractive models and the potential money at stake for those at the top. I remember back in the 80s when Linda Evangelista, one of the new band of supermodels, hit the headlines for saying "We don't wake up for less than $10,000 a day." Exploitation reaches far wider though, with much of the clothing produced overseas by people paid a pittance to work long hours in terrible conditions. And if that's not bad enough, there is the huge amount of damage done to our environment in producing a totally unnecessary mountain of soon-to-be-discarded clothing.

But that's the extreme side of the fashion world. We all need clothes, and that need is met by an industry that provides employment to many while being a confidence-building source of fun and enjoyment to its fans; it's just that I'm not in that group. To many people, the huge variety of cheap clothes available now means things are better than in my day, while others will focus on the costs incurred both by people and the environment and say things are worse. Yet another draw I think.

28.

The City, Commuting and a New Millennium

My travel adventure over, I was home and in need of a job so, once again, I turned to the national papers, this time quickly finding something of interest in the Telegraph. A health insurance company was looking for trainee system analysts to move into computing, no technical knowledge required, would suit someone who likes to solve puzzles. Worth a try I thought, and to my surprise I got through the interview to join a team of seven other trainees for a spell of induction lasting about three or four months. This was not a particularly taxing time; all eight of us were of a similar age and background, with many things in common, we weren't exactly driven hard and all got on well to the point that I am still regularly in touch with two of the group, one of whom did me the honour of asking me to be godfather to his daughter. Training over, we were assigned to various teams and the real work began.

I didn't really appreciate it at the time, but I was going through a huge lifestyle change; I was now a commuter, and for the rest of my working life would be a slave to train timetables. At each end of every day, depending on the location of my office in relation to Waterloo Station, I would spend between an hour and 90 minutes commuting. On a good day that is. Still, I got to read a lot, and the company could be entertaining, although there was an unwritten rule that conversation time was limited before everyone got down to whatever they were doing. Many commuters used this time for extra work, but that was a pleasure I usually chose to forego.

Commuting has been the subject of many comedy sketches but it's no laughing matter I can tell you, it's a jungle out there. You can never be sure when or even if you will arrive. Most common cause of delays is the wrong type of weather; rain and wind bring down leaves on the line causing train wheels to slip, rails buckle in the heat, snow blocks the line, ice interferes with power supplies and rain causes landslides. Weekend engineering works regularly overrun, causing travel chaos on Monday mornings, often compounded by staff shortages. Then there are the technical issues; train failures, points failures and power problems to name but three. Sadly, there is also a growing number of 'incidents' on the railways, a euphemism for suicides or serious accidents.

During the morning rush hour of 12th December 1988, a crowded passenger train crashed into the rear of a stationary train, waiting at a signal outside Clapham Junction, then sideswiped an empty train travelling in the opposite direction. 35 people died and 484 were injured. I was in a train a few minutes behind. We were diverted all around London and I finally arrived at work around 1 o'clock, oblivious to the events that had unfolded, this being before the age of the mobile phone.

Clapham again, and in December 1991 the IRA exploded a small bomb; nobody was injured but the rail network in London was closed down for five hours as all stations were searched, causing misery for around one million commuters and costs in lost business somehow estimated at £46 million.

Commuting aside, this was an enjoyable spell of my working life. It was the 80s, the economy was recovering and not only did companies have more to spend on their employees, but actively did so in order to retain them. People were even paid to wander through offices cleaning the phones, a job satirised in The Hitchhiker's Guide To The Galaxy, where the Golgafrinchans sent their Telephone Sanitiser population, together with another third of the planet's population who were also considered useless, away to colonise a remote planet saying that the rest would be along later; unfortunately the Golgafrinchans who stayed at home were subsequently wiped out by a nasty disease picked up from unsanitary telephones, so perhaps there's a deep and meaningful Covid-age message there.

We were paid reasonably well, lunch was heavily subsidised as were outside social activities like treasure hunts around old City of London pubs; at Christmas we each received a bottle of spirits or a turkey, and the Christmas party was always well funded. Work could occasionally be challenging but pressure was rare, and we had the added bonus of flexitime whereby any additional hours worked outside of our normal 9 to 5 could be banked and put toward extra holiday. There were a number of marvellous old pubs in the vicinity and, this being an age when lunch still meant lunch, we would often while away a happy hour or so in historic establishments like Ye Olde Cheshire Cheese in Fleet Street. My colleagues and I had similar tastes in music, shared albums and occasionally attended live performances; David Bowie's album 'Let's Dance' was popular then and always conjures up memories of those times, so this is my theme music for the period.

278

Then, in 1983, my life changed completely; I was on a course when I met my wife-to-be. Fate must have taken a hand; as a system programmer her technical knowledge was far greater than mine and we would not normally have found ourselves on the same course. It was Sunday evening, and we were all gathering in the hotel bar for a pre-course introductory dinner; she arrived late and I saw her coming down the stairs dressed in a white t-shirt, pastel green pleated skirt and a cardigan; just back from holiday she had a healthy tan and 80s-style soft perm.

It would be nice to say that as our eyes met it was love at first sight, but that's not quite true. She was beautiful, intelligent and great company and we clicked, but I don't think either of us was actively looking for love at the time; we kept in touch, and it was a little while before I came to the conclusion that this was the lady I wanted to spend the rest of my life with. My dear kids still ask what she saw in me, but I can't remember her ever answering. It definitely wasn't money she was after; my finances were still recovering having been plundered for my travels two years earlier, and my beaten-up VW Beetle was the most expensive thing I owned. But we met up again after the course, and pretty soon she was lucky enough to join my beer-swilling colleagues and I in the Lyceum in the Strand on Friday nights; the age of romance was not dead. Within a couple of years, we were married.

In the City, Big Bang was fast approaching and, if you worked in computing, the finance industry beckoned. I took a job at the Stock Exchange. Those were exciting times. We were at the heart of unprecedented change and because of the nature of the project we knew that, for once, deadlines had to be met; no slippage. It was manic, particularly as many stockbrokers and financial institutions were totally unprepared and had to be coaxed over the line, but in the end, we made it. While the Exchange was fairly conservative, madness reigned outside as institutions paid exorbitant salaries to attract the best teams and threw away millions trying to build computer systems to give them one over on their rivals.

In July 1990 the IRA exploded a bomb in the Exchange, in the men's toilets behind the visitors' gallery. They had given a telephone warning, as was usual then, and there were no injuries but quite a bit of damage to the building. In 1993, in response to a number of other IRA bombings in the City, the 'ring of steel' was introduced. Roads entering the City were narrowed to slow down traffic, CCTV cameras were installed and there was often a sentry box where armed police stood guard to monitor traffic.

Other changes followed; station rubbish bins were popular with the IRA as receptacles for small bombs so, in 1991, following the explosion of a device in a bin on Victoria Station concourse, the police removed all bins from London stations. Shortly after, bins were removed from all London streets. Bikes, too, became objects of suspicion as small explosives could be concealed in the frame. The Troubles finally ended in 1998 and the streets of London became a little safer for a few years until the next wave of terrorist-inspired attacks.

In the late 80s and early 90s, as the roaring economy started to slow, we experienced a new phenomenon, mass redundancies. In the City there were many tales of unhappy workers throwing computers through windows, or of company cars, usually Porsches, being left jammed up against the office door, locked but with alarm activated, and with the keys thrown down a nearby drain. Happy times indeed.

The Stock Exchange IT department, me included, was outsourced to a consulting company in 1992 and, just a year later, thirty-six of us were made redundant. Not too bad an experience for me though as I didn't really have the mindset to work for a consultancy company. To help us get through the experience, the company arranged counselling. So there we were a few days later on a bright sunny day, wearing summer casual clothes, shorts, Hawaiian shirts and the like, waiting to be counselled. It started something like this; "I would normally begin by telling you not to worry, you will get over this horrible experience, but I don't think I've seen thirty-six happier looking people, so we'll skip that bit." In a couple of months, I had another job, the redundancy money was stashed away, and the world looked rosy.

January 1st, 1999, saw the introduction of the euro; from that date computer systems had to recognise and process transactions in the new currency although it would be three years before coins and banknotes came out. For a year or two before, considerable effort was focused on preparing computer systems to be euro compliant. As with Big Bang, the date was set in stone with no chance of an extension, so the work took priority over non-essential projects.

As the date drew near, the complexity of the problem became clear, companies fought to get or retain key staff and the bill rocketed. The consultancies magnanimously offered to help, at a cost of course. In the end most people managed, although many system enhancements were necessary well after the event. The technicians gave themselves a pat on the back while the non-techies felt aggrieved that so much expense had been necessary for what seemed a simple request. This set the scene for the year 2000.

As the new millennium was fast approaching, people were considering ways in which the momentous event could be celebrated. The Millennium Commission was set up to allocate National Lottery funds among projects deemed suitable, the result being a variety of schemes as diverse as Cornwall's Eden Project, the National Space Centre in Leicester and the Millennium Seed Bank in West Sussex.

In London we had the Millennium Bridge, a steel suspension number crossing the Thames to join Bankside, handy for the Tate Modern and Shakespeare's Globe theatre, with the City of London just south of St. Paul's cathedral. Being greedy, we also had the Millennium Dome, located on the Greenwich Peninsula. If that wasn't enough, a privately funded project saw the Millennium Wheel, or London Eye, constructed on the south Bank opposite the Houses of Parliament.

Needless to say, none of these constructions went up without incident, and we had plenty of entertainment as work progressed. Foe example, an unfortunate design fault meant the Millennium Bridge tended to move too much in the wind and its opening was delayed until the fault was fixed; to many, this construction will always be known as the Wobbly Bridge. But despite the usual arguments, incidents, dramas and delays, all were completed in the end and stand today, a testament to British something.

But it was not only construction projects that were inspired by the approaching new millennium. In all walks of life fears grew over the potential impact on a society that had become so dependent on computers. Many programmes stored the year in just two digits, so when the year went from '99' to '00' how would they react? Would they recognise the year as 2000 or 1900? Would they carry on as usual or perhaps add one hundred years interest to an outstanding debt? Or just get totally confused and crash?

The media had a field day and were awash with stories about the risk of planes falling from the sky, traffic systems grinding to a halt, banking systems imploding, hospital life support systems turning themselves off and so on. But it genuinely was a problem. Millions of lines of code had to be analysed and changed, and there was a real potential for chaos.

Billions were spent worldwide on ensuring that computers would continue to function correctly after the stroke of midnight on December 31st, 1999, and all but essential changes were put on hold as computing staff efforts were focused on Y2K as it was now known. Salaries for the techies went up and many were offered bonuses for staying to see things through. This work was essential but of course, human nature being as it is, some took advantage. Once again consultancies offered their specialist services, at specialist prices, and some key staff used the situation to ratchet up their salaries. Technical staff around the world spent New Year's Eve in the office, nervously waiting for the stroke of midnight.

There were a few stories of computer issues but, generally speaking, the event passed without too much drama. We survived. Once again, the techies gave themselves a pat on the back but the moneymen felt aggrieved. It was a bit like complaining that you'd wasted money on house insurance when your house hadn't burnt down.

As the new millennium got rolling I made a a big decision, resigning from my permanent job to become a freelance consultant, and that's how I saw out the remainder of my working life. During the next eighteen years I would work on a variety of projects for a number of firms, British, French, American, Japanese and South African, all still based in The City. They were rollercoaster years; when I was working I earned good money but that would then be followed by spells, sometimes long spells, when I would be chasing work while earning nothing. But for me I think it was the right thing to do.

A year before Covid struck, I decided I had been retired. Freelance work depends on work coming from clients, and the flow had dried up; possibly my age and jaundiced cynicism didn't help. Bertrand Russell once said "one of the symptoms of an approaching nervous breakdown is the belief that one's work is terribly important"; that was never a problem I faced. I could have run around searching for another way to make an income, but that path had limited appeal and so I hung up my boots and took to a life of ease.

So that's my working life over. The question is, are things better or worse for kids today? Without doubt, some things are better. Regulations around health and safety, minimum wage schemes, workers' rights and the like mean that, in theory, employees are treated better. With more emphasis on work/life balance we now have such innovations as paid paternity leave, jobshare schemes and flexible hours. Working from home, a concept that appeals to many, has gained traction courtesy of Covid; and before the pandemic struck, the unemployment rate was lower than it had been for 45 years.

But look a little closer and you see a slightly less rosy picture. Change is far more rapid than in the past; technology has replaced humans in many jobs, and industries such as retail are under pressure, meaning workers need to gain new skills and move outside their comfort zone in order to make a living. I recently heard on the radio that, having spent three or four years at university, some 34% of graduates don't achieve 'graduate-level' jobs. Many jobs are now part-time, workers on zero-hour contracts don't have the benefits or stability of a guaranteed income and, in many industries, availability of overseas labour has led to high competition for jobs while wages have remained low. The number of people in employment who are on such low pay that they still need benefits to earn a living wage is disturbing, and in these challenging times stories abound of a growing dependence on food banks, even among the employed. Following Brexit and Covid, we are currently experiencing a shortage of labour that, together with the effects of the Ukraine war and other factors, has generated a cost-of-living crisis and double figure inflation.

Challenging times ahead and, all things considered, I think perhaps the Oldies probably did have things better.

29.

Keeping a Roof Over our Heads

For approaching thirty years, with occasional breaks in between, 'home' was a three-bedroom detached house owned by Mum and Dad. It had been built in the early fifties by Mum's brother, who was also responsible for the other fifty or so houses in the road, and Dad always said that a large part of the house was material left over from other jobs. I doubt that they would have been able to afford the house otherwise, and they regularly told us how it was some time before they owned any real furniture, orange boxes standing in for a lounge suite.

There were three bedrooms, two doubles and one very small single. This last room started as a nursery, then became Big Brother's domain when it was felt that the eldest needed some privacy. After Big Brother left home for the first time, Little Brother moved in there, and I kept the larger bedroom to myself, so never actually occupied that space.

At the time, we pretty much took everything for granted, and it was only in later years that I truly came to appreciate just how great a home Mum and Dad had created. We didn't have a lot of money but never went without, everyone was welcome, and the house was always full of laughter.

By modern standards things were basic; with no central heating we relied on an immersion heater for hot water, a coal fire in the lounge and a coke-burning stove in the kitchen. Cooking, including boiling a kettle for a cup of tea, was all by gas. Most food was kept in a brick-built pantry, although we did have a small fridge. The bathroom was of a reasonable size, no shower though, just a hand-held extension. We did have the luxury of two toilets, one upstairs and one down.

There was a garden large enough for football and cricket matches, a single integral garage and a drive. Outside the back door was a brick coalbunker, a regular hiding place. It was a quiet road so we could play football outside with few interruptions, and it was a couple of minutes' walk to the Woods. What more could anyone have wanted?

It was a happy house, often ringing with music and laughter; right from the start our friends were always welcome despite the tendency for our play to cause mess and destruction, particularly in Dad's beloved garden, and as we got older it was often the meeting point for our friends both before and after a night out; Big Brother often brought the local scooter boys home for some of Mum's bread pudding. But it wasn't just the kids; Mum and Dad had occasional parties well into the night and were able to make their own mess too. They would always joke about how many people would say "this is great we must have our own party", but then, somehow, never did.

In my final year at Uni, I had an interview with an aerospace company based in the North and Midlands, with just one southern site in Acton. When asked where I would prefer to work, being a Surrey boy I of course said the South. My interviewer expressed surprise, saying that in his view, the South was an amorphous splurge covered with concrete, with no discernible space between one town and the next, and no decent countryside. At the time I felt quite offended but have since come to realise what he meant. True, we do have the Surrey Hills, without doubt a beautiful patch, but at less than a fifth of the area of the Lake District not quite so impressive. The green belt, created after the War as "the lungs of London" in response to growing congestion and urban sprawl, is continually under attack by developers out to make a buck. With inadequate infrastructure the South seems to be pretty much full, covered in concrete, yet the building never stops.

During my lifetime, the economy of the UK has changed dramatically with a move from industry to services. The deregulation of the finance industry accelerated further the trend for people to focus on London and the South East in order to earn a living. To be fair, if you look back over the last thousand years you will find regular references to London being overcrowded and unable to grow further, but somehow it always does. The appeal is understandable as London's site is hard to beat, docks on a wide river just a short trip from the English Channel and the markets of Europe. Since I bought my first property in 1984, the population of London has increased from 6 to 9 million and that of the South East has increased at a similar rate. They all have to live somewhere.

Little Brother was first to marry, and that was when he bought his first house. I can't remember whether it was he or Big Brother who actually took the first step onto the property ladder, but I do know that I was a slow starter. The early 80s were a great time for property buying with various policies introduced by Margaret Thatcher to increase home ownership. My wife-to-be had her flat, and I finally bit the bullet and bought my own.

A particularly huge salary wasn't essential in order to afford a flat back then, and most of my workmates already had one, both for the independence it gave them, but also to save on time and money commuting, while enjoying the London social scene to boot. On the other hand, my home friends tended to stick with parents until matrimony beckoned.

Like everyone else, I had sleepless nights over my first mortgage; had I taken on too much debt? Inflation at the time was in double figures, not a good thing, and we were all blissfully sleepwalking into a recession; but while there were rocky times ahead, salaries often went up with inflation, and as a result, my mortgage payments soon became more manageable.

My wife-to-be sold her flat and moved in with me, we married, and in 1987 moved into our first family home. It ticked most of the boxes: nice location, local pub, short walk to the station and, most importantly, still fairly local so our social life could continue unaffected. We had to decorate throughout and make minor changes but nothing drastic. Then Daughter came along, followed seventeen months later by Son, so now we truly had ourselves a family home. We were happy there making many wonderful memories, but soon felt more space would be nice and started looking around.

But there were storms on the horizon in the form of the economic recession of 1990/91. Unemployment rose from 6.9% of the working population in 1990 to 10.7% in 1993, and the housing crash saw house prices fall 20 per cent between 1989 and 1993. For the first time we heard of negative equity, a property being worth less than the mortgage owed, a situation that would affect some two million properties at the peak. Between 1990 and 1995,

289

around 345,000 homes were repossessed, and as these came up for sale at bargain prices, house values dropped further.

We put our house on the market and received an offer the following day. Yippee, what could possibly go wrong? Quite a lot actually. This was the start of the recession, and within days the offer was withdrawn. For years we tried to move, but events conspired to frustrate us.

It was seven years before we finally moved, but it was well worth the wait. We moved a few miles down the road and have been here ever since. The house has a reasonable sized garden with a wonderful outlook over open fields. On our first visit, the kids ran wild in the garden and we both fell in love with the place, although Wifey did feel some of the rooms were a bit small. I promised that we would extend, and she only had to wait another twelve years before her wish came true. All good things come to those who wait.

Property ownership in the UK has developed into a key ambition for many, yet more recently this goal has been harder to reach as more and more people compete for an inadequate supply of housing. At the same time successive governments have cut back on council housing, turning instead to the private sector to meet the housing needs of those who can't support themselves. This might have been done for perfectly sound reasons at the time but, unfortunately, it's not that simple, and the papers regularly feature stories of unscrupulous landlords exploiting the situation or of local governments paying extortionate amounts for temporary accommodation.

The shortage of property has provided opportunities for those with money to become landlords. Depending on your perspective, this is a good thing increasing the stock of property to rent, or bad as landlords price locals out of the property market and profit from their misery.

Meanwhile, as the economy focuses on services at the expense of manufacturing, mining, fishing and the like, whole communities have gone into decline. With few local job opportunities, kids gravitate towards London, or other large cities, and the decline continues. Then, adding insult to injury, if the community is in an attractive area, outsiders buy up property as holiday homes thus pushing prices up and further out of the reach of the locals.

In England and Wales, home ownership peaked in 2001 when just under 70 percent of homes were privately owned. The figure has since fallen to around 64 percent, and social and financial factors suggest it is unlikely to rise in the foreseeable future. This position has come about as a result of a number of factors: the population then was significantly smaller; the economy was booming, and people felt they had a more secure financial future; banks were more willing to lend money, and council house tenants were able to buy their homes.

There can be no doubt that my generation had it better than kids today when it comes to getting on the property ladder. Kids claim that the Oldies have messed it up for them, but it's not really anyone's 'fault'; in the face of changing circumstances people have just taken the actions that seemed sensible at the time.

Left to its own devices the situation can only get worse. The population in the South continues to increase, pushing property prices up further as, despite a building boom destroying what precious countryside is left, demand still exceeds supply. I can think of three initiatives that might help address the situation, but they all need to be government-led, and I have little hope of that in the near future.

First, the appeal of the South, and particularly London, needs dampening. Post-Brexit, industries like fishing could possibly provide more local opportunities but more help is needed. Boris Johnson talked of 'levelling up' the country and encouraging businesses to locate in more depressed areas; time will tell the extent to which the new government adheres to this. The Covid pandemic has both proven to some firms that working remotely can be a viable option and highlighted our dependency on overseas suppliers for goods we could easily produce ourselves. Just maybe, we will see an increase in both UK manufacturing and working from home that could benefit regions other than the South.

Next, a particularly thorny one this, we might reconsider our views on second homes, making them less attractive. While these can bring welcome cash and visitors to depressed areas, it often means that locals are priced out of their own area; possibly a harsher tax regime would make them less appealing. I don't expect any significant change here though; it probably doesn't help that policy makers are likely to be among the owners of holiday homes.

Finally, as the number of vulnerable people requiring support continues to grow, the issue of housing them needs addressing; surely a scheme whereby councils, in partnership with private enterprise, build and maintain accommodation for the vulnerable, would be better than our current situation. Sadly, any change along these lines requires long-term planning and cross-party commitment, something our leaders don't excel in.

30.

Shopping and Consumerism

Shopping was easy in my early years. Taking the five-minute walk to junior school, I would pass on the opposite side of the road, the Toy Shop, the ABC cinema, the Pet Shop, the Sweet Shop (not only sweets but comics and tobacco products too), and finally, the Book Shop. All obviously had names, but we rarely bothered with that. Thinking back, we were well served for shops; in the High Street there were the likes of Boots, Smiths and Sainsbury's, although they bore little resemblance to stores of the same name today. There were three barber shops, butchers and bakers, a fishmonger, a couple of menswear shops, Dorothy Perkins, Burtons, a fishing tackle shop, a cycle shop, shops selling furniture and carpets and many more. With the exception of the occasional present or luxury item, most things were available just a short walk from home.

One common feature of shopping, introduced in 1958, was Green Shield stamps, a concept that, like so many, had been imported from America. Customers paying for goods would receive a number of stamps to be stuck in books and later redeemed in shops or through the gift catalogue. But in time, customers showed a preference for lower prices and interest in the scheme waned, until it was finally withdrawn in 1991. The catalogue remained however, although cash only, and was rebranded as Argos.

On a similar line, I remember gift certificates given with Kensitas cigarettes. An old lady, Mrs. Chapman, lived on her own over the road from us and would often ask Mum if one of her boys could pop down to the Sweet Shop to buy her some cigarettes. One or other of us would do the honours; I didn't mind, it was a bit of an adventure. I would do this on my own from the age of about four or five, imagine that today.

Anyway, the packets each included a printed certificate, points again, for redemption against goods. We were unaware of this until one day when Mrs. Chapman presented us with a large bag full of them, to show her appreciation for the help we had provided her. There is no irony intended in those last words as, at that time, the health risks associated with smoking were virtually unheard of. However, I recently saw a few pictures of these gift certificates on the Internet, and they did bear a health warning that I think is a further sign of the times:

> "ADVICE BY H.M. GOVERNMENT
> If you do smoke cigarettes
> Leave a long stub.
> Remove from mouth between puffs.
> Inhale less. Take fewer puffs."

Perhaps not quite as effective as "Smoking Kills"?

Mrs. Chapman was a heavy smoker and had been collecting for years, and it was like receiving a huge bag of money. We sorted and counted the certificates before making piles wrapped in rubber bands, and a few days later, made a bus trip to the Kensitas gift shop in London, possibly Kensington. The place was like an Aladdin's Cave, a large shop full of glass display cases containing all sorts of wonderful gear. We all had our share of certificates and chose whatever we wanted. I have no memory of what we got, but the experience obviously impressed me.

The beginning of the end for the High Street came in the mid-60s with the arrival of our first Supermarket, Safeway. This was greeted by excitement for some, but others warned that local businesses would be forced to close as they lost out to price-cutting stores. Other supermarkets have followed, and the number of independent shops has radically declined.

Without doubt, consumerism was not a factor in my early life. In the fifties the war still had to be paid for, and a shortage of resources such as timber, metal and bricks meant priority was given to the essentials. Houses were built using as little material as possible, and only utility furniture was available unless you were rich. The lack of things to buy was only matched by the shortage of money people had to spend.

The swinging 60s brought a little respite, but economic gloom continued through the 70s. In comparison to modern society, we had few possessions. Thinking back to my more expensive assets I can remember: a secondhand racing bike, a secondhand Ilford Sportsman 35mm camera and a secondhand acoustic guitar.

But things picked up in the 80s, a time of economic boom, yuppies, the idea that greed is good, and you can have anything you want. Consumerism had truly arrived. And I can't think of one good thing to say about it. While there are billions in the world struggling to feed themselves, far too many people now consider that the most important thing in life is to upgrade their iPhone, Xbox or trendy trainers to the latest model, despite there being nothing wrong with the one they have.

No thought is given to the environmental damage caused in satisfying their cravings, let alone the economic and psychological pressures they put themselves under. And for what? Producing and transporting tons of unnecessary stuff has a horrendous effect on the global environment as we gobble up finite resources and unnecessarily generate mountains of rubbish, much of which is then re-exported to poorer countries so as not to pollute our own, which in itself is surely wrong. Consumerism has led to globalisation to the extent that you can't get away from the likes of Starbucks and McDonalds anywhere in the world; and in some cases, companies are more powerful than governments. It's depressing, and I don't want to talk about it anymore.

After supermarkets came the out-of-town retail parks and shopping malls applying more pressure on the High Street. Then the final blow as Internet shopping has really taken off, particularly during the past months when it has proved to be a real lifesaver in Covid times.

I remember the High Streets of my youth as great places, the heart of any community. Shopping was a social event as you communed with fellow shoppers and were made to feel wanted by the retailers. I'd love to see a revival, but must accept my share of the blame for their decline as I, too, now regularly shop in supermarkets and on the Internet. You reap what you sow. Kids will wonder what all the fuss is about anyway; without stepping outside, they can buy just about anything they want from anywhere in the world, with the chance of bargain prices to boot. What's not to like?

So, I suppose that the answer to the question "which was better?" once again depends on where you are coming from. Personally, I think the whole experience of shopping in the old days was better by far; but modern kids would bemoan the lack of choice, limited opening hours and the need to venture out in all weathers to complete their purchases. A draw once again, I think.

31.

Language and Its Use Thereof

"It's enough to give your arse the earache!" This has to be one of my favourite phrases, but perhaps I should explain. Dad regularly spoke these words and, as with other phrases he'd use, they are, well, nonsense; yet when he used them it was immediately obvious how he was feeling: annoyed, frustrated, angry or fed up. I also have great fondness for a marvellously evocative four-letter word beginning in 's' and ending in 't'. In the old days use of such language would have been considered truly offensive, yet today it can regularly be heard on TV, causing hardly a raised eyebrow; more to the point, the way the word is used leaves the listener with no doubt as to the speaker's feelings. Language is not an end in itself but serves a purpose, to communicate. When referring to 'bad language' people usually mean words that are offensive, but in my view bad language is that which is ambiguous and open to interpretation, while good language leaves the listener fully informed of the speaker's message.

Both the variety and usage of language in the UK has changed in my lifetime. I was born in a time when people generally didn't stray too far from where they were born, meaning they tended to be surrounded by folk of a similar background using the same language, dialect and phrases. If asked, we would all probably have said that we spoke 'normal' English, and of course with no accent, both claims that would have been mocked by people from just about anywhere more than fifty miles away. I recently read an article suggesting there are 14 different indigenous languages used across the UK, including Cornish, in which some 500 people are fluent.

At school we were taught how both to speak and write English 'correctly'. Knowing the difference between, and how to use, nouns, adverbs, adjectives and the like, when to use capitals and punctuation. All pretty tedious but we stuck to it, we had no choice, although I seem to remember reaching my limit trying to understand gerunds. We were regularly told never to start a sentence with 'and', 'but' or 'so', rules that you may well have noticed I tend to treat rather as guidelines. And of course, spelling correctly was hammered into us from an early age; I can still remember the shame of losing a junior school spelling competition when I forgot the 'd' in handkerchief.

Language is a huge and complex thing and over the years the lessons seem never to have stopped. Many years ago, a colleague of mine mildly rebuked me when I talked about the alternatives we had for a computer system we were working on. "There cannot be a number of alternatives," she told me, "the word comes from the Latin alternatus meaning one or the other of two. You can have many options but there is only one alternative." To be honest this was not the usual type of conversation we had at work, but the lady was ex-BBC after all.

I had never really taken this kind of stuff seriously at school, but that particular nugget has stayed with me ever since and I can't keep my mouth shut when people talk of alternatives. Similarly, the misuse of other words (it's 'myriad', not 'myriad of'), poor spelling, grammar or punctuation seems to raise a flag in my brain. I was going to use the word 'bugbear' in that last sentence but felt that, in the circumstances, I should check its meaning first. Lucky I did, as 'something that causes terror, especially needless terror' might have been slight overkill. Honest, I'm not a pedant.

"The United States and Great Britain are two countries separated by a common language." This quote, generally attributed to George Bernard Shaw, identifies one of my gripes with modern English. With spellchecking software generally favouring the other side, I fear the war has been lost with regards a lot of our spelling, although I have tried to stick to British spellings throughout; there is currently a red line under the word 'favouring' as Microsoft order me to remove the 'u', but I will resist and fight on. The quote probably refers less to spelling and more to the use of words; why invent new ones unnecessarily, like 'faucet' instead of 'tap' or 'trunk' instead of 'boot'?

But when it comes to pronunciation, I have to admit that we do have our own idiosyncrasies; I mean where's the 'f' in lieutenant (reminds me of an old joke), or why the differences in pronunciation for bough, bought, dough and rough? But where the Americans really get up my nose is when they completely scramble 'our' words. When did it become acceptable to mangle our language using nouns as verbs? Use of words tends not to be the greatest concern among techies, but it did grate when people at work stopped building systems and instead 'architected' them.

But we are quite capable of scrambling our own language, thank you very much. People whose aim is to give the impression that they are far smarter than average, or who wish to ensure that their words are not fully understood, possibly because they are trying to mislead or, Heaven forbid, because they actually have nothing meaningful to say, often fall back on a proliferation of acronyms and jargon. Business leaders and politicians are particularly adept at this although you don't have to look beyond your local pub to find a few lesser mortals skilled in the art.

Since my childhood, the number of people living in the UK, but for whom English is not their first language, has increased considerably. One article I read suggested a million people in England and Wales speak little or no English, while over 300 different languages are spoken in London alone. This in itself presents a huge challenge. At uni in Wales, I became aware for the first time of the need to produce bilingual signage and the challenges and costs involved, yet this is nothing compared to those faced by modern day companies and institutions who, for both regulatory and commercial reasons, need to produce much of their documentation in countless languages.

The English language is continually evolving. A few years ago, if you had talked of googling for a meme, you would have got rather strange looks; and I love it when a wonderful word like omnishambles comes along. In recent years we have developed a whole pandemic lexicon, 'lockdown' and 'bubble' being words that will never be the same again. But words also go out of use. A Collins English Dictionary team that tracks public usage of words in the media, recently came to the conclusion that 40% of people under 30 are unlikely to be familiar with a number of words commonly used by Oldies; words like cad, bonk, sozzled, betrothed, nincompoop, wally, bounder and swot.

Change is good if it helps further understanding, but it is not without risks. Texting has generated a whole new language, a subset of English pared down to the minimum number of keystrokes, which is often ingenious and can be

301

amusing. In itself this is great, but as people communicate more by text, they tend to forget the longhand version. "What's wrong with that?" you ask, "old fogeys just can't stand progress". Well, what's wrong is that you still need to communicate with people who may not be so tuned in. Applying for a job still generally starts with a written application giving the potential employer a first impression of the applicant, and the process is likely to go no further if the impression is of someone unable to communicate. Unfair perhaps, but life's like that.

In recent years there has been a worrying trend to ban the use of words that some might find offensive. Many of these words are only offensive when used in a particular context, and banning their use outright is draconian and offensive in itself. Personally, I consider the whole thing to be a load of cobblers, a phrase which presumably risks causing offence to workers in the shoe industry.

So, our use of language has changed considerably in my lifetime. I have no problem with change, but if it happens too fast people can't keep up. It seems to me that in my day, the chance of a random group of people all leaving a conversation with the same understanding as to what had actually been said was probably greater than it is today. If that is a measure of successful use of language, things were probably better back then. So, with no further ado, let the dog see the rabbit, eyes down for a stuffed mouse and on to the next chapter.

32.

On Tying the Knot

When it comes to marriage, I suppose things were different in 1955. My parents had married four years earlier, both in their early twenties. They often talked of the day; church service, reception at the local pub and a short honeymoon on the south coast with barely enough money for a bus ride. It was a time of austerity, but they didn't care, they were happy and were still happy at their Golden Anniversary in 2001. This was a time when marriage was supposed to be for life and divorce was frowned upon as bringing shame to the family. If they managed to live long enough, many of their family and friends celebrated Golden anniversaries too.

There was a downside, of course, in that people in unhappy or abusive marriages had little chance of escape, but things were made much easier with the introduction of the Divorce Reform Act 1969, and then the Family Proceedings Act 1984, making it possible to apply for a divorce after only one year of marriage. Marriage was no longer a lifetime commitment but something you could try and then cancel if you didn't like it.

I was thirty when I decided it was time to take the plunge, quite old compared to my folks, but relatively young for today, it seems. The decision wasn't taken lightly, my view being that there was little point in bothering unless the intention was to stick together for life. Up till then I had pretty much done what I wanted when I wanted, so was I ready to give up that freedom? The answer was a resounding "Yes!".

Little Brother had led the way a few years earlier and Big Brother, a confirmed bachelor at that point, felt I was being hasty and had let him down, leaving him 'exposed' in his unmarried state. Prince Charles had been forty when he married Diana, and Big Brother's view was "if 40 is good enough for Prince Charles it's good enough for me", although he eventually managed to hang on a couple of years longer before he too succumbed.

Now, I must admit to never having been one for the grand romantic gesture, so the proposal wasn't a hugely impressive event. My preference is for understatement, and as a result I never actually proposed in the classic sense of the word. I had a plan though; I would gaze into my darling's eyes and say something along the lines of "why don't we take a trip to Hatton Garden to look at rings", at which point she would first look a little puzzled before the implication of my words sunk in, her eyes would light up and she would tearfully throw her arms round my neck in delight. Unfortunately, that's not quite how it went though, and to this day I'm known to my kids as the bloke whose proposal went "I suppose we better get a ring then".

Having made the decision, there was no point in delaying; it would be a registry do and we knew where we wanted the reception, so it was just a case of finding an available date. The 'proposal' was in April, and we were offered August Bank Holiday Saturday, four months later, as there had been a recent cancellation. Perfect, a long weekend for anyone who wanted to party. Let the preparations begin. Of course, with such a short engagement there were many who thought wife-to-be must be pregnant; she wasn't, shame on them.

Wife-to-be had in mind the type of dress she wanted and, going against tradition, the pair of us went out together to find it. We searched the West End in vain before returning home to her flat in Snaresbrook. Not for the last time in our lives, Fate took a hand and, as we traipsed home rather dejectedly from the tube station, there in the window of a small shop just yards from the flat, was The Dress. White, off-the shoulder, knee length with a lacy finish to it. It was perfect and looked truly wonderful on the day.

We booked the honeymoon through a local travel agent whose specialty was the Greek islands; that's the way we did things back then, no Internet. Two weeks in the tiny, picturesque, unspoilt Greek island of Paxos.

By modern standards the stag do was a very tame affair, beers with a small number of friends at my local. Two days later, on a hot sunny August Saturday, the ceremony took place in the registry office, after which we all repaired to a nearby hotel for the festivities, a sit-down lunch with the family and an evening disco for our friends. It was a wonderful day.

Best man was my car-owning friend from swimming club days and, as so many grooms have done before and after me, I sat cringing while he made his speech, expecting any number of lies or exaggerations at my expense. I needn't have worried as he said nothing but nice things, truly the Best Man. With good company, not bad food and an adequate supply of drink, I sat through lunch between my new wife and my Mum, at peace with the world. There followed a stroll in the hotel grounds and more drinks before moving on to the disco.

On Tying the Knot

Not exactly the epitome of romance, but my theme tune for the day is 'Hands Up' by Ottowan. We had been determined not to do the traditional thing and head off on honeymoon leaving the party behind, after all this was the largest gathering of family and friends that we were ever likely to have, and we wanted to stay and enjoy it; and enjoy it we did. Friends who just didn't 'do' dancing happily moved around the floor, some gracefully some not so, and this tune characterises the joyfulness of the occasion and memories we will never forget; in particular the performance, brought on by this song, of a hitherto non-dancing Irish friend. And the Marine demonstrated a rather dapper turn of foot too.

The evening finally came to an end, and people were leaving when the manager asked where the best man was, as he was needed to organise the removal of our presents to a secure room. Some chance. We discovered later that he was out cold in his car, so Wifey and I found ourselves lugging all the stuff around before finally heading to bed.

Mum and Dad hosted a gathering on Sunday for family plus, of course, a few others. We left late afternoon to pack for our honeymoon and then went to the pub across from my flat for a quiet meal.

Next morning, the best man turned up punctually to drive us to the airport. After a flight to Corfu and a long ferry ride stopping at various islands, we finally arrived at our destination. We had an apartment with a boat thrown in, not quite as extravagant as it sounds, it was a rowing boat with a tiny outboard engine, but it was great for exploring the coast. Affectionately known to us as the 'pop-pop boat', it's limitations became clear when, unaware of an imminent blow, we set off round the coast only to find ourselves in a rather choppy sea, too rough for us. We beached the boat and walked home, totally oblivious to the fact that, on realising we had not returned, the locals were looking for us. But all ended amicably.

Considering myself a bit of a photographer, I was determined to have a good honeymoon album. Those were the days before digital photography; no multiple exposures and discard the rubbish, each picture cost money, so you had to be a little frugal. I had a couple of rolls of film and planned a limited number of pictures, not just snaps of course, but 'real' photos; moody portraits, glorious sunsets, artistic landscapes the lot. I finished the film already in the camera with half a dozen photos of Greek fishing boats and Wifey paddling, before installing a new film for the real stuff. It was a 35mm camera with a quite bulky telephoto lens, and I lugged it around, trying painstakingly to keep it out of the sand, only uncovering it for the occasional masterpiece. It was on our last day that I discovered that I hadn't actually loaded the film correctly and had, in fact, taken no pictures. Nil. Zilch. To my kids' amusement, I am now not only the man who didn't propose, but also the man too incompetent to take honeymoon photos.

But the honeymoon had to end, and in no time at all we were being picked up at Gatwick by the best man. "Thank God you're back", he said, "perhaps now we can finally stop toasting the bloody bride and groom every five minutes!" It's nice to be missed. Real life as a married couple was about to begin. And 37 years later it continues, frighteningly only thirteen years to go before we too can celebrate our Golden. Crikey, suddenly I hear Sandy Denny singing "who knows where the time goes?".

So, what about marriage today? Since 1955, the number of people choosing to marry has decreased significantly. According to the IOS, some 358,000 couples married in 1955, rising to a peak of 426,000 in 1972 before dropping to around 236,000 today; this in a period when the population rose by some 15 million. There has also been a significant decrease in the percentage of church weddings, and it was in 2014 that laws allowing same sex weddings came into force. In 2017, the average age for marriage in opposite-sex couples, was 38.0 for men and 35.7 for women. While the number of marriages may have come down, the price certainly has not. One website suggested an average cost of £31,974 for weddings in 2019 and that's without the cost of hen/stag parties that seem to last longer and be held further afield in places like Vegas, Mexico and Thailand. Things have definitely changed.

When I was younger, I noticed the tendency for married couples to preach about the wonders of matrimony and to urge their single friends to take the leap, saying how great life was. I was always a tiny bit sceptical at the time that, just maybe, they wanted others to get hitched to endorse their choice and stop having fun. Today, excepting the impact of religious or cultural background, the social stigma of remaining single or 'living in sin' has largely gone, and the need to get married is far less pressing. This, together with the potential cost of the whole process can create a powerful case for not tying the knot. Things have definitely changed, but I don't think this is really a subject where I consider the situation to be better or worse than in my day, just different, so time to move on.

33.

Great British Humour

1941, dark times indeed. The military might of the Third Reich had swept through Europe, and the British now stood alone with only the English Channel keeping the marauding hordes at bay. With invasion expected at any time, there was no option other than to release the secret weapon, satire.

In later years, Dad would occasionally quote catchphrases from the BBC radio series 'It's That Man Again', a morale-boosting satirical take on issues that concerned the population under siege, apparently compulsory listening for much of the population. The character of incompetent German spy Funf, "the enemy agent with the feet of sauerkraut", is credited with ridiculing German propaganda broadcasts to the extent that, apparently, they became more a source of fun than of fear, as catchphrases like "This is Funf speaking" were commonplace up and down the country.

Not only were the Nazis targeted, but also the competence of government agencies as they implemented seemingly petty war-time regulations; one character being the Minister for Aggravation at the Office of Twerps. This aspect was quietly dropped as the war continued, replaced by other targets including the Squire of Much Fiddling, and for a while the setting for the show was a rundown seaside resort called Foaming at the Mouth.

"So what?" I hear you say. Well, to me this illustrates our very unique British sense of humour, a characteristic that I fear we might be losing. The son of the ex-pat who befriended us in Rio ran a record shop, and he was particularly proud of their marketing approach. I still have a keyring from the shop, a logo of a man standing in the sea dressed in shorts and shirt with braces and a knotted handkerchief on his head. This was inspired by the Monty Python sketch where a Gumby stands in water while saying he would put a tax on all people who stand in water. On the back of the keyring, in Portuguese, are words that roughly translate to: "Foreigners. The English. Drink warm beer, poor lovers, eat horrible food, talk about the weather, invented football yet play it badly. But they really know music." This apparently caused great confusion among the macho Brazilians who couldn't understand why anyone would take the mick out of themselves, and they are not alone in misunderstanding British humour.

Someone once coined the term 'The Cynic Factory' for my senior school. If they meant that nobody was immune from being mocked, then I guess they were right. One small incident or mistake could leave you with a nickname that stuck with you throughout your stay; guys in our year earned sobriquets they would probably have preferred to be without, like 'Bubbles', 'Blossom' and 'Dan D Ruff'. Years later, in the bar after an old boys' football match, mistakes on the pitch would be the source of mockery as a player might be invited to 'take the chair' to explain why, exactly, he decided not to tackle that nice opposition player, instead gifting him with a goal.

An Irish university friend once complained about the number and tone of Irish jokes doing the rounds and said that I wouldn't like it if he told English jokes, of which he knew many. So I asked him to tell me one. This was the 70s, a time of high inflation and crippling industrial action causing us to be labeled the sick man of Europe, and the joke went like this: "How do you get 100 Englishmen in a Mini?" answer "Send a shop steward in first and the other 99 will follow." I genuinely thought this hilarious and asked for another, but he never did tell me any more. I'm not sure whether he thought I was just being patronising, or whether I'd somehow deflated his indignation.

When Son was about 15 or 16, he had friends round and they wanted to watch a film, so I recommended 'Blazing Saddles'. Well, that wasn't such a good idea. They were shocked by it and left convinced that their mate's dad was a closet racist. Can you believe it? The Jewish director, Mel Brooks, had built his reputation producing works that mocked racists and the like; the hero was a black sheriff who outsmarted the dumb racist rednecks at every turn, and the scene where he's wearing Ku Klux Klan robes and hood while standing in line with a bunch of reprobates waiting to sign up with the KK is a killer. Yet the boys apparently couldn't see the satire and took the whole thing at face value. I can't help feeling that something has gone horribly wrong.

Dad was a bit of an amateur ornithologist, a trait he passed down in varying degrees to Mum and his boys. Not twitcher level, he just took pleasure from watching and learning about our wonderful birdlife. He particularly liked to visit Norfolk or Suffolk in the spring as millions of migratory birds return to British shores. Occasionally, one or other of us would accompany him. Some seven years ago, both brothers and I went with him to Blakeney Point in Norfolk, a particularly lovely coastal site with a number of RSPB reserves nearby. Dad was getting old, and we all knew he was unlikely to have the energy for many more such outings. We had a great time, but I particularly remember how, when we came back, a friend in the pub asked him whether it had been a good trip. "I don't think I've ever laughed so much in my life" he said, before adding "although most of the laughs were at my expense", and then he roared with laughter again. True, we had laughed at some of the things he said or did, but we all took our turn when it came to being mocked, at times for things we hadn't actually said or done, but as Big Brother would say, "never let the truth get in the way of a good story".

What I'm getting at here is that I see satire, mocking banter and the ability to laugh at oneself as a strength of the British character going back years. Of course, we are not unique. Many American programmes like 'The Simpsons' happily take pots at numerous aspects of American life. But forces are afoot to curtail such evil and malignant attacks. In days gone by television comedy was often "anarchic", revelling in the ability to shock. Nobody was immune as programmes like 'Spitting Image' lampooned the high and mighty; even the Queen and royal family were regular targets. I personally found it a bit depressing when programmes depended solely on swearing and toilet humour to raise a laugh, but people find different things funny, and I could always just turn off the TV. Yet today comedians run the risk of being fired, their career ruined, if they produce material considered 'offensive'. Things have gone too far, and I think that, although they might not think so, or even understand why I say it, this is one area where the younger generation definitely has it worse than we did.

34.

In Praise of the Much-Maligned Public House

Public houses, taverns, inns, all have played a big part in British history. To some people they are places of comfort, succour and companionship, places where you feel wanted and people are happy to hear your views on all aspects of life; to others they are but dens of iniquity where unsavoury characters gather to plan evil deeds, and where the innocent are led astray.

Dad liked pubs. In my lifetime, and as landlords came and went, he generally moved between four main locals, two Courage establishments, one Youngs and one Ind Coope, although he was not averse to visiting others when duty called. Initially pubs were his domain, but in later years Mum would join him, and together they developed a fairly active social life. Big Brother likes pubs and has dedicated much time, effort and money in a personal and selfless crusade to support local hostelries in their attempt to stay afloat in challenging economic times. Little Brother likes pubs, but is showing worrying signs of sophistication now, and probably prefers a good bottle of wine over a foaming pint of ale. And it will come as no surprise that I like pubs too. Son likes pubs. When recently searching with his partner for their first home, a major priority was that it be within walking distance of at least one good pub. While happy to visit pubs on occasion, neither Wifey nor Daughter share the same love for them, so I guess it must be something to do with the male genes of the family. It's in my blood.

I visited my first local at the tender age of 13. My friends were all older than me, and I was large for my age, so we thought we had the landlord fooled, but obviously we were kidding ourselves; as long as we behaved, he was just happy to take our money, lack of which would usually have restricted us to a single pint anyway. I graduated from there to two other pubs, the common denominator being that these were establishments never frequented by Dad. Until, that is, one evening when, as we were playing darts in a walled off area, one of my mates told me my old man was in the bar next door. I kept my head down waiting for him to leave but, unbeknown to me, my car-owning friend sent a pint round for 'the man with the grey hair' who, needless to say, came round to identify his anonymous benefactor. Oops. He was alright about it though, just as long as I didn't start drinking scotch or smoking, he said; oops again.

When I first started visiting pubs, opening hours were limited; Sundays between noon and 2 pm for lunch and then 7pm to 10.30pm in the evening; opening times for the rest of the week were 11am to 2pm then 5pm until 10:30pm, extended to 11pm on Fridays and Saturdays. In my Welsh university town, pubs weren't allowed to open on Sundays, but this was a joke as alcohol was available at the Students Union bars and various 'clubs' with very cheap one-day membership. It was no wonder that overseas visitors seeking refreshment got confused.

For a number of years our swimming group adopted a Watney's house as its local, almost a second home. Ale drinkers didn't hold Watney's beer in high esteem, but we were still lager drinkers then so that was of no concern. I drank Skol costing 3 shillings and 4 pence a pint until decimalisation arrived on February 14th, 1971, at which point the price changed to 17p, less than £2.50p in today's money.

The landlord and his wife were naturals, providing the perfect blend of conviviality and authority, making you welcome while always aware of who was in charge. Due to the pub's proximity to the local courts, the clientele was a strange mix, and lunchtime on court days would find the pub bustling, with defendants drinking in the public bar, the local police taking a pint in the saloon bar and the judiciary eating in the lounge bar. I assume that it was this connection that led to the local constabulary's rather relaxed response to the landlord's interpretation of licensing hours. It was often the case that, well after closing time, a policeman on his beat would drop in for a coffee that he would drink while determinedly failing to notice a group of us gathered around the fruit machine.

While I concur that graffiti can often be pretty unpleasant, both in content and visual effect, I have to admit to being a fan of good graffiti, and one of my all-time favourites, reflecting the eclectic mix of clientele at the pub, was in the Gents of the saloon bar: "Why go to Burtons when the CID will stitch you up for free?"

By this time Dad's local was a Youngs hostelry, frequented by yet another group of colourful characters. One, an ex-RAF pilot with a moustache and accent to match, was always immaculately dressed, with a tie worn in a way I have never seen before or since. He would tie it as usual except for the last move when, instead of tucking the long bit into the knot he left it outside hanging over the knot. He could easily polish off a bottle of scotch in a session before walking out apparently sober, well almost. We had numerous other regular haunts in the area and were generally served by a variety of, what we considered to be, good pubs.

As a particularly dedicated supporter of licensed establishments, Big Brother could get quite animated on the subject of children in pubs. He was perfectly happy for them to be sitting outside with a bag of crisps and a bottle of Coke, as had on occasion happened with us, but a pub was no place for children. This might not always have made him universally popular, but he stuck to his guns and wouldn't back down. Until, that is, twenty-three years ago when he arrived at his favourite local, baby in hand, to ask rather sheepishly if he could possibly bring her in. Needless to say, he hasn't been quite so vociferous on the subject since.

Anyone visiting a pub will realise pretty quickly that they are places of much wisdom, full of people packed with knowledge about nearly any subject in the world; and they are always happy to share their knowledge. This leads me to a great lesson from US sitcom 'Cheers' on the positive effects of drinking. Know-it-all postman, Cliff Clavin, explains The Buffalo Theory, describing how the strength and speed of the buffalo herd increases as predators pick off the slowest and weakest members. He goes on to explain similarities with the brain. We know that alcohol destroys brain cells, but Cliff tells how, here too, it is the weakest that are targeted first, thus leaving the brain stronger, which is the reason why we do some of our best thinking after a couple of pints, even if we can't necessarily recall those great thoughts later. Makes sense to me.

Working in the City of London, I was spoilt for good old-fashioned pubs, many dating back centuries. We regularly visited Ye Olde Cheshire Cheese in Fleet Street. Rebuilt shortly after the Great Fire of London it has been

316

frequented by writers like Charles Dickens, Alfred Tennyson, Sir Arthur Conan Doyle and Mark Twain. Another rebuilt after the Great Fire is The Old Doctor Butler's Head, named after a self-proclaimed specialist in nervous disorders whose treatments included holding consultations on London Bridge, during which the client would be dropped through a trapdoor into the torrent below.

The Seven Stars is one of the few City buildings to have escaped the Great Fire. Ye Olde Mitre is famous for having a cherry tree around which Queen Elizabeth the First is said to have danced with Sir Christopher Hatton, although English Heritage records suggest it wasn't actually built until 1773. Then there is The Blackfriar, The Old Bell Tavern, The George in Borough High Street and the Lamb & Flag in Covent Garden. And there are many, many more that are well worth a visit. These establishments also make great film locations. The Blackfriar appears in 'Men in Black' as a secret entrance to the MIB London headquarters, and The Market Porter was turned into the 'Third Hand Book Emporium' in the film 'Harry Potter and the Prisoner of Azkaban'.

Before we married, on many a Friday evening my wife-to-be would drive over to join me, together with a few workmates, in the Lyceum on the Strand. Waiting for her arrival, I'd buy a copy of the Evening Standard and peruse the adverts for films and theatre, while planning the evening's entertainment; somehow we managed without the Internet. Perhaps we would dine out, or maybe take in a cinema or theatre; the world was our lobster.

More often than not though, one beer would follow another, banter would abound, I'd get comfortable and any chance of us moving on would go out the window. The

317

upshot being that we might take in a late meal before she drove us home. What a lovely lady. The chances of us getting away early were even longer in the winter months, when I needed to stay near a phone in order to keep in touch with the guys responsible for football team selection. I was captain of the 4th XI and if anyone from the higher teams dropped out I would lose a player and had to decide who came up from the 5ths. If there were a number of dropouts, this process could take half the evening, and with no mobile phones the whole exercise was challenging.

After we married, we moved into a more rural area of Surrey with a host of good pubs. A couple are just about within walking distance, but most are a short drive away; my attendance at such institutions has become more infrequent over the years but I still force the occasional pint down.

As tastes in society have changed the popularity of pubs has declined. Apparently, between 1990 and 2020 the number of pubs in the UK fell from around 64,000 to some 40,000. In 1990 there were 111 pubs per 100,000 people in the UK, falling to 73 pubs for every 100,000 in 2017. To address changing tastes, and in order to survive, pubs have adopted various strategies with many focusing more on food and offering café-style services. More imaginatively, I have heard of pubs offering a variety of services such as lessons for Oldies in how to use the Internet, cookery courses and the like, shop and library facilities; basically, anything to attract customers through the door. Good luck to them all I say.

But all is not lost as apparently, for the first time in decades, 2019 saw an increase in the number of pubs in the UK, driven at least in part by the surge in craft beers and microbreweries. Beer seems to be becoming trendy, if more expensive, and perhaps announcements on the death of 'the pub' may yet be premature, although any good news is offset by the impact of Covid and the current cost of living crisis on the hospitality industry. Only time will tell how many pubs will survive.

Moving on to the question of whether things were better then than they are today. For people who genuinely like old-style pubs, things are definitely worse; there are still some great ones, but the number is dwindling. On the other hand, if your preference is for large screens showing various sporting events, if it's for live entertainment or loud music, if you want pubs that specialise in gin or if you are a fan of gastro pubs, then there is a much larger choice of venues, most types of which didn't even exist when I was young. Perhaps, once again, another draw I feel.

35.

Parenting, Perhaps the Only Job for Life?

Back in the days when they lived in caves, Mum and Dad decided they wanted to have kids, so they did. Nowadays it's not so easy; you have to master 'Parenting', which has managed to turn an instinctive natural process into something more formal and scientific, and a whole industry has evolved with websites, social networks, books and countless experts giving advice on how it should be done properly. I suppose this different approach reflects the way society has changed; we all need help sometimes, but many people no longer live in communities where their neighbours are happy to chat and share experiences about just about everything, and families, who you could always turn to for advice and support, now tend to live further apart than when I was a lad. So the availability of advice from 'experts' can be a blessing, although it can also lead to unnecessary stress, expense and confidence-sapping worries over whether the newbies are 'doing it right'.

I can't help thinking though, that treating child rearing like a school subject seems to suggest a path to producing 'better' children, a bit like a cake recipe or a car repair manual. You can't make the perfect child by following an instruction manual; they're all different. Kids develop at different rates, both physically and mentally, they may show a natural talent in any number of areas, or they may show none, ability may be latent, coming to notice later in life, perhaps never. But they start as a blank canvas, and the approach taken by parents, particularly in their early years, largely dictates the type of individuals they grow into. They benefit more from a parent's time, care, love and attention than any amount of pushing. I have to smile when I hear so many parents speaking proudly of how advanced their child is; it seems we are overrun with geniuses. Why can't people just be happy that their child is 'normal'?

Anyway, I admit that I too approached parenthood with some trepidation. Life was going to change but I couldn't really envisage by how much. As so often in life, Wifey took the lead. If she could be so happy with all that pain on the horizon, the least I could do was smile. In all honesty, I was looking forward to the experience. I was thirty-three years old and ready. Maybe.

We didn't know whether we were having a girl or boy and had prepared the nursery in neutral pastel colours with bits of pink and blue. Almost everything came from Mothercare, and there was tons of the stuff; cupboards, cot, changing mat, nightlight, musical mobile, cuddly toys, clothes, nappies, high chair, baby bath and things to clean the baby, food, bottles, sterilising gear, playpen and much more; not to mention the necessities should we ever manage to venture out of the house, like pushchair, travel cot, car seat. The list was endless. Quite a bit came as gifts but the whole exercise would probably have bankrupted us had we not suddenly undergone a dramatic decrease in other outgoings as our social life took a nosedive.

People would ask whether we wanted a boy or girl, and I gave the obligatory answer; "I don't care so long as it's healthy". I was lying of course. Coming from a family of boys I knew what you did with them; a bit of football and tree climbing was all you needed, but what would I do with a girl? What did I know about Barbies and girl stuff? Needless to say, my first was a girl. And I couldn't have been happier. One gurgle and she had me twisted around her tiny finger. And regarding that pain so manfully shared with Wifey? It was a little noisy at the time but within hours she was talking about our next one, so I have to assume that it wasn't that unbearable after all.

We drove home from the hospital uncharacteristically slowly, even for the 2CV, me scouring the road ahead for potential hazards while Wifey sat in the back nursing our priceless cargo. I was terrified I'd do something wrong, but against all the odds we made it home safely. With nobody around to make sure we were doing it right, there followed a series of nerve-wracking unassisted firsts; first home bath, first home feed, first nappy change by Dad, first night at home. When the baby slept, I'd continually get up to check that she was still breathing.

Sleeping patterns took a bit of a bashing and we were soon pale and black-eyed. One night, when Daughter was teething and wouldn't sleep, I took my turn carrying her while singing quietly in an attempt to get her settled. It was winter, about three in the morning and pitch dark outside; I was exhausted and started thinking about the position people can find themselves in. I was in my thirties, employed and financially comfortable, living in my own home, happily married and holding the daughter I loved and had been waiting for. And yet I was still getting frustrated with her crying. So how would a young, unemployed, new dad with few prospects living in a less comfortable environment be feeling in the same situation? Trapped maybe? Angry? Violence against children can never be condoned, but suddenly I could understand how, in some circumstances, it might be triggered. Quite a sobering thought.

On a lighter note, it wasn't long before number two came along. We had planned a second, but he turned up ahead of schedule. At the time this seemed a bit unfair as we were just beginning to get some normality back in our lives, but in retrospect it was for the best for us all; the nappy phase just continued rather than starting again, which might have been a bit painful, and at only 17 months apart, the kids provided each other with good company of a not-too-different age.

But from the perspective of convenience, the actual delivery was a pain. A few days before the baby was due, I was in the New Forest, best man at my globe-trotting university chum's wedding. Wifey felt it better to stay at home, and I was permanently on edge assuming that the call would come at the most inconvenient time. So, primed to drive home at a moment's notice, I delivered my best man's speech stone cold sober, probably the only person present who was. But all passed uneventfully, and it was not until a few days later, while at work, that I got the call, rushed home and we drove to the hospital. Where we waited. And waited. Until finally we were told that, yes, the baby appeared to be on its way, but things had somehow stopped so we should go home. Not for the last time, one of our kids was messing us around. But after a few more days things started rolling again and Son made his way into the world.

We were veterans now, so things came a lot easier than the first time round, although we soon came to realise that 1+1 does not necessarily equal 2 when it comes to the impact a baby can have on life. With one child to care for, Wifey had been able to catch up on sleep when the baby slept, not so easy with two. They approached sleep as a tag team, each ensuring the other was awake before they dozed off. While one slept the other wanted attention. Tiring times indeed. But we got through them, or at least Wifey did as I was out of the house for about twelve hours a day.

Shortly after Son was born, Wifey's family visited for an audience with the new arrival; we still have a short video of the proud occasion. As the tiny, wrinkled bundle of joy is being carefully passed around, Daughter stands to one side in front of one of my loudspeakers; she is keeping a careful eye on things while dancing along to music playing in the background; it's 'Real Gone Kid' by Deacon Blue and that's my soundtrack for this phase. Holding a biscuit while staring into space and rocking from side to side, her moves seem strangely similar to the way I dance now.

We had both agreed that it would be better for one of us to stay at home with the kids, at least for their early years, and I was happy to fill a househusband role. This made economic sense as Wifey was earning more than me, but she announced that she wanted to be at home with her babies, so decision made. At the time, I honestly meant that I would have stayed at home with the kids, but in retrospect I realise that this would probably not have been a wise move for any of us, and as it is, Wifey did a superb job of bringing the children up while I went off to earn a crust.

One outcome of this setup is that, to this day, the kids will always go to her first with their problems, and they seem almost to have a psychic link with her. Once, when Son was away at uni, he phoned, a little worried as it turned out that he'd lost his student ID card that he needed in order to sit an exam that morning. Not a lot we could do

200 miles away, I thought, but Wifey calmed him down and suggested he look in his shoe; and there it was! He was understandably gobsmacked and asked how she knew so she explained, "I just knew."

Nothing can beat the pleasure of watching your kids growing up and developing their own characters. I spent many hours in the cold and wet on the touchline as Son played football or rugby, and I wouldn't have missed it for the world. Daughter took to dancing, and I loved watching her practice and perform, although there was one embarrassing incident during a competition in Epsom. While Wifey was helping with preparations backstage, Son and I were seated out front watching the other competitors, when a young girl in a bright pink leotard came out and immediately started rolling around the stage, some modern artistic dance interpretation presumably. All was going OK until Son said, quite loudly and giggling, something like "what on earth is she doing?" We were surrounded by proud mums, any of whom might have been with the girl, and I had to fight hard to stifle a laugh before telling him to keep quiet and enjoy the performance. This was not the last time that my kids would embarrass me by giving voice to something that I too was thinking.

Our kids have always been strong on fairness; in a good sort of way that is, not the whining "it's not fair!" way. Both gave indications of this at an early age. At nursery one day Wifey was told that Daughter had missed playtime as a punishment for fighting; the teacher explained that during break she had assaulted a boy in the sand pit. Serious bit over, teacher smiled and went on to say that the boy was the biggest bully in the class and got what he deserved. A year or two later, Wifey was embarrassed when, on arriving to pick up Son, his teacher announced loudly in front of the other mums "wherever there's trouble, your boy is in the middle of it". It transpired that he had actually been trying to stop a fight at the time, a fact of which the teacher was totally unaware. There have been many incidents since where this characteristic has shone through and we're proud of them both for standing up for their principles

Birthday parties were always fun. We tended to invite all the classmates, which could be challenging. I will never forget one early party for Son. I think it was his fourth or fifth birthday, and we had a whole gang of children in the local village hall; Wifey was in charge of catering while I handled the entertainment. What could possibly go wrong?

I had a list of party games that would easily fill the time we had. "Who wants to play musical statues?" I asked. Everyone of course. They jumped up excitedly and I started the music, but unfortunately it soon became clear that they had no idea how to play. I explained, but still they didn't get it. So, "who wants to play Simon Says?" Everyone of course. They jumped up excitedly but again it soon became clear that this too was new to them, and they weren't in the frame of mind to learn new things. I was in deep trouble. We worked through my whole list with similar results; no games left and still a long time to food.

I was desperate and tried one last ploy. "Who would like to sing a song?" They all did and jumped up and down excitedly. I chose one and asked the others to sit on the floor and listen. Amazingly, they all sat quietly listening to a rendition of some song or another. At the end I asked if anyone else would like to sing. Same response, so I chose another performer who sang exactly the same song, but nobody seemed to care. That song was then sung over and over again by a variety of kids, but they seemed happy enough. Food followed, parents turned up for their kids, party bags were distributed before we waved off the guests and turned, exhausted, to clearing up. An experience never to be forgotten.

Both our kids like music and have worked their way through a variety of instruments. I love listening to them, but early days on the violin, drums, piano and guitar tended not to be terribly melodic, and things could grate at times. I taught both of them guitar basics, but they soon mastered my repertoire; other than that, and an early couple of lessons, they're pretty much self-taught. As his drums were less portable than a guitar, Son found it easier to invite his friends to our house for 'band practice', something the other parents were presumably quite happy about. Things would get pretty noisy, but they were good times.

I think, on the whole, that my kids were both happy at school. Wifey ran most of the school things; taking them in, picking them up, making sure they had the right books and PE kit, following up with teachers about homework, school trips and the like. I did very little other than attend parent meetings and sporting events when I could get time off work. Occasionally there were issues requiring liaison with the school and Wifey handled most of these too. Although I did get involved when Son had problems at junior school with a group of kids who kept taking his basketball away. Wifey had talked to the teachers about it, but they hadn't taken much notice and Son was pretty miserable. This had gone on long enough, so I gave him some advice along the lines of: "Don't tell your Mum, but as a last resort, if someone won't give your ball back, whack him. You will get in trouble with the teachers but don't lie, tell them exactly what you did and why." It happened again and he responded as suggested. He did get into trouble, but the kids were far friendlier from then on. Doubtless today I would be reprimanded for 'bad parenting' and encouraging unacceptable behaviour, but sometimes the old-fashioned ways work.

One of the perks of being a parent is being allowed, expected even, occasionally to embarrass the kids. One such occasion occurred when Daughter was about ten; Wifey was ill and so I took over the school run for a while. One day Daughter announced that she didn't want to go in and just stood rooted to the spot at the school gate. After a protracted and unsuccessful attempt at negotiating I changed tack, and it went something like this. "If you don't go in, I'm going to start dancing." "Don't be so silly, I don't want to go in." "Duh de dum dum, duh de dum dum…." "What are you doing?" "Getting the music started for my dance. Duh de dum dum, duh de dum dum.." My feet started moving to the beat and began what I thought was a pretty cool dance move. Other kids and parents were starting to take notice. "Stop that, you're embarrassing me." "Duh de dum dum, duh de dum dum….". It wasn't long before she huffed and went into school. Result. And to a number of her friends, I would forever be known as the Dancing Dad.

One thing I hadn't expected was the extent to which parenting is a competitive sport. Mix with other parents and you find many who are looking for their child to be first or best at doing something. Tiger parenting is a term I heard a while back regarding people who push their kids to be high achievers, not only in their academic labours but in extra-curricular pastimes, particularly cultural subjects like music and dance, but also sport. The term apparently originated with Chinese-Americans, but it doesn't seem miles away from the methods used by many parents today who will tell you they want their children to be 'winners'. I recall talking to parents on the touchline of a football match. "What point is there", they asked, "in playing sport if you don't win?" "Fun?" I asked, but this seemed a concept they couldn't grasp.

Of course, I don't want my kids to be 'losers', but I have to wonder the extent to which these people are trying to re-live their lives through their children. A while back I was with someone who started talking about his kids when it soon became clear that his son was a bit of a disappointment. After an expensive education the lad had opted not for a 'meaningful' profession as a doctor, lawyer or such like, but instead had chosen a less impressive career path. His dad obviously had problems understanding this, and with a sigh concluded "but at least he does seem very happy". It was my turn to be confused, as happiness is the first thing I want for my kids.

The impact that competitiveness has on the kids is open to interpretation, but it definitely brings out the worst in the parents. I have witnessed many touchline incidents where parents have loudly made their feelings known regarding just about anything that occurs on the pitch. One in particular springs to mind. Son was about nine and we were at a rugby festival in Godalming where a little girl playing for the home team was running rings around the opposition. Suddenly, one of the opposition parents yelled to his son that he was useless and was being beaten by "just a girl". Both his son and the girl were visibly upset, but this oaf obviously saw nothing wrong in his behaviour. As an example of 'good parenting' I think this left a bit to be desired.

Once the parenting thing has got you it doesn't let go. It doesn't matter that you are getting older and slower while your kids are in their prime, blossoming and perfectly capable of looking after themselves, you still worry about them and give advice that isn't necessarily wanted, needed, believed or appreciated. But that goes with the job. Always has done and always will, so no change there. Paul Simon sums up parenting in his song 'That was your Mother', as he recalls how great life was before he became a parent, but ends with how much he loves his son and, like me, wouldn't have missed the experience for the world.

I'm not really in a position to say whether it's better or worse being a parent today compared with the old days. While all the natural things are pretty much unchanged, the social and economic side seem miles apart so I think I'll just call it yet another draw and move on.

36.

The Fourth Estate and Freedom of Speech

In school History lessons, we learnt of the use and impact of propaganda during wartime and periods like the Russian and Chinese revolutions. I naively thought that propaganda had had its day, democratic governments would have no desire to mislead their citizens. Besides, modern-day people were far better educated and had access to much more information than in the past, they would easily see through any lies and no longer be duped. Well, what can I say?

At some point in time, most people like to know what's going on, at least in areas that affect them personally. Regardless of whether their interests are local, national or global they face the same problem; where to find a true account of what is happening. In our technology-enabled world we have access to a veritable tsunami of 'news', yet much of this at best gives a hugely biased version of events, and at worst comprises downright lies.

It was quite a while before I started to take much interest in the news. We were encouraged to follow 'current affairs' at school but I don't think many of us did. If we wanted to find out what was going on, we had a limited number of sources; the papers, local and national; the TV news, broadcast a few times a day on our three TV stations; or the radio, usually BBC. With such limited resources it is certain that we weren't always told the whole truth.

It didn't take long for me to realise the extent to which unbiased reporting is a great rarity. Even a journalist who wants to report the truth can find it a career-limiting move to chase stories that go against the views of their editor or proprietor. By my late teens I was a fan of the TV programme What the Papers Say, launched in 1956 and running for fifty-two years. The format was simple; a guest reviewer, often a newspaper editor, would take a few news stories and provide examples of the way they were reported in different papers. I soon came to realise that journalists didn't need to lie in order to mislead their readers; they just had to be economical with the truth. This remains a common problem today where, for example, the BBC and Channel 4 are regularly accused of portraying liberal-leaning views in a far more sympathetic way than those of anyone with opposing values. Although to be fair to the BBC, they are often accused of bias by just about everyone.

Nowadays we can get news 24-hours-a-day from a plethora of sources both domestic and foreign, plus the veritable flood of views and opinions broadcast over the Internet and presented as 'fact'. I recently read an interesting article summarising a report published by the Oxford Internet Institute concerning the role of social media in influencing online public behaviour. They came to the conclusion that in the last four years "social media manipulation has evolved from a niche concern to a global threat to democracy and human rights". In 2020 they claim to have identified social media manipulation campaigns in 81 countries, up from 70 in 2019, and refer to 'cyber troops' run by governments, the military or political parties in order to manipulate public opinion on social media; they talk of 'Troll armies' deployed to suppress political activism and the freedom of the press. Further, they claim to have evidence of state actors working with private computational propaganda companies in 48 countries in 2020, even after the Cambridge Analytica scandal that revealed how data illegally farmed from Facebook was used in an attempt to influence opinions and meddle in democratic elections.

This whole issue highlights the problems we face today in getting to the truth. While I have no reason to doubt the fundamentals behind the Oxford Internet Institute piece, I have neither the time nor the inclination to check who the authors are, whether they actually exist and the extent to which their report is true. The article featured on theconversation.com, an allegedly independent website that I quite like and often visit, but can I really depend on the veracity of their articles?

And another problem now raises its head. Whether the miscreants are state sponsored, industrial or just morons with nothing better to do, social media platforms definitely provide them with powerful tools to carry out their dirty work, and calls are regularly heard for these networks to police the messages they broadcast. It is generally accepted that any truly democratic society must allow its citizens to speak freely without fear of reprisal. The concept goes back to Ancient Greece, and the underlying principle is encapsulated by the views of Voltaire expressed as "I disapprove of what you say, but I will defend to the death your right to say it." In 1689, freedom of speech for Members in Parliament was incorporated into the England Bill of Rights and still stands; after the French Revolution it was affirmed as an inalienable right in the Declaration of the Rights of Man, and it features in the First Amendment to the United States Constitution. Winston Churchill gave a slightly more nuanced view when he said, "Everyone is in favour of free speech. Hardly a day passes without its being extolled, but some people's idea of it is that they are free to say what they like, but if anyone else says anything back, that is an outrage."

But freedom of speech cannot be an absolute right, even in democracies, and laws have been passed making it illegal, for example, to slander a person's reputation or incite violence. I have no problem with that, but we are seeing more and more restrictions simply because people might not like what they hear or might be offended. This is a slippery slope. In all walks of life people with genuine views to express are unable to do so for fear of instantly being labeled sexist, racist, homophobic, ageist, anti-Semitic; the list seems endless. It is worrying enough that the result of this censorship can badly distort the news we see and hear, but just as worrying is the influence this is having on schools and universities. By definition, these must be places where all views can be freely aired and examined in order to achieve a balanced evaluation, and yet more and more institutions are veering away from topics that students might consider offensive.

A related incident recently made the headlines. As mentioned earlier, in this digital age with many people turning to social media to air their views, there is growing pressure on platform providers to moderate the content distributed across their networks. They find themselves between a rock and a hard place; blamed for failing to act when it transpires their networks have been used to circulate criminal information, but accused of censorship

334

when they take down accounts. In January 2021, Facebook and Twitter both suspended Donald Trump's accounts on their platforms on the basis that some of his posts were false and incendiary. There is a world of difference between closing accounts linked to criminal activity and closing those of users whose views are deemed unacceptable.

Now, I am no great fan of Donald Trump, or of social media for that matter, but I am concerned that we have a situation here, where a commercial organisation is restricting the ability of the President of the United States to get his message out. Surely, regardless of the merits of the message, this state of affairs is questionable? In an age when so many depend on social media to communicate, isn't this denying an individual's freedom of speech? I don't know the answer, but I do believe that, at the very least, any move to restrict freedom of speech must be made on the basis of decisions taken by elected representatives and not be at the whim of a commercial outfit.

Another key facet of western democracy is freedom of the press. Throughout history the rich and powerful have often been able to act with impunity, but a free press can help counter this; one claim commonly made today is that they can 'hold the government's feet to the fire' by, for example, exposing such things as dodgy arms deals with Saudi Arabia; MPs' personal interests in government contracts; abuse of the MPs' expenses system to furnish their own homes; or reporting on ill-conceived mismanaged projects that lead to a huge waste of public money.

This is not a new thing; I remember as a kid hearing, but not understanding, many stories on the TV and radio concerning the aforementioned Profumo affair involving the British Secretary of State for War, model and showgirl Christine Keeler, and a Russian spy. The scandal was pivotal in the eventual downfall of Prime Minister Harold Macmillan and helped the Tories to lose the 1964 general election. But it's not just the politicians who can be targets of the press, they also like to keep us informed of the, occasionally questionable, behaviour of the rich and famous 'elite', sometimes questioning their behaviour, or how they actually came about their wealth and fame.

In recent years, our press have done themselves no favours by infringing on individuals' privacy to an unacceptable degree. The News International phone-hacking scandal revealed the extent to which newspaper reporters would go to get a story; stealing mobile phones, hacking into computers and voicemail accounts on mobile phones and making illegal payments to public officials. Some resorted to breaking and entering, blackmail and entrapment. And these methods weren't restricted to big stories on the rich and powerful; the phones of 'ordinary people', like the victims of the 7/7 London bombing and murdered schoolgirl Milly Dowler were also hacked as a matter of course.

The scandal led to the closure of the News of the World tabloid in 2011 and an eight-month trial costing some £100m. One of those convicted was Andy Coulson, by then David Cameron's official spokesman, who had been editor at the time the offences were committed. In the end the whole thing rather fizzled out; it was believed by many, but never proven, that such practices were common throughout the industry; nobody senior was convicted and Ipso, the Independent Press Standards Office, replaced the Press Complaints Commission, although whether they are any more effective than the PCC remains to be seen.

Freedom of the press has come under more violent attack outside the UK. In January 2015, in response to the publication of cartoons of the Islamic prophet Muhammad which they considered to be blasphemous, two armed Muslim extremist brothers attacked the offices of French satirical newspaper Charlie Hebdo, murdering eleven journalists and security personnel; the death toll reached seventeen as they escaped and were hunted down. Charlie Hebdo had a reputation for satirising everyone, but their main targets were French politicians and subsequent analysis of its front covers over the ten years previous to the attack apparently showed that a little over 1% had any relation to the topic of Islam. On the day of the attack, despite the terrorists still being at large, thousands took to the streets in Paris and other French cities demonstrating solidarity with the journalists through the slogan "Je suis Charlie". This message was quickly taken up around the world, becoming a rallying cry for freedom of expression and freedom of the press.

We must not underestimate the value of good investigative journalism, nor the risks that these journalists take. For three decades, the International Federation of Journalists has been keeping count of the number of journalists murdered for carrying out their job. By 2021, 2,658 had been killed, 42 of them in 2020; at the time these figures were published a further 235 journalists were in prison as a direct result of their work. Such extreme events tend to be most common in unstable countries, or those with dictatorial governments, countries like Russia, China, Mexico, Pakistan, Afghanistan, India, Iraq and Nigeria. But they can also happen nearer home, as was the case with Lyra McKee, a young Irish journalist murdered in Derry in 2019. We must not become complacent and take our journalists for granted.

I realise now that, in my early years at least, most of us probably lived in blissful ignorance of the world outside the UK and were often unaware of what was going on closer to home too. In contrast today, the availability of global 'news' 24/7 can be overpowering, and the task of filtering genuine news from the other stuff is daunting. The golden rule remains, as it was in the old days; try to ascertain the source of any article.

If you are in the conspiracy theory camp, believing the media to be part of an establishment plot to keep us all down, that's your choice. Personally, I believe that, on the whole, the media are generally trying to keep us informed, even if the views they are peddling might be somewhat biased at times. I tend to follow mainstream media in the belief that, at least to a degree, they are regulated while the Internet is like the Wild West. At the same time, I accept that they too may have been misled, or choose to present articles in a biased way, so I will always look for confirmation of an interesting article; if the same story features in both the Guardian and Telegraph, with a similar slant to both, then there's a possibility it might just be true.

Whether or not things are 'better' today is open to debate. There is obviously considerably more information available now, but the distortion of the truth seems far easier and can be much more extreme. Where someone actively seeks an objective view of events, I think things are better; but there is a common tendency for people to filter their news in order only to receive topics of interest to them, and then only through sources that reflect their own views; from this standpoint the modern world is decidedly worse.

37.

Environmental Awareness

There is no doubt that in my early days very few people took notice of the environment or the problems we might be storing up for the future. But to be fair, the problem is hardly new; polluted fog caused by the burning of coal was an issue in London as early as the 13th century. Thick yellow fog was a common London phenomenon, and during The Great Smog of 1952, visibility was so poor that people were unable to see their feet. Lasting 5 days, it was attributed as the cause of death for some 4,000 people, although double that number may also have died prematurely from related respiratory illnesses. London's air pollution was finally identified as a serious issue, and in 1956 the Clean Air Act was passed; smoke-free areas were established throughout the city, and restrictions were placed on the burning of coal in domestic fires and industrial furnaces. Grants were introduced to encourage homeowners to change their fuel sources to electricity, oil or natural gas. The 1968 Clean Air Act followed, focusing, among other things, on introducing taller chimneys to speed up the dispersal of pollutants. So change is possible.

We should probably forgive earlier generations for the mess they made. I imagine that, with the exception of a few scientists who would have been labeled as barking mad doom-mongers, nobody had any idea about what they were doing to the environment; besides there was probably

340

no obvious alternative to fossil fuels, and the idea that the earth's resources were finite and could one day run out would have appeared laughable. But there is no excuse now. Of course, there are those who say human activity has little effect on the climate, that the earth is just going through a temporary phase as it did during the Little Ice Age, which started around 1350 and lasted some four hundred years during which mountain glaciers expanded, average temperatures across the Northern Hemisphere fell, livestock froze to death, the Thames froze over and famine killed thousands of peasants; all apparently preceded by an unusually warm spell.

While I accept that climate change might not necessarily have been started by humans, we have at least added to the problem and can still take action that may possibly alleviate some of the effects. But here we immediately come across a major challenge, human nature. Identify any action causing environmental damage and a whole host of people will crawl out of the woodwork to argue on its behalf; the charge is false, the activity is essential or unavoidable. They rarely mention the main reasons behind their arguments; that the activity concerned is profitable, convenient or fun.

But whatever the motives, the effect of non-stop claims and counterclaims is that changes that might possibly help the environment, move at a snail's pace, giving people the perfect excuse for doing nothing; if the scientists can't agree what we should do, why should I change anything? We need guidance but, unfortunately, it's not that easy. In the early 80s, I shopped regularly at Safeway supermarket where they used brown paper bags rather than plastic, each stamped with a logo proudly claiming that the paper used was recycled and

341

environmentally friendly; so far so good. Then another supermarket, possibly Sainsbury's, printed on their plastic bags the message that producing recycled paper bags used far more electricity than did plastic bags, their bag was ultimately 'greener'. It has taken nearly forty years for the argument to move on and for restrictions to be placed on the production and use of plastic bags. But the problem is that they are so convenient.

The challenge Joe Public faces is how to get at the truth. The tobacco industry is notorious for its 'playbook', a strategy developed in the 50s to deflect growing evidence of health threats linked to smoking, with the aim of maximising profits regardless of the impact on public health. They didn't aim to prove smoking was safe, instead they simply planted doubt in people's minds by paying scientists to rubbish anti-smoking reports; by broadcasting messages that appeared to come from grassroots supporters, hiding the fact that they actually originated from sponsors with financial interests in the industry; and by investing massively in lobbying politicians to slow down any regulation. All this while claiming to be self-regulating, and denying that tobacco was harmful, addictive and being marketed to children.

In 1954, the first lawsuit was taken out against a US tobacco company claiming compensation for health problems caused by smoking. Eight hundred or so further lawsuits were taken out over the next 40 years, of which only two prevailed; and they were overturned on appeal, so it seems the strategy worked. It was not until the Tobacco Master Settlement Agreement (1998), that the tobacco companies finally had to pay out, after 46 US states took the companies to court in a joint attempt to recover their tobacco-related health-care costs; they knew exactly what they were doing, but had stalled for over forty years. Money talks, and these are the same tactics, sometimes even the same people, now being used by the fossil fuel industry, among others, to cause doubt among the population and hold back any call for change.

So, while the big decision makers are mired down in slush, what point is there in us doing anything? After all, what impact can one individual have compared with the billions of tons of carbon pouring out of power stations, factories, car exhausts and the like worldwide? Well, there are over 60 million individuals in the UK alone, so surely if we all made a tiny impact the overall effect might be noticeable. Nothing drastic, simply recycle and use less. Ask yourself "do I really need the latest phone/laptop/trainers etc. while what I already have is perfectly OK?" Perhaps leave the car at home occasionally and walk or cycle. If the population of the world were to take similar actions, surely it would have some effect?

But the big stuff has to come from our leaders, and it is nigh on impossible to persuade national governments to address the problem, let alone implement a global strategy. By nature, politicians look for short-term wins, preferably things that don't cost much and cause minimal disruption; not to mention the possibility that some may even gain financially from blocking change.

But there is still hope, and global cooperation is not totally impossible. During the 60s and 70s, scientists became aware of a hole in the ozone layer causing a 40% reduction in atmospheric ozone over Antarctica. This decline resulted in increased exposure to UVB radiation causing skin cancer and cataracts, while also harming marine life and plants and reducing the productivity of crops such as rice and wheat. It was confirmed that the hole was a direct result of human activity, and emissions of certain gases were identified as the culprit, in particular CFCs widely used at the time in things as diverse as fridges, air conditioning units and aerosols.

Time passed before, in 1985, the existence of 'the hole' and severity of the threat it posed became known to the public. The issue wouldn't go away, and after huge publicity, numerous campaigns and the like, something was actually done; in 1987, the UN's Montreal Protocol to regulate the global level of ozone depleting gases was signed by 197 countries, an unprecedented moment as no other treaty had achieved universal ratification. The size of the hole has greatly reduced since 1987, but full recovery of the ozone layer is still expected to take decades. So, despite the cost and inconvenience, major change is possible.

1995 saw the inaugural United Nations Climate Change Conference, an event repeated annually since. A good thing perhaps, but progress has been at a glacial pace and self-interest again takes the wheel, as in the creation of schemes whereby industrial countries make no changes themselves, instead funding emissions reduction activities in developing countries. A news report from the 2006 Kenya convention illustrates the problem. It refers to Yvo de Boer, then the new executive secretary of the United Nations Framework Convention on Climate Change, speaking of countries seeing climate change policies as opportunities for enhancing economic growth in a sustainable way. Many more such conventions followed before anyone seriously started to talk about reducing emissions. Hmmmm.

In recent years many kids have started taking an interest in environmental issues, making headlines in 2018 when 16-year-old Swede, Greta Thunberg, called for climate strikes and students around the world walked out of class demanding action on the climate crisis. Around that time a new group, Extinction Rebellion, arrived on the scene. A global organisation established in the UK, their stated aims are to compel government action on environmental issues through the use of nonviolent civil disobedience.

While I applaud the motives and aims of these and other groups, I'm afraid that they are fighting an uphill battle until they gain support from an overwhelming number of people as happened with the ozone hole. Think back to the tobacco playbook. People who like things as they are can undermine these movements by rolling out their own scientists to question any claims, they can churn out figures to prove proposals are economically unviable and, easiest of all, they can cause Joe Public to doubt the motives of the individuals involved; a tactic referred to by Sir Humphrey Appleton as playing the man instead of the ball. XR did itself no favours when it transpired that celebrities giving their support to a London demo had flown in First Class, or even by private jet, thus generating an unnecessarily large carbon footprint. And by disrupting flights and trains they probably alienated more people than they attracted.

An Australian politician launched a blistering attack on the striking kids, suggesting that they lived a spoilt existence and could not complain while they lived an energy-consuming lifestyle: perpetual streaming of music, film, social media and the like; home comforts such as air conditioning and central heating; being driven to school when they could walk, the list was long. True, the kids only have these things because their parents provide them, but this won't stop their detractors using it to cast doubt on the sincerity of their campaign.

So far, I have only mentioned the impact humans may be having on 'our' environment, but of course we are not the only ones living on Earth. The International Union for Conservation of Nature (IUCN) maintains a list of mammals they believe to have become extinct since 1500; while total extinction is impossible to prove, the list comprises some eighty species. The most common cause identified is loss of habitat through urban sprawl, deforestation and the like, while other factors such as exposure to poisonous chemicals and overhunting have a significant impact.

In the UK we have 47 native species of mammal and the conservation status of each is categorised on the Red List based on analysis of their populations, threats to their survival and threats to their habitats. Eleven species, just over one quarter, are identified as 'at risk of extinction'. Two of these, the wildcat and greater mouse-eared bat are critically endangered; the beaver, red squirrel, water vole and grey long-eared bat are classified 'endangered'; and the hedgehog, hazel dormouse, Orkney vole, Serotine bat and Barbastelle bat are 'vulnerable'. Another five of our native mammals are classed 'near threatened'.

And that's only the mammals. Over-fishing and pollution are devastating aquatic species, bird populations have declined, and countless insect species have been wiped out with hitherto untold consequences; witness current concerns over the devastating impact on crops that a reduction in pollinators may well be causing. I also recently heard of a study suggesting that earthworms, the gardeners' friend that generate so much compost while providing food for birds, mammals and the like, are in significant decline. The human race has certainly managed to make a mess of the world.

So, I have little faith in our politicians implementing significant changes for many years, and the cynic in me doesn't expect too much from the various movements we hear about in the news, although I do admire their sentiments. Can anything be done?

Well, yes and no. On the positive front, these groups should learn from the ozone hole and plastic bag episodes. Both have achieved a level of success by galvanising public support, forcing politicians to respond or risk losing their jobs. But these were both single issues where the public could understand the problem, the potential solution and the cost to themselves. In contrast, the plethora of current environmental campaigns with differing goals and priorities plays into the hands of those profiting from the status quo, giving the opportunity to divide and conquer. So I suggest they need to work closer together, agreeing bite-size targets and coordinating their efforts to achieve these. Youthful idealism needs to be tempered with more jaundiced realism in order to identify practicable goals. But of course, this is unlikely to happen as human nature again takes control; who will be in charge and how will they agree on what is most important?

I recently read another depressing news snippet of interest. A study by Oxfam suggested that the richest 10% of the world population produce half of the planet's individual-consumption-based fossil fuel emissions, while the poorest 50% around 3.5 billion people, contribute only 10%. Yet those same 3.5 billion people are "living overwhelmingly in the countries most vulnerable to climate change". Human nature dictates that the richer countries are less likely to take significant action while the greatest threats are faced by the others.

By now you probably get the idea that I am not very optimistic about the future; that in terms of the environment we're all doomed. Well not so fast matey. True, we are not in a good place, but all is not lost. Like a scene from Lord of the Rings, battle lines are being drawn and the baddies are indeed powerful. Like a dark cloud spreading across the world, the forces of evil are strong; destroying our forests, polluting our seas and poisoning the very air we breathe. Theirs is a large army of conscripts comprising Bad Business seeking profit at any cost, indifferent and sometimes corrupt politicians and an ignorant, self-centred and lethargic human race.

But hang on there, an army of resistance is stirring. The antics of the various activists are gaining some attention and, with leadership from the likes of David Attenborough in the role of Gandalf the White, the little people of Middle Earth are beginning to wake to the threat facing humankind. There is a limit to what they alone can achieve through recycling, installing solar panels, making their gardens wildlife friendly, leaving their cars in the garage and turning their heating thermostats down, but they are not alone; supporting them is a veritable army of scientists investigating a vast array of potential solutions and together they make a stronger team. We were all vaguely aware of the presence of unsightly plastic waste strewn hither and thither, but it needed the scientists to confirm the extent of the pollution, to raise awareness of the impact of the waste and to identify the presence of the ubiquitous microbeads in our food chain before the activists, and in particular Attenborough through his series 'The Blue Planet', could galvanise the people into action.

But while these guys investigate and come up with a variety of proposals from green energy and electric vehicles through changes in diet to behavioural changes, that in itself is not enough without another key participant, Good Business. By definition the driving force behind business is the need to make a profit and any scientific proposal is unlikely to succeed unless it is economically viable; electric or hydrogen powered cars will only be the norm when they're sufficiently cheap, reliable and appealing to the public while, at the same time, generating a good profit for the manufacturers. But if that can be achieved, they will prevail. And there is one last player for the good guys, environmentally aware politicians. Though we have yet to see many of them, these lawmakers have the power to bring about real change but will only do so if it suits them and wins them votes.

So, there we are. The current, rather sad, position we are in today is that the Earth we are passing on to our children is in a far worse state than when our generation took stewardship of it. But a lot of the problems have arisen through ignorance, and little will be achieved by trying to pin the blame on any one particular group of people, we must instead look to the future. We might still have time to improve things, but this can only be achieved with good leadership and global cooperation. To date this has not proven to be the strongest characteristic of the human race, but just maybe, in the face of such dire threats, something good may arise.

But with the exception of a few Oldies, it is the next generation who need to take the reins. Perhaps they will be able to galvanise a global response where the Oldies have failed miserably. Their chance of success will depend on what changes they are willing to accept and what luxuries and conveniences they are willing to forego; what price are they prepared to pay to get a better, cleaner world?

38.

Want to Bet on it?

Throughout history, society has tended to view gambling as wrong, sinful; so I guess that makes me a sinner, as I must admit to being partial to the occasional flutter. I can still remember the look given me by the mum of one of Daughter's friends when she saw me coming out of William Hills one Saturday morning; a fairly conservative type, she obviously did not approve.

I'm not talking big money here, just a few bob now and again, usually on the horses; something I must have inherited from Dad. There's no logic to it, in the long run I will lose more than I win, but that doesn't matter; the buzz when my horse comes in is gratifying, particularly if it's at long odds and I can tell myself that few people have been as clever as me. In today's world there is very little enjoyment available that doesn't cost, so why should giving my money to a bookie be any worse than spending it on a trip to the cinema, a sociable evening in a pub or expanding my music collection?

Gambling was not made legal in the UK until 1961, when the first casino and high street bookies were opened. By law, bookies had to have "dead windows", blacked-out or shuttered to minimise their appeal to prospective punters. Conservative MP Rab Butler said the aim of Parliament was to make betting shops "as sad as possible, in order not to deprave the young, that they ended up more like undertakers' premises". I remember the bookies in the High Street as a dark, uninviting place with a plastic strip curtain hanging in the doorway; the occasional man, after all this wasn't a place where women were encouraged, would furtively slink in or out. It took twenty-five years for the rules to be relaxed, allowing betting shops to provide comforts like better lighting, comfy chairs, refreshments and, most important of all, televised live racing.

Slot machines, or 'one-armed bandits', were around in my youth but were often seen as 'amusements' rather than gambling, a view Dad disagreed strongly with as, while decorating the local Comrades Club, he had witnessed a number of women visiting during lunchtime to empty their purses into the machines before leaving, looking decidedly unhappy.

These machines became common in pubs during my late teens although jackpots were limited to £2; in clubs, however, jackpots of £100 or more were waiting to be won. On our uni Rag trips to Blackpool we would join my friend's family in the Blackpool Bowling Club for a sociable beer; the club was not particularly large, but it had a whole bank of such machines, the profits from which funded numerous days out; trips to the races and sporting events for example, where not only transport was provided but tickets, food and drink were all paid for, and members might even be furnished with a little stake money. These machines were big business.

Bingo, once an innocent pastime for the old or a seaside holiday novelty, has blossomed. Games were held in local council halls and the like, before purpose-built venues arrived on the scene. Technology then allowed these to link up so larger numbers of players could compete for bigger pots. Bingo was already big business before the Internet and that business has since grown exponentially; and it's no longer just the realm of the Oldies as more and more kids get involved.

1994 saw the launch of the National Lottery, although government emphasis was on the generation of cash for good causes rather than the gambling element. I can remember winning on my first attempt; eagerly clutching my ticket as I queued for my winnings, I had no idea how much to expect, but was a trifle disappointed on receiving about a fiver.

Online betting first became available in the UK in 1996 since when it too has blossomed. You can now bet on just about anything; not only final football scores, but who scores when, the number of corners, number of fouls, number of shots on target; the options seem endless. And if sport isn't enough, you can bet on the outcome of elections and TV shows. In case we forget, we are continually bombarded with TV adverts encouraging us to bet and participate in online bingo and other games that are strangely portrayed as 'social' events. The betting companies are aware of their social obligations however, and their adverts show their concern, warning us to be aware of the pitfalls of gambling, "when the fun stops, stop". Hmm.

We have definitely become a nation of gamblers. For the majority, this is probably not a concern, nothing wrong in a little fun. But the number of problem gamblers, those addicted to the point where they lose far more than they can ever afford, thereby wrecking not only their own lives but those of their nearest and dearest, is large and growing. The sensitivity of the issue means estimates of the number of problem gamblers in the UK vary widely between some 0.4 and 1.4 million people, but it's growing. Even taking the lowest figure, add in the side effects on family and friends and this is a big and rising problem. Recent changes in regulations mean, for example, that betting companies now have 'know your client' checks for account holders. These and other changes make it harder for a problem gambler to access the systems, but none of the restrictions are truly insurmountable.

Personally, I can see no real practicable solution that doesn't involve the banks and betting companies sharing client information thereby breaking all sorts of data protection and rights laws. That being the case, we can either have a society where the freedoms of the many are restricted to protect the few, or where we can go on enjoying our pleasures and let the vulnerable suffer. A gambler myself, I still think we have rather lost control here, and that things are definitely worse than they were.

39.

The Years Keep Rolling On

Well, I can't say I wasn't warned, so why did it come as such a surprise? After all, it's a long time since I realised my barber was paying as much attention to my eyebrows, ears and nose as he was to the rest of my head. And I remember chuckling as Jack Dee talked of the shock of reaching forty; his mum, he said, was always asking "does anyone else feel a draught in here?" then suddenly he'd become draught-aware. I laughed, but smugly; I was six years older, but draughts were never a concern.

Then there was Billy Connolly describing how, when you reach fifty, it's obligatory to grunt or make some sound at every energetic action like bending down to pick up a newspaper or tying your shoelaces; he may be thirteen years older than me but, unlike the draughts, this sounded unnervingly familiar.

Victoria Wood talked of browsing those slightly odd adverts that appear in the weekend papers and wondering whether it was possible to buy a CD player driven by flatulence; this was really getting close to home. I've seen the impact age had on my parents, grandparents, uncles and aunties, yet still it came as a surprise when things I had always found easy suddenly weren't.

The beginning of the end came one day in the bookies with Dad. True, the light wasn't particularly good and the print in the newspapers attached to the wall was quite small, but as I scanned the all-important information essential for choosing those winners, I realised all was a blur until I stood back slightly and squinted. Off to the opticians for the first of a series of ever-more-powerful reading glasses. A brief aside; who decided that at a certain age your toenails turn to concrete?

I've never been one for big parties, a nice quiet pint with select good company is more my bag. But I couldn't let the 'Big 5 0' go by without doing something to mark the event, so we spent the weekend at the Sandbanks Hotel with Mum and Dad, both brothers and their families, and a jolly time was had by all. It was April but the weather was good, so we walked a fair bit; we visited a number of pubs, guided as usual by Big Brother who is very fussy about his drinking establishments, often passing many suitable-looking places and travelling miles to reach his desired destination. Son, who was ten at the time, had to swim in the sea that, it being April was freezing. Needless to say, we watched from the shore and he wasn't in for long. The food at the hotel was good. And we laughed, a lot. What more could you ask for?

My extended family always seems to have embraced large parties. Cousins from Mum's side lived in Cornwall, Shropshire, Wales and Liverpool, and all have been willing to travel when my brothers staged parties for various reasons. We in turn would jump in our cars and trek off for a long weekend whenever anyone declared a party.

Birthdays, weddings, anniversaries all called for a party. We decamped to Cornwall when my cousin, yes the only girl member of the Mars Bar gang, held a belated 50th birthday as a joint event with her brother's 70th; and again to Center Parcs in Longleat for her 60th, before back to Cornwall for her son's wedding afew years later. Then it was off to Welshpool for a 70th and a Golden Wedding anniversary and Shrophire for another Golden Wedding.

But by far the largest number of events has taken place in Surrey, and they would all turn up. Various weddings, my brothers' 50th and 60th birthdays, Mum and Dad's Golden Anniversary, Dad's 80th and 90th and so on. So, by my 60th I felt obliged to have a party.

My original plan was for a garden party but, being April, we couldn't rely on the weather, so I decided to delay until June. Then we dropped the garden idea and opted for the hotel a short walk from our house, so no reason why we hadn't gone for April in the first place, but there you go.

Do you know how much it takes to organise a party? No wonder I hadn't had one before. So many things to think about. Who to invite? Getting the invitations out. What food do we want? What music? There was a bar, but I wanted decent beer so that had to be ordered in. And some people wouldn't be going home and would need rooms. Mainly thanks to Wifey's organisational skills, we managed. Catering for family and friends of all ages, the result was more akin to a wedding reception, but I thoroughly enjoyed myself nonetheless, and as far as I'm concerned it was a great success.

Holding the party in June meant my actual birthday weekend was free, so Wifey, kids and I took off for a weekend of luxury, returning to l'Horizon in Jersey, twenty years after our previous visit. The weather was less reliable this time, but that didn't stop us enjoying ourselves. At the end of the gloriously long sandy beach was the ancient and characterful Old Smugglers Inn where we ate one night; when the sun shone the beach and surrounding countryside provided good walks and I remember spending a wet lunchtime on the covered terrace of The Tenby in St

Aubin, just sipping ale, chatting with my nearest and dearest while watching the wet world go slowly by. Priceless.

For most of my life I have been reasonably fit, just the usual childhood maladies, an occasional cold, annoying hayfever, but little else. Days off school or work due to illness were almost unheard of, and I hardly ever visited the doctor. That all changed when, at the age of 60, I had a problem and headed off to the health centre. My doctor listened sympathetically before telling me it was nothing to worry about, perfectly normal as "everything starts to fall off at sixty"; and he wasn't wrong. In the following eighteen months I was in hospital for three separate reasons. Some years earlier, I had read in a novel a lovely phrase describing one of the characters as being "in the foothills of middle age"; it suddenly felt like I was no longer in the foothills but hurtling down the piste.

A couple of days ago, out of the blue, I had a call from my swimming club car owning friend; our Royal Marine chum was coming to town, and we had to meet. Now, over the years I have observed a definite difference between men and women when it comes to friendships; please forgive the generalisation, but it seems to me that women can get upset if they're not regularly in touch with their friends while us chaps can go years without seeing each other, and then continue as if one of us had just popped out of the room for a few minutes. This is how it was with our Marine chum who I hadn't seen for six years.

True, we are at an age where it took a few minutes to mock our changing appearances; after all, he was sporting a rather impressive military-style moustache, my hair is pretty much all grey and the driver's hair has gone AWOL;

and catching up on medical issues took a depressingly long time, but after that it was as if he'd never been away.

We took it in turns to mock and be mocked, all sticking to Big Brother's guidance about not worrying overly much about the truth. We had to endure politically incorrect tales of life in the forces and regular complaints about how unreliable and generally useless civvies are; and I took considerable stick over my chainsaw maintenance skills until the Marine inadvertently let slip his technical incompetence when it came to looking after his own lawnmower. They both thought it hilarious that I was bothering to write this book and I confirmed, to myself at least, both the wisdom of keeping it anonymous and my inclusion of the warning as to the unreliability of the facts, as we regularly needed to help each other recall what actually did happen in times gone by.

We discussed our families and old friends and, like the true Oldies we've become, we moaned about the changing world. Somehow, with no lead from me, we managed to cover half the topics in this book. As kids, we always knew the Marine's dad as Grumble, and now we had all matured to fill that role; we had become our fathers. Before parting, we agreed to get together again soon. Who knows when that will actually happen? But it was a great reminder of how lucky I am not only to have a wonderful family but also such good friends. After all, it was some fifty-five years ago when the three of us met, not bad at all.

I hadn't really noticed my folks getting older, there were just points when suddenly they'd aged. One day, when I was in my early twenties, Dad came in from work on a cold October day, he'd been working outside all day and he looked grey, haggard and suddenly old; it turned out he had an ulcer but hadn't gone to the doctor for fear of being told he had cancer. Another time, I brought round a bag of peat for his garden, and he used a wheelbarrow to move it when previously he would just have hefted it.

It's come to my notice, that in old age everyone seems to develop similar characteristics. They become creatures of habit, incredibly reliant on their routine. Dad would complain if he felt he'd been ignored for a while, but woe betide if I turned up and interrupted his routine; 'cantankerous' is a lovely word that seems fitting for so many people as they grow older.

Then there's the stories; anyone who has been in the company of someone growing old will tell of the same tales being told and retold, often many times in the same day. In some cases the details are exactly the same, other times they may change a little over time. My kids tell me that this is a trait I am already developing; oh dear. But be patient and look interested as they relive their memories of these key parts in their lives.

And no disrespect here, but old people also become naturally selfish. Life has gone full circle; as babies, our instincts for food and attention focus all our actions, then as we get older, becoming more aware of our vulnerabilities, survival instincts kick in once again as food, shelter and attention become priorities. Oldies become devious too, trying to manipulate events to their own liking while not being too direct, in order to avoid causing offence. But before you get all uppity, let me say that this is not a criticism, just an observation on human nature and a warning for my kids of times to come; or already here.

Dad was ninety when he died; not a bad innings as they say, and he'd learnt to look after himself since Mum died; no mean feat bearing in mind he had played little or no part in domestic chores for most of their married life. He was independent, living in a flat within walking distance of the bookies, pubs, shops and coffee bars, which was ideal, and he developed a fixed routine such that we usually knew where to find him at any time of the day. He was well known in town, and there always seemed to be someone around to help him out if needed. My brothers and I all lived reasonably close by and, together with our wives and families, were able to keep an eye on him and keep him company; Wifey and Daughter dropped in regularly to clean and help with the shopping.

As he became less able to look after himself, we suggested he try a live-in carer. Dad was surprisingly responsive to the idea; we had expected him to be against having a stranger move in. Big Brother and his wife made the arrangements, and after a few false starts, we ended with three good carers who took it in turns to live with him. Up until the last few weeks, he was able, with the aid of his trusty shopping trolley, to walk the short trip to the bookies, returning to a cooked meal and some company before falling asleep in front of the telly. He got to know about his carers' lives and their families, and even became a regular viewer of programmes like Strictly Come Dancing and Eastenders. At ten o'clock he'd be tucked up in bed to be woken the next morning with a nice cup of tea.

It was sad when Dad died, but not unexpected. A few years earlier he'd been hospitalised and we thought he might not come out then, so those years seemed a bonus. It was the end of an era, but his quality of life had taken a distinct downward turn to the point that he could no longer get to the bookies without assistance; I think he probably felt there was little left to hang around for. The same can't be said of Mum who died unexpectedly sixteen years earlier at the age of 75. She went into hospital for a routine procedure and didn't come out. We were all shocked, Dad in particular, and it took a long time for some sort of normality to resume.

At least both Mum and Dad knew they had a whole network of family and friends that they could rely on; although to be fair, we did occasionally discuss with Dad cultures like the nomadic red Indians who would move on while leaving their oldies behind, or eskimos leaving their old parents outside the igloo. He didn't seem particularly impressed.

But for a lot of old people, a combination of social and economic factors means the impact that both family and community have on their lives has declined considerably through my lifetime, and many Oldies now don't have the level of support common in the past. Whole communities have been devastated as their livelihoods have been taken away, as is the case with the mining and fishing industries. In London, the South West and many other areas, locals have been driven out as a result of government policy, gentrification or rocketing property prices as more affluent outsiders buy up property, often as second homes. This particularly affects the youngsters who have to move away from home to look for employment and affordable housing. People are also far more likely today to move away from their home area, even their home country, in order to pursue career choices. Many other factors are also at work; a shortage of council housing means people can be moved out of their home areas to get accommodation, and a significant number of overseas arrivals has also had an impact as, too, has a growing number of divorces and single parent families.

The outcome of all this upheaval is that, while people get to live longer, they don't necessarily have access to the type of support that they could have expected in the past, and they instead become reliant on the state. In recent years it has become painfully clear that this support is far from adequate and, not to put too fine a point on it, in crisis. Age UK have identified four particular issues that urgently need addressing, namely: underfunding, with significant cuts in spending on adult social care despite a rapidly increasing demand as people live longer; big differences in levels of care depending on where people live; the fact that more than 1.5 million people aged over 65 don't receive the care and support they need with essential living activities; the dependence society has on unpaid care workers and the ever-growing pressure these people are put under as a direct result of government policy.

So, where am I going with all this? During my lifetime our life expectancy has increased by some 11 years and the number of old people who need caring for has gone up considerably; meanwhile changes in society mean that they are less likely to be cared for by family and friends than might have been the case in the past. All this is happening at a time when state care is woefully underfunded and dysfunctional. Unless this problem is addressed somehow, for today's kids growing old in the future is going to become an even less enjoyable experience than it has been for some in the past. The youngsters are right to turn their attention to issues like the environment, but if they don't also focus on care for the elderly, they themselves will pay the price in the future.

40.

Big Brother is Watching You

A couple of decades ago, had you asked just about anyone what surveillance was, they would probably have described a scene from a crime or spy film involving a character being tailed by a team of trackers, with perhaps the occasional hidden microphone or camera thrown in. But no more. Sci-fi novels like '1984' depicted dystopian societies with citizens under continual surveillance; we never really imagined such a thing would come about, and yet suddenly it doesn't seem so fanciful. CCTV is a permanent feature in our lives now, and pretty much taken for granted. An article I read recently stated that the British Security Industry Association believes there to be between 4 and 6 million CCTV cameras in the UK, meaning throughout the world only the US and China have a higher rate of cameras per capita.

You can of course see this as a good thing, the government working to keep us safe and reduce crime; if you're doing nothing wrong you have nothing to fear. On the other hand you may view it as infringing on your personal liberties; why should anyone be allowed to track your every movement and action?

Traffic offences can be caught by roadside cameras; the first you realise you've been done, is when that notice drops onto the mat, complete with picture of you at the wheel and a demand for instant payment or dire consequences to follow. Arguably a cheap and easy way to police our roads, but maybe a bit draconian, taking away the chance for a police officer to assess the situation and give a warning rather than a fine if they consider there to be mitigating circumstances. Always in the back of motorists' minds is the thought that these devices are less concerned with keeping our roads safe and more with milking the cash cow to swell the coffers.

Automatic Number Plate Recognition is a useful tool for the police in fighting crime. The registration number of every vehicle passing an ANPR camera can be read and instantly checked against database records of vehicles of interest, with officers dispatched to intercept a suspect vehicle if necessary. As a national system, it is particularly helpful in tackling situations where criminals move outside their home patch in order to commit a crime. There are some 11,000 ANPR cameras capturing around 50 million ANPR records for processing daily; sounds impressive if you're a law-abiding citizen, but the fact that, without you knowing it, your vehicle, speed and parking habits are regularly being monitored may not sound quite so good.

Automatic face recognition has become a bit of a hot topic of late; surely if police cameras are able to identify 'people of interest' that's a good thing? But what if your facial structure is similar to that of a wanted miscreant, and while innocently going about your life, just because of a computer mismatch, you must interrupt whatever you are doing just to prove your identity. Imagine, you have managed to get your hands on tickets for the FA Cup Final and you're eagerly making your way to the game when the Police intercept you because a computer thinks you look like someone suspect. They whisk you off, and it takes hours to prove that you are who you say you are, by which time the match is over. Hmm.

Whenever you use a card to remove cash from an ATM, the chances are you're being photographed, recording exactly where you were at the time.

The majority of the population now uses mobile phones that provide a vast pool of information regarding the user's travels and habits; do you have any idea who can access this information and to what end? Not only that, but phone apps are available to enable tracking; good if you and your friend are meeting up and want to know how close each of you are, but not so great if it's loaded surreptitiously by a coercive partner wanting to monitor your movements.

People are buying more and more smart devices for the home, giving the ability to remotely change heating settings, turn lights on and off, answer the door, open and close curtains and doors, let you know what food is in your fridge and much more; all via their home Internet hub. All these gadgets may be great for improved comfort and convenience, but all increase the risk of the home hub security being breached. Doubtless many of the scare stories circulating about devices listening to or watching you are rubbish, but where the technology is capable someone will be devising ways to abuse it.

I have only scratched the surface here; with rapidly developing technology our society has become one where a large part of our lives is routinely monitored and recorded. Views on this state of affairs vary; to some it is a price worth paying to keep us safe while to others it represents too much of a threat to our personal liberty. Personally, I feel things have gone way too far. There may possibly be an age split with the youngsters more likely to accept that this is just the way of the world, while perhaps the Oldies only acquiesce because they don't actually understand how much all this new-fangled stuff puts them under the microscope.

Governments of both persuasions regularly consider introducing a national ID card, a way to address a large number of societal issues that would at the same time enable much greater levels of surveillance. Public opinion has blocked such proposals to date, but it seems inevitable that some such thing is not too far away. My globe-trotting friend has lived in France for many years, and he carries an ID card that he has no problem with; it does what's required but includes far less data than those regularly proposed by British governments. Perhaps that's the answer.

41.

The Nation's Health

Since its introduction by Nye Bevan in 1948, the NHS has been the jewel in the crown of our welfare system, providing medical and dental treatment free at source to all. Lovingly satirised in films like 'Carry on Matron', the service was seen as being run by doctors who were to be treated like gods, their judgment never questioned; wards were run with military precision by fearsome matrons and their army of nurses, most of whom were female.

Like supernatural shamans, doctors were versed in the great mysteries of life far beyond the understanding of us mere mortals. The vast majority were men of course. Our doctor personally tended the family for some twenty or thirty years; it was him we saw whenever we needed medical advice; he knew the history of each family member from birth and would happily visit if called upon. This was a truly personal service. You only visited the doctor if you felt unwell, even then worrying that you were wasting the great man's time. His purpose was to make you feel better, and this he did with a bit of soothing talk, often accompanied by a prescription for antibiotics, whether or not they were really necessary.

Group medical examinations were held at school, as were the dreaded mass inoculation sessions where we lined up for our various jabs. Polio had been defeated recently, but there were still kids wearing leg irons and using crutches to get about; at least the polio inoculation came in a sugar cube rather than a needle. The bogeyman of the time was cancer, the big C; the oldies talked about it in whispers and there was little that could be done if you were unlucky enough to get it.

Dental treatment was free for all, but not a particularly pleasant experience; drills were mechanical and slow, belt-driven devices. My current dentist talks of how, in the 70s, decay was treated like a cancer by dentists who would drill out far too much tooth for fear the decay would spread. Fillings were all the old metal amalgam type; I had a mouthful. Anaesthetic was rarely used. Cosmetic dentistry was unheard of, unless you were rich, but it was commonplace to have all four wisdom teeth yanked out.

Eye examinations and glasses were free on the NHS. The glasses were mass-produced and tough rather than fashionable; those for children included arms that curved inwards with ends made from wire that circled around the child's ears in a bid to keep them from sliding off during play. This might have been effective, but it didn't make them very comfortable. I started with tortoiseshell glasses complete with wire bits, progressing to more grown-up black types with solid arms when I moved to senior school, then ended with the gold-rimmed model in an attempt to emulate John Lennon.

Mum already wore glasses, so we had our family optician; we'd visit his home for an eye test comprising not much more than reading letters on a chart, reading script close up and checking for colour blindness. That said, there seemed something mystical about the process, like being in a wizard's study; he would take orders for our glasses which we would pick up a number of weeks later.

Mum was a keen blood donor, with an enamel brooch identifying her long-term service, and on reaching the age of eighteen, we were expected to join the party. It tended to be a bit of a family outing; all shepherded to the local hall by Mum where we joked nervously, regularly quoting from the marvellous Tony Hancock Blood Donor sketch. We would each give our pint of blood, then sit briefly with a cup of tea and a biscuit before heading to the pub for a well-earned pint.

The medical world has taken huge steps forward in my lifetime, with life expectancy for men in the UK growing by more than 11 years, which I find truly amazing. Knowledge and understanding of the human body have grown, as has the supply of available drugs, technology and treatments. Cancer is no longer the guaranteed death sentence it was in the past; it is still scary and claims many lives, but while we are now told that 1 in 2 of us will get cancer during our lifetime, a large number will, at least to a degree, be treatable; I have many friends who remain alive and kicking after treatment for various cancers.

With greater understanding we are in a much better position to fight new diseases like AIDS, and the speed with which Covid vaccines have been developed is truly impressive. Various types of scan are commonplace, looking inside the body to detect problems; and robotic surgery is used in many cases. People think nothing of having a new hip or knee fitted and, with vastly increased knowledge of the brain's workings, operations on the brain are an everyday occurrence.

Dental treatment is far less painful and more effective than in my youth, although it can be hard to find an NHS dentist, and opticians are far better at identifying and curing eye problems; Dad had a cataract operation that took less than an hour, during which a lens was removed from his eye and replaced with an artificial number, and all with no need for anaesthetic. Opthalmic technology not only facilitates much better eyecare but can also provide warnings as to serious health problems elsewhere in the body, for instance through inspecting the condition of blood vessels in the eye. Things have come a long way since my youth.

But it hasn't all been plain sailing and the future is far from clear. The NHS has grown considerably in my lifetime; the number of people now employed by the NHS approaches 1.2m, making it the fifth largest employer in the world. In the early days they employed 80,000. It has become a huge, incredibly bureaucratic organisation, and we are continually being told how they are under pressure and near to breaking point, which is hardly surprising.

Their aim is still to provide medical care for all, free at source, although over the years there have been unpopular moves to recoup some of the costs by charging for prescriptions, eye tests and the like. In response to soaring demand, the National Institute for Health and Care Excellence, or NICE, was created with a remit to promote clinical excellence in NHS service providers in England and Wales by developing guidance and recommendations on the effectiveness of treatments and medical procedures. NICE has the unenviable task of deciding whether potential treatments warrant expenditure from public funds; they recently announced that the NHS would no longer perform procedures deemed 'ineffective', such as inserting ear grommets or removing varicose veins.

The truth is that we now have far greater expectations of the NHS; treatments are available for things that in the past we would never have dreamt of, or just had to put up with; but this all comes at a cost. Add in the fact that we have an aging population requiring regular and long-term care, plus a lower percentage of the population paying the taxes needed to provide the services to support them, and we have a problem; unless we are willing to put up with significantly higher taxes, something has to give.

While it is a noble aim to offer free medical care for all, this is becoming economically unviable. Dad would get quite heated when discussing the subject, telling how he had "paid his stamp" and all his healthcare costs should be free. The fact is that the money he contributed in his lifetime probably covered the cost of a small number of his many trips to doctors, hospitals and dentists during his later years; the rest has to come from somewhere else.

The original NHS bore no resemblance to the huge industry it has evolved into today; its aim was to look after people, to get them back out and about as quickly as possible. Complex and expensive surgery rarely came into it, and there was a limited number of drugs available, most of which weren't particularly expensive. Contrast that with the huge variety of treatments and the plethora of new, sometimes eye-wateringly expensive drugs available today, many of which are prescribed long-term, and the problem is obvious.

The NHS is particularly under pressure at the moment for its lack of support in the mental health arena. For whatever reason people, and particularly kids, seem to have far more mental health issues than in the past, and the NHS just doesn't have the funding to address them; yet if they don't, we're in big trouble.

Lack of investment in the care sector by successive governments has exacerbated problems faced by the NHS as valuable beds are taken up by oldies who should be in a home rather than a hospital; an issue that has been raised regularly over the years only to be kicked down the road by whoever is in power at the time. The pandemic has highlighted this matter, giving rise to a number of successful local initiatives whereby care and health services have collaborated; perhaps one good thing that could come from Covid is a review and overhaul of the system using knowledge gained from these initiatives. Perhaps.

The NHS are fantastic when it comes to trauma; if you have a heart attack, or are involved in a serious accident, you couldn't be in better hands once the medics take over. Costs for this service must always be covered by the public as should those for, say, maternity services; but I can see no option other than for patients to be asked to pay in some way towards other medical treatment. Measures will be necessary to ensure that those who can't afford it receive the treatment they need for free, but for the rest some contribution will be necessary. It will doubtless be heralded the thin end of the wedge, but asking patients to pay a small amount towards procedures, akin to an insurance excess, is unavoidable.

Whatever the answer, this is too big a question to be left to politicians alone and can only be successfully addressed by a cross-party body led by experts from the health sector and given the remit to come up with a viable long-term solution that won't be immediately tinkered with come the next election; and I'm not holding my breath for that.

Another problem that has come to light in the past few decades is the arrival of superbugs. Antibiotics used to be handed out willy-nilly by doctors regardless of whether they were actually necessary, anything to make the patient feel they were receiving treatment. Unfortunately, like all living things, bacteria evolve to survive and unnecessary exposure to antibiotics has led to an increasing number developing a resistance to them; there is now talk of returning to the Middle Ages, as far as medicine is concerned, with a frightening number of people dying from infections picked up in day-to-day life, minor hospital operations and the like. Not so good.

In laboratories around the world, an increasing number of scientists have been beavering away in an attempt to understand better the workings of the human body. But, of course, it's not that easy. Research costs money and there is a need to prioritise effort; in the private sector, ideas offering the most profit are likely to be given priority while in the public sector those most likely to win votes get pole position, so countless good ideas fall at the first fence for lack of funding. And the scientists themselves don't always help. Like so many highly intelligent people, they can be prima donnas at times, believing that they always know best; sometimes being less than totally honest about their pet project while trying to drum up interest and financial support; fighting for the recognition they feel they deserve; claiming the credit for discovering just about everything while continually undermining the ideas and work of the opposition.

It's twenty years since Bill Clinton announced that the sequencing of the human genome had been completed, describing the achievement as "the most important, most wondrous map ever produced by humankind". He predicted that within twenty years, by understanding which genes lead to which illness, we would be in a far better position to prevent, detect and treat illness. Exciting times indeed, but not quite yet the panacea

374

hoped for. True, greater understanding has led to changes, but progress has tended to be slow, raising further questions, highlighting what we still don't know and emphasising the need for far more research. As a sideshow, there have also been a number of arguments on the legality and ethics of the potential to play God or use genetics to discriminate where, for example, armed with this knowledge, insurance companies could refuse to insure perfectly healthy people on the grounds that they are more likely to get ill in the future.

The use of vaccinations was first noted in 1721 before Edward Jenner refined the process making it less risky. Since 1796, the basic principles remain pretty much unchanged. Daniel M. Davis's eminently readable book 'The Beautiful Cure' describes the evolution of immunology and the potential it has to revolutionise our approach to dealing with illness.

Davis describes how every immune system is different and in a continual state of flux, suggesting a need for personalised treatment rather than the one-size-fits-all approach currently employed. The aim of immunologists is to introduce a completely new approach to illness whereby, instead of introducing agents into the body to kill disease, the immune system is stimulated to attack and destroy all offending baddies while keeping the ability to put the brakes on when necessary, in order to avoid autoimmune reactions.

Understanding of this hugely complex, multi-layered system with all its inbuilt checks and balances is progressing apace, but there is still a long way to go, and the wider medical world tends to be far happier keeping with long-standing practices rather than introducing anything new. Maybe Covid experiences of the past few years will stimulate interest and funding and speed up the process. Maybe antibiotics will become a thing of the past. Maybe.

Scientists are also starting to understand how a number of mental conditions such as depression can be kicked off by an infection in the gut affecting the enteric nervous system, known by many as the body's second brain. This might possibly not only explain the growing number of people with mental health issues, often coming out of the blue, but it also may offer a solution; wipe out the offending bacteria in the gut. More research is needed here too, but possibly grounds for optimism.

The regard in which doctors are held has also changed during my lifetime. While generally still highly respected, they are no longer automatically treated as gods, rather as well-educated humans who have chosen a particular career path. Doctors are human body mechanics and, as with car mechanics, there are good and bad ones, and you generally get a better service when the mechanic is dealing with something they see regularly. With so much more information available, we are able to understand our own bodies better and query advice given, and if that isn't bad enough from the doctors' viewpoint, there are regular salacious stories in the media of medical malpractice and even of doctors assaulting or murdering patients. More than ever, doctors today need to earn our respect rather than just treat us all like morons.

One final, admittedly controversial observation; at times the NHS seems to spend inordinate time and money keeping alive patients who, given the choice, might prefer to slip away. People live so long now, often only with considerable support that can take away their privacy and dignity, and their quality of life has to be questioned. I appreciate the counter arguments and concerns, but genuinely believe there is a good case for voluntary euthanasia; where the person concerned is of sound mind, that individual should have the right to call it a day.

Anyway, time to bring this subject to a close. With huge advances in understanding, drugs and technology during my lifetime, when it comes to health and medicine, things today are far better than in the old days. And yet, strangely, people are probably less happy about the subject now than they were then. Without doubt, as we dutifully accepted anything the doctor said to be true, we were in a blissful state of ignorance; but what's wrong with an occasional bit of bliss?

The NHS is in crisis and 'something has to be done'. At the moment there are some 40,000 unfilled frontline vacancies and this number will grow considerably as many leave the service as a result of Covid burn-out, or in response to the latest salary proposals; NHS staff, including doctors and nurses, have voted to strike for a large increase in the face of the ongoing cost of living crisis. The NHS is totally dependent on agency and overseas nurses, and we have to ask why we are unable to meet more of the demand domestically, and also to acknowledge the moral issues around the detrimental effect the drain of medical expertise from abroad could be having on their home medical services.

Nurses seem to be seen as dedicated individuals who get so much job satisfaction that they don't need to be paid as well, but that's not good enough; the pandemic has highlighted the importance not only of nurses but also of care assistants, and the total dearth of home-grown talent wishing to fill these roles. We need to make these jobs more valued and appealing to youngsters seeking a career path, otherwise things can only get worse. To add to the joy, we are told to expect further pandemics down the line, which is hardly cheering. But it's not all gloom; if the immunologists are on the right path, we could be on the cusp of a revolution leading to far more efficient and effective medical services; I hope they're right, but only time will tell.

42.

And The Award Goes To

At some point during my labours, I decided that I should attempt to identify the single factor or innovation responsible for the greatest changes in our world during the last sixty-eight years; but, once again, it's not that easy. The shortlist quickly came down to two, and there I got confused. True, computers alone have had a huge impact, but how much less that impact would be without the Internet; then again, the Internet is just a network of connected computers. So, after lengthy deliberation I have come to the conclusion that the single innovation to have had most impact on my life is the computer.....and the Internet.

The first mechanical computer was created by Charles Babbage in 1822, but the birth of modern computing can be traced back to World War II, although it was not until the 60s and 70s that they started to become more common, and even then their cost and size generally limited usage to government departments, large companies, universities and the like.

Writing code was truly a scientific art form in those days; storage capacity was both very limited and expensive, and processing was slow, so programmers had to write code that was efficient in minimising both processing time and storage requirements. Code would be written by hand on coding sheets and passed to a team of typists for 'punching' to create computer input in the form of punch cards or ticker tape, then delivered to computer operators for feeding into the computer. Output from programmes would be hardcopy only, often reams of continuous form, green-striped, 'piano paper'. The whole process was tortuous. For my Uni computing course, I had to write code by hand, deliver it to the punch room, then wait 3 or 4 days to find out whether the programme had run as planned; if not, the process had to be repeated. And this type of setup was in place wherever computers were used.

With the launch of the Apple II and Commodore PET in 1977, home computing was born and things never looked back. Computer processing speed and data storage capacity grew exponentially; computers became smaller, faster, cheaper and ever more powerful, while screens got bigger, brighter and clearer. Mobile phones followed, and there were computer chips in more and more domestic products, even, as my car-owning swimming club mate found, in breathalysers. Gaming consoles, music players, iPads, the list is ever-growing as computers have become an essential part of virtually all aspects of our lives. Your doctor will keep your records on a computer and likely need a computer to diagnose your ailments; I personally have experienced robotic surgery. Your car is probably dependent on computer technology. Medicine, transport, sport, government, industry, policing, defence, all rely on the truly ubiquitous computer, a dependency that has increased massively since the birth of the Internet.

Most of us now use the Internet in one way or another, but do you ever stop to think about what is actually happening when you do? I just did a search "when was the Internet invented?" Top of the list was an article from history.com, but in small print above that was the message, "About 5,950,000 results (0.67 seconds)". Do what? In a little over half a second my little question had gone off somewhere and something had identified nearly 6 million articles that might be of interest! Through the use of web crawlers, my search engine has identified a huge, ever-changing, repository of web pages, noted where these can be found (their URL addresses) and identified key words in order that they can be indexed. So, all that happened was that my request was routed to one of the browser servers where it was matched to an index in order to identify anything that might be of interest. Oh, there's more; it then used an algorithm, probably based on the number of web pages linking to it, to sort these into the order it thinks most useful. Simple. My mind remains boggled.

But enough of that. How has this changed our lives? We now have access to almost unlimited reserves of information from all around the world. You want to know the population of Guatemala in 1955? Easy. Want to wish Grandma in Australia a happy birthday? Simple; perhaps a video chat would be good. Then there are everyday functions such as shopping, banking, buying insurance, booking a holiday, or applying for a job, passport or driving license; the list seems never-ending. Want to place a bet, play a game, listen to music, read a book or see a film? It's all there. Anyone under thirty will find it hard to imagine a world without the Internet. And that's not to mention the fact that, for many people, it has become the font of all knowledge, the go-to for any information. To them, newspapers and books are anachronisms.

Your views on the efficacy of the Internet will likely depend on your age and personal experiences. Is it a benign tool or a malignant weapon? It was 1988 when the first major virus infected computers connected to the Internet.

2020 was a horrible year as we came to grips with Covid19; around the world, people locked indoors for weeks at a time turned to the Internet to maintain their sanity. Whether working from home, looking for information on the virus, seeking inspiration for physical workouts, learning new skills like cutting hair or making banana bread, streaming music and films, or keeping face-to-face contact with friends and family through Zoom calls, the Internet has been there. Truly a lifesaver.

But critics paint a slightly different picture. True, the Internet can be a lifesaver, but a growing number of incidents concerning psychological issues and even suicide have been attributed to Internet usage and experiences. Internet fans describe it as 'inclusive', yet it can only be so for those with access; whole swathes of people are excluded from key functions. Government departments and many businesses like banks and insurance companies now start with the assumption that everyone has online access, which can be particularly trying and stressful for those without; notably the Oldies and those who can't afford the relevant kit. The Internet can be empowering, but it can also be enslaving, for example where people go to incredible lengths to give the impression on social media that their lives are perfect and that they have numerous 'friends'; how does a social media addict respond when their 'like' count falls?

The Internet provides a huge store of valuable knowledge and yet also assists in the rapid dissemination of fake news and conspiracy theories that can easily be mistaken for the truth. Burglars can case a joint, or at least the surrounding area, remotely. Billions are lost through scams every year. The dark web is a tool utilised by many legitimate users such as solicitors and journalists wishing to retain anonymity in order to protect their sources or client interests, but at the same time it provides a forum for criminals to broker illicit transactions whether in drugs, arms, people or just about anything they wish to hide from the authorities. If not for the Internet, cyber-crime would exist only in the realm of sci-fi stories. The proliferation of smart devices in the home leads to increasing security threats and problems in the event of a power cut. Further, the Internet enables governments to spy on their population, to identify and suppress opposition and to censor the information they can see or distribute.

So, I have decided on the innovation that has brought about most change during my lifetime, but has it made things better or worse? Not an easy one really. I am no Luddite; I've willingly embraced technology and it has provided me with a good living for over forty years. And yet computers are a bit of a Pandora's box, bringing both good and bad; they have fuelled industrialisation and population growth, exacerbating several of the environmental issues we face today and yet, for many, they have also helped significantly to improve living standards.

My concern is that while computers have become an integral part of life, we are now too dependent on them. People's lives are regularly affected in ways they don't expect or fully understand, and they can be easy prey to criminals, can be misled through fake news and conspiracy theories and are unaware of the degree to which governments can monitor and control their lives. After careful consideration, my personal opinion is that during my lifetime the ubiquitous computer has achieved too strong a grip on our lives and led to too many changes too quickly. On balance, I would say that the costs have outweighed the benefits in many ways reducing our quality of life, and maybe things were better then. But doubtless this is a view with which both a large number of my generation and most of today's kids would not concur..

43.

That's All Folks

Well, that didn't go quite how I expected. Prone to distraction, it took me longer than planned to complete, and I'm now officially Old, I've now been a pensioner for two years.

When I started this little exercise, it was with a reasonable idea as to where I was going, but I do seem rather to have wandered off into uncharted waters more than once; as consolation I suppose that if you're still with me you must have found at least something of interest, so thank you for that. One challenge has been the speed of change, with some of the content becoming out of date even before I finished.

In my introduction, in an attempt to justify my self-centred nostalgia fest, I suggested a few objectives that I might address. My aim was to provide a brief summary of changes in the world around me since my birth, in order to unleash memories in readers who have similar experiences, while at the same time trying to give younger folk a bit of an insight into how we got to where we are today. I suspect I might be more successful in the former than the latter.

Rather grandly, I suggested that the book might address a few of life's mysteries, but regarding my achievements here, for one last time, I have to say it's not that easy. Let's begin with the question of whether life was better back then. I may well be fooling myself, but in my memory at least, the world of my youth was a better place than it is today. For a start, the air was cleaner, we had more space, there were fewer people, and it was quieter; anger wasn't ever-present, and the most trivial of disagreements tended not to flare up into a violent verbal or physical confrontation. People seemed to care more, whereas today looking after Number One seems often to be the guiding principle, and the idea of helping others is seen as a sign of weakness. Every stranger wasn't viewed suspiciously as a potential mugger or paedophile.

Life was less stressful too; we weren't continually being bombarded by one bunch or another commanding us to think or act in a particular way. Society was far less polarised compared to today, where every disagreement results in opposing camps digging in their heels and slagging off the other side while not giving them a chance to get a word in edgeways, and compromise or appreciating anyone else's views is unheard of. And people smiled and laughed more. It didn't seem as if everyone was out to relieve you of your hard-earned cash and incredibly, some things like parking a car for instance, were still free.

But I know that's just my rose-tinted glasses view as a somewhat jaundiced pensioner; I'm sure that many people today, and not just the youngsters, would find life unbearable and boring without all the modern-day comforts and luxuries now taken for granted, so things may or may not be better.

Then there's the question of whether kids today are the horrible, undisciplined, work-shy layabouts that some of the Oldies claim them to be. Well, yes they are, and then again, no they aren't. Without doubt there are many spoilt brats, but they tend to be the product of the society we have created; what can you expect when consumerism and waste is god; where looking after Number One trumps everything else; and where people believe they don't have to earn the things they want, they just deserve them. After all, it's often parents just wanting the best for their kids that create these little darlings. Then there's the feral packs of wild kids who think plunging a knife into a stranger for no real reason is a perfectly normal act; kids have definitely gone the wrong way.

But hang on a minute matey, let's not get too excited here. Quietly working away to get through school, land a job and basically get on with life, is a whole army of kids with just the same kind of worries and cares that you and I had. Look back through time and you'll realise that the younger generation has always been a bit of a disappointment; people just have a tendency to forget that they too were young once. So it's inevitable that, at least in some ways, kids are different today as they evolve to deal with an ever-changing world that we don't understand, but that doesn't make them generally any worse, just different; there have always been bad apples and there always will be.

So now to the £1,000,000 question; if things really are worse than they were in my day, then whose fault is it? The human race is incredibly resilient in the face of adversity; after wars, plagues, natural disasters and the like, the survivors just carry on. I'm sure it won't be long before Covid-19 is just added to the list of unpleasant things we have to deal with, mentally filed away as people continue living as if it never happened. Historians recognise six distinct cradles of civilisation, namely Egypt, Mesopotamia, the Indus Valley, China, Mexico and Peru; places where our very first cities were built, where language developed alongside social structure and where technology had its roots. We're talking some five or six thousand years ago; while these guys were building their pyramids, coming to grips with mathematics, mastering astronomy and coming up with a basic legal structure for trade and commerce, life in Britain and surrounding areas was, to say the least, relatively primitive.

Yet from the 1500s it's Europe that has provided the rulers of the world; the great early civilisations and empires have all gone. The Buddhist doctrine of Impermanence, anicca or anitya, sums it up; nothing lasts forever. If you are going through bad times take strength from the fact that they won't last forever, but also enjoy the good times while you can as they too have a limited shelf life. The status quo won't last and inevitably power will move in time, probably eastwards. Change unleashes irresistible forces and individuals can only go with the flow.

Unless you are the likes of Albert Einstein, Louis Pasteur, Alexander the Great or Adolf Hitler, it is unlikely that your actions will significantly affect the way of the world. That being the case, the kids are being a little unfair in blaming their parents for the current state of the world; things just happen, and you deal with it. When I began this exercise, words from the 1988 Mike and the Mechanics song 'The Living Years' came to mind. That's the one about how every generation blames the one before for the state of things. But now, considering the bigger picture and our role in it, I've come to the conclusion that a more recent offering, Rag'n'Bone Man's 'Human', seems far more appropriate; we are after all only human, going with the flow, and none of us can really be blamed for that.

That's me done. Thank you, and goodnight.

Printed in Great Britain
by Amazon